THE REFLECTION OF THEOLOGY IN LITERATURE:
A Case Study In Theology And Culture

THE REFLECTION OF THEOLOGY IN LITERATURE:

A Case Study In Theology And Culture

By
WILLIAM MALLARD

Trinity University Press, San Antonio

Grateful acknowledgment is extended to the following publishers for permission to quote from: Sophocles, *Oedipus the King*, trans. Kenneth Cavander. New York: Chandler Publishing Company, copyright © 1961. Richard Wright, *The Long Dream*. Doubleday & Company, Inc., copyright © 1958 by Richard Wright. Flannery O'Connor, *Mystery and Manners: Occasional Prose*, ed. Sally and Robert Fitzgerald. Farrar, Straus & Giroux, Inc., copyright © 1969 by the estate of Mary Flannery O'Connor. *Interpretation: The Poetry of Meaning*, ed. S. R. Hopper and D. L. Miller. Harcourt Brace Jovanovich, Inc., copyright © 1967 by Drew University. T. S. Eliot, *Essays Ancient and Modern*. Harcourt Brace Jovanovich, Inc., copyright, 1932, 1936. Richard Wilbur, "Epistemology," from *The Poems of Richard Wilbur*. Harcourt Brace Jovanovich, Inc., copyright, 1963. Flannery O'Connor, *A Good Man Is Hard to Find*. Harcourt Brace Jovanovich, Inc., copyright © 1955, by Flannery O'Connor. Robert Frost, "Stopping by Woods on a Snowy Evening" from *The Poetry of Robert Frost*, ed. Edward Connery Lathem. Copyright 1923, © 1969 by Holt, Rinehart and Winston; copyright 1951 by Robert Frost. Elie Wiesel, *The Town Beyond the Wall*, trans. Stephen Becker. Holt, Rinehart and Winston, copyright © 1964 by Elie Wiesel. Wallace Stevens, *Collected Poems*. Alfred A. Knopf, Inc., copyright, 1954, by Wallace Stevens. Franz Kafka, *The Trial*, trans. Willa and Edwin Muir. Alfred A. Knopf, Inc. © copyright, 1937, 1956. Jean Toomer, "Song of the Son," from *Cane*. Liveright Publishing Corporation, copyright 1923 by Boni & Liveright, copyright renewed 1951 by Jean Toomer. Ezra Pound, "In a Station of the Metro," from *Personae*. New Directions Publishing Corporation, copyright 1926 by Ezra Pound. Jean-Paul Sartre, *What Is Literature?* trans. B. Frechtman. Philosophical Library, Inc., copyright, 1949. Erich Auerbach, *Mimesis: The Representation of Reality in Western Literature*, trans. Walter R. Trask. Princeton University Press, copyright, 1953. William Faulkner, *The Sound and the Fury*. Random House, Inc., copyright 1946. Franz Kafka, *The Great Wall of China*, trans. Willa and Edwin Muir. Schocken Books, Inc., copyright 1946; copyright renewed © 1974 by Schocken Books Inc. *Faulkner in the University*, ed. F. L. Gwynn and J. L. Blotner. The University Press of Virginia, copyright, 1959. *The Martin Luther Christmas Book*, trans. and arr. by Roland H. Bainton. The Muhlenberg Press, the Westminster Press, copyright © 1948 by W. L. Jenkins.

Opening sections of chapters VII and VIII appeared previously in *Transcendence and Mystery*, ed. Earl D. C. Brewer, copyright © 1975 by IDOC/North America, New York City, N.Y., whose permission to reprint has been kindly granted.

For
 Gatra, Reid, Winn, Rob

Preface

This study builds primarily on two concerns. First is the general crisis of the theological discipline in contemporary Western culture. Certainly it is clear that the intellectual foundations of the modern world have been less than supportive towards classical Western theology. The second concern lies with literature and theology as an interdisciplinary field. A significant amount of my own classroom teaching has pursued the possible relation between theology and imaginative literature, and reflections on this relationship comprise the greater part of the book. In addition, I have intended the pursuit of the second interest to serve the first. That is, a critical study of literature in its relation to theology may serve as a case study (broad though it is) of theology's relationship to modern Western culture generally. I certainly intend no extensive generalizations from the limited scope of this brief study. Nevertheless, I believe that the outline of a theological structure emerges, which may be suggestive for further work on both dogmatic theology and the theology of culture.

Initial work on the book was made possible by a cross-disci-plinary award (1969–70) from the (then) Society for Religion in Higher Education, New Haven, Connecticut, and it is really to the character of that award that the book owes its nature and impetus. That year Professor Hans W. Frei of Yale University was more than generous with his time and thought. The debt that I owe to him is significantly plain, more particularly in Part III. Also during that period Pro-fessors Don Saliers and David Kelsey of Yale were helpful and kind. Several colleagues read parts or all of the material in an earlier version and were essential to its progress at that time: Manfred Hoffmann, Hendrikus Boers, William Beards-lee, and Thomas and Alma Altizer made long and careful readings, with many invaluable notes and suggestions. (More recently Professor Boers read the Introduction.) Neverthe-less, my own responsibility for the finished work is even great-er than usual, since none of the above had opportunity to respond to the final recasting of the work during the past year. In particular, the point of view adopted overall attaches only to myself. I feel this responsibility especially in relation to Professor Frei's work, to which I am much indebted, yet with most important divergences. Conversations with my col-league, Professor Walter J. Lowe, were also most helpful, as becomes clear in the text.

I wish to recognize my editor, Professor John H. Hayes, without whose thought and patient guidance the volume would likely never have seen the light of day, certainly not in its present form. The Candler School of Theology has also been specially supportive. Dean James T. Laney and Dean Jim L. Waits generously provided summer opportunities for seeing the work to completion. Finally, Mrs. June Caldwell ably typed most of two separate versions of the manuscript; helpful contributions in typing also were rendered by Ms. Keren Humphrey and Mrs. Phyllis Bishop.

William Mallard

Candler School of Theology
Emory University
March, 1976

Contents

THE REFLECTION OF THEOLOGY IN LITERATURE:
A Case Study In Theology And Culture

Introduction:
Literary Foundations Of Theology

Everyone familiar with the general field of Western Christian theology has known something of that discipline's severe dilemmas during the last one hundred fifty years. Modern critical study, historical turbulence, and the uprooting of tradition have taken a heavy toll of theology's strength and viability. Nor have matters on the contemporary scene been improved by the passing of theology's twentieth-century "giants." Surely the very stature of people like Barth, Bultmann, Tillich, Bonhoeffer, and the Niebuhrs has played a part in the malaise that has followed them. How do you overcome "the fathers" when they have achieved so much at such a high standard? On the other hand, how can you remain content to be only their faithful disciples? Younger theological figures have thus been caught between revolt and submission. Yet there have been more reasons than just the "father-son" ambivalence for the problems of current theology. Indeed, the entire drift of Western society has seemed inimical to the theological enterprise.

Certainly the broad intellectual community of the modern West has not grounded itself upon theology or specific religious commitments. In America, colleges and universities once founded for pointedly Christian reasons have produced countless specialized scholars whose fields correlate in no particular way with theology, if indeed they are not hostile to it. Meanwhile, vast numbers of active churches in this country have but a blurred notion of their intellectual task. Most agencies of the social order have become "secular." The various arms of government and much of business are presumably sympathetic to religious aims and presuppositions, but their "official" sympathy does not contribute to thoughtful religious reflection. Indeed, the universality of "civil religion" in America is an obstacle to creative considerations of Christian meaning. At the same time, protest against conventional attitudes has resulted in a wide variety of informal religious expressions throughout the society, especially among the young. Such protest has challenged theology at the point of its disciplined, historical lines, which have been conceived as oppressive. The picture is not simply that of an academic discipline in difficulty, but of a culture turning against its previously normative foundations.

The erosion of theology may be summarized as arising from four areas. (1) Pluralism. The diversity of religious and ethical commitments in American society has tended to relativize theological meaning. Speaking of God appears to arise less from revelation, an independent source of reliable knowledge, and more from the accidental circumstances and preferences of the speaker. When all theological speech appears to become contingent, then confidence in it obviously wanes. (2) "Religion." The effect called "religion" easily follows upon the impact of pluralism. When all creeds seem contingent in their precise claims and forms, many observers will nevertheless decide that they must have some common underlying cause; they impress as different versions of a single broad activity. That common activity is called "religion," and investigation of religion then replaces theology. Now it is true that human response to the sacred, however that sacred

2

is understood, is a discernible activity that may be called "religion." The term is nevertheless more a matter of modern convenience and need in no way replace theology unless the latter is shown to be unfeasible. (3) Humanism. Surely no one objects to the affirmative implications of the term "human." But in respect to the demise of theology, the concept and the affirmation have their problems. Pluralism in "religion" suggests that even the God-relation is primarily a human function or venture. God or ultimacy is located by following clues inherent in general human experience; worship is essentially a self-projected expansion of human awareness. The difficulty with an expanding or self-contained humanism lies in maintaining the subtle dialectic of the human *per se*, its outreach *and* its limits, apart from the traditional religion that nurtured the meaning of "human." Even Cicero's humanism did not forget the Roman gods. Hellenistic Platonism in a somewhat different manner set out to disclose the human, and ironically ended in seeing the human soul itself as divine! (4) Secularism. Humanism that does not elect "religion," or becomes weary with it, moves to secularism—the notion that since human utility is the final reality, the best procedure is always to manipulate circumstances to best advantage. Among the circumstances to manipulate are God, religion, theology, as occasion may require. At least in America secular humanism appears thus manipulative; the European tradition of humanism may offer wider possibilities.

Reason enough exists for genuine, serious theological reflection to have receded sharply in the mid-twentieth-century West. The general conditions have intruded subtly upon many who have no wish or desire to reject an essential factor in their heritage. Thus a pervasive set of images has arisen from the general culture that suggests the unreality, indeed the absence of those objects theology discusses, including God himself. In much common parlance, to become "theological" means to introduce solutions out of nowhere, without regard for the facts. The loss of theological vitality thereby correlates with the rise of a certain contemporary "honesty" that may indeed be a virtue, but only a half-virtue. Bonhoeffer, for example, spoke in his *Letters and Papers from Prison* of the apparent "honesty" or "enthusiasm for truth" that is actually a mark of cynicism.[1] Thus direct candor about one's own state may illicitly be offered as the truth of things generally. In particular, many do not realize that their sense of the "unreality" of God, faith, worship, may actually be the beginning for them of a more sophisticated theological understanding. Very often no leadership or guidance is nearby to indicate that serious questioning can be the beginning of religious wisdom.

Guidance is important, for there is much about Western religious faith that simply has to be learned. Direct "experience," feeling, or vision is not enough. Thus theology can be thought of as the intellectual discipline of Christian faith. (I am specifically concerned with Christian theology, although it seems that Jewish theology maintains very special parallels.) In this definition of theology as discipline, notice that the double sense of the word "of" gives the statement two important meanings: first, theology is of Christian faith as belonging to it, serving as its instrument and expression. The implication is that theology rests on a foundation of faith that includes both emotional and cognitive elements, and that this special merger needs further explaining and clarifying. Second, theology is the discipline *of* faith in the sense that faith needs discipline and does not emerge apart from discipline. The point is that thinking not only expresses a commitment, but actually recoils upon that commitment, testing it, pressing it, and setting up the conditions for its renewal.

The disciplined task of theological learning becomes more complex with each passing decade; yet the tendency towards theological meandering continues. Under such conditions, is it appropriate to offer another study in theology and literature, such as this book purports to be?

Obviously, I have no intention of trying to elaborate a full theological system. What limited contribution is therefore in view? The problems of theology that we have outlined above essentially focus the question of theology's relation to cul-

ture. Expressions of Western culture tend to be pluralistic, humanistic, "religious," secular, in baffling combinations, while theology traditionally owns an allegiance singular, exclusive, revelatory, and by implication unifying. It would be helpful if some light could be shed on a feasible relation between such a theology and such cultural conditions.

Yet this relation itself is far too complex for limited treatment. Therefore, the aim of this volume will be simply to present a single case study within that relation, namely, the relation of theology to imaginative literature—a relation that will ultimately be designated by the image of theology's "reflection" in literature. (I am aware, too, of the pitfall of generalizing about an entire culture on the basis only of its literature. Literature is clearly a rather specialized cultural product.) Such an aim is itself a tall order. Indeed, since my interest falls primarily upon theology, the result will be to consider simply what theology is and does, but from one particular angle or perspective, namely, the literary or poetic. The procedure will not include detailed work on theological and biblical materials in their literary phase (many books already do this), but will begin with observations on modern language studies and literature to discover what potential for theology they contain, or how theology is "reflected" in them. Then theology proper will be considered in relation to its peculiar New Testament literary foundation. While the venture into theological exposition will be limited, the central affirmation of theology should come clear, as well as a position on the doctrine of revelation.

To reflect on the poetic aspect of theology is not easy; but to ponder theology's "central affirmation" in the light of that aspect is more difficult and controversial still. Something further, then, should be said about these tasks.

Modern Theology and 'Earth'

A certain commonplace about modern theology notes that since at least the eighteenth century, the mainstream of Western theology has become more "earth"-centered and less "heaven"-centered. To remember an early American colony

like Jamestown or Plymouth and the small, brief lives that
hurled themselves against the Atlantic and the wilderness is
to realize how the hope of a better after-life sustained those
settlers. Yet already in the 1600's, in the work of Spinoza and
others, general human philosophy and historical study—not
heaven—were beginning to be the point of reference for religious truth. By the eighteenth century, the arena of human
history, rather than the inspired biblical text, was the locus
where revelation "happened," even if the Bible were still
considered literally true. Concern with philology, history,
science, and philosophy, ordinarily pursued, quietly began to
assume a more *normative* role in the meaning of Christian
revelation.

In countless ways, theoretical and practical, "this world"
became increasingly a treasury of criteria and insights for illuminating Christian faith. That development has continued
up to the present and has brought both weal and woe. To
consider just one side of it, modern Christianity has been far
more sympathetic, even in its sectarian and pietist movements, to including "things of earth" as furnishings of the
Christian life. That means not only wealth (and crusades
against poverty), but marriage and human love, varieties of
vocation, social protest, and democratic rights and liberties.
Meanwhile, scholarship on Christian origins has in its own
way added support to the "earth" focus. Late studies have
shown that primitive Christianity was cradled in an apocalyptic outlook Jewish in origin; and apocalyptic hardly favored
abstraction, but looked for the concrete goods of earth to be
finally achieved at the end-time. It is interesting to see recent
Jewish scholarship honoring Albert Schweitzer for his insistence on Jesus' apocalyptic consciousness. In the view of
Lou H. Silberman, apocalyptic, the power of the powerless,
realistic hope projected against the clouds, should always
remind later Christianity that eternal values may not be separated from concrete forms, that an emphasis on individual
vision must not commit the disaster of severing all social
bonds, i.e., "of being outside of history."[2]

Thus modern theology has reversed what our Protestant

parents and grandparents learned about Christianity when they were children: that Bible stories present supernatural happenings, that Christianity is a special set of beliefs and rules divinely given, that God is a present Father who intervenes "from above" to help "spiritual" persons, and takes them to heaven when they die. Nor has the weight of conventional supernaturalism been any lighter a burden for Roman Catholics, as Joyce's Stephen Dedalus so painfully learned in his schooling by Jesuits.[3] The Christian intellectual community has thus determined that the Christian life must be in accord with many aspects of natural experience and feeling, otherwise God's creation is violated and Christ's honoring of the flesh would be pointless.

Much of this modern development has been unqualifiedly good, some of it severely troublesome. Our point for the moment is a limited one: a theology that comments on concrete life rather than on abstract doctrine must keep its own language responsive to concrete expression. That means that theology must respond to the phenomenological, the metaphoric, the poetic. For, contrary to lingering popular sentiment, poetry is not rarefied and abstruse. That is, poetry's language may on occasion be difficult and "dense," but its concern is nevertheless with the "here and now." Thus a literary work expresses the concrete, immediate presence of its subject matter. Indeed, literature resonates with extraordinary meaning just because it arranges concrete objects in fresh and surprising ways.

Theology as Poetic and Metaphoric

The important relation of theology to poetry is hardly a new development or a new discovery in theology's long annals. Modern theology's concern with "earth" rather than with "heaven" has not introduced that relation as a novelty. Rather, the modern period has provided an opportunity *for one perennial side* of theology again to be noted, again to be dealt with. Any theology maintains, at least implicitly, two sides: the imaginative or poetic, and the logical or abstractive. Neither is pure, since neither side can come to expression without some element of the other; at some level, they remain interdependent. Nevertheless, for various reasons, during the high and waning middle ages and much of the Reformation and post-Reformation time, the logical, abstractive side of theology was uppermost. The modern period, by broadening the individual and experiential elements in theology, gave new breathing room for the concrete, imaginative functions of theology to take place. In doing so, modern theology found itself surprisingly at home with many features of early Christianity, prior to the towering logical developments that set in.

Jesus himself taught in parables, and his own story was rehearsed as narrative literature in the early church's Gospel accounts. Paul of Tarsus was literary not only in that he wrote letters, but in a more important way, since a view of human destiny was opened up for him and his circle through a cluster of images, metaphors, and symbols: ". . . he emptied himself, taking the form of a slave . . ."; ". . . I live no more, but Christ lives in me . . ."; ". . . the just shall live by faith . . ."; ". . . when I am weak, then am I strong . . ."; ". . . that God may be all in all . . ."[4] Certainly no one accuses Augustine of Hippo, despite his neoplatonist and dialectic refinements, of being closed to sensuous, poetic language.

> Belatedly I loved thee, O Beauty so ancient and so new, belatedly I loved thee . . . Thou didst call and cry aloud and didst force open my deafness. Thou didst gleam and shine and didst chase away my blindness. Thou didst breathe fragrant odors and I drew in my breath; and now I pant for thee. I tasted, and now I hunger and thirst. Thou didst touch me, and I burned for thy peace.[5]

Francis of Assisi was not a theologian, but his movement produced many "lesser brothers" who indeed were theological, and his child-like vision of a concretely loved world set the motif of their abstract reflection.

It is important to note—and this will be considered in detail later on—that using language of the poetic imagination is not a mere decoration for a fixed structure of reality, as if one were to resort to images for a kind of flourish over the perfected whole of things. Rather, primary metaphoric language signals and effects a certain shift in the general state of affairs, indeed is the medium in which the passage from old to new realities takes place, and in which the movement of history occurs. Metaphors and parables cannot be reduced to simple propositions, for in and through themselves they summon the world into new dimensions of meaning. It is not surprising that the turn of affairs in history called "Christian" should have been characterized by a set of terms and narratives that recalled an older world ("Messiah," "Israel," "Kyrios," "Logos"), but in such metaphors as to call forth a new world ("Jesus Messiah," "the New Israel," "Kyrios Christos," "the Logos made flesh"). Such images and stories must endure if Christian vitality remains, precisely because they are not a code for certain abstract indicatives, but in some way bear in themselves the reality about which they speak.

The later addition to Christian stories of elaborate analytical language, as theology developed, was obviously a significant turn. Theological doctrine became expressed in language that certainly built upon images (e.g., one God-Creator "over" the world, a son of God who came "down," Jesus on the cross), but commented on these biblical figures in generalized, universal concepts ("being of the same substance," "two natures in one person," "unconfused union"). Then constructive theology, which elaborated the received doctrines for particular times, places, and cultures, became increasingly conceptual in nature in order to delineate precisely their meaning. For example, the medieval method of biblical study borrowed heavily upon the allegorical conceptualizing of ancient hellenistic Alexandria. In effect, allegorizing enabled the Bible to be translated readily into received doctrine (e.g., the biblical Jerusalem as an allegory for the church catholic). In addition, the high middle ages introduced into biblical commentary certain conceptual *quaestiones* for discussion ("Is God simple or complex?"); the manifold responses to these *quaestiones* enabled the theological systems of Thomas, Bonaventura, Alexander of Hales, Scotus, and others, to develop.

Systematic theology dealt with contemporary questions, presumably intending to keep its responses within the classical boundary lines of received doctrine, which in turn commented upon the Gospel account of Jesus Christ. Theology's typical function thus employed language in its power to interpret, to analyze, and to generalize in systematic order. But at the beginnings of Christianity, in story, metaphor, and symbol, lay the general capacity of language to "open up" and disclose reality in concrete fullness. A movement to recover this side of theology took place at the Reformation, especially in Luther's work. Luther was adept in theoretical scholasticism, but the core of his dialectic, "At once justified *and* sinner!" was a metaphoric announcement that opened a different perspective on the God-self-world relation. Prophetically, Luther's design to confront the ambiguity of the earthbound human self called for theology in a metaphoric, and therefore dialectic, key. Medieval in temperament, Luther nevertheless anticipated modernity's "earth" allegiances.

> He is not worth calling a theologian who seeks to interpret "the invisible things of God" . . .
> But he is worth calling a theologian who understands the visible "backsides" of God to mean the passion and the cross.[6]

Luther's disturbing metaphor of divine and human "backsides" pressed hard against classical lines of doctrine in an attempt to renew religious vitality within those lines. (Opponents declared his dialectic blows had broken them.) His poetic evocation of the Christian world, as an act of reform, produced inevitably a theology of and for preaching. The Word, whenever proclaimed, was presumed to effect what it declared. The engaging power of the Spirit's "presence" in the message translated the hearer and his or her world; in such a manner faith found renewal.

There is no need to rehearse here the unhappy misappropriations of Luther (some by Luther himself!) in his lifetime and after. Nor will it be necessary to outline the somewhat different poetic Reformation bases of Calvin and others.[7] The point is that post-Enlightenment Protestant theology, whether liberal or dialectical, has made much of the Reformation's poetic fundament, which in turn looked back to the language of the New Testament founders.

It is true that in expressing its at-homeness with "earth" modern Protestant thought has shown a scientific, abstractive side at times dominant over the literary element, or that of "engaged" metaphor. An example is the late nineteenth-century "new theology" (responsive to evolution), as is the recent "process" theology of John Cobb, Schubert Ogden, and Charles Hartshorne, grounded in Whitehead's philosophy of nature. The roll-call on the other side is nevertheless significant. Schleiermacher built his theology out of a peculiar component of affective and cognitive factors that he called "feeling," more particularly a feeling of absolute dependence. While the term itself is obviously abstract, it very closely derives from a certain imaginative sense of the religious world and its foundations. Older metaphysical structures were laid aside in favor of a primal religious posture Schleiermacher found implicated in the Jesus story. Hegel's dialectic, though philosophical, methodologically influenced a host of nineteenth-century theologians and biblical scholars, most prominently Kierkegaard. Yet Hegel's dialectic, by his own intent, is a generalized reduction of the crucifixion-resurrection story, a narrative which immediately informs the movement of his thought. Hegel's conceptualizing is consequently notoriously difficult. The dialectic moves, not by commonplace logical inferences, but more by a richness of poetic insight, a certain logical "fitness" rather than strict necessity, as John Findlay has helpfully noted.[8] Thus metaphor, which precisely includes a logical "gap" between the dissonance of its components and, on the other hand, their unity, has its place in the essentials of Hegel's thought. And the foundation of his metaphor-dialectic is the story of Christ.

Another preoccupation of Protestant thought has been Christology and "revelation in history," closely accompanied by much scholarship on the historical Jesus. Invariably, this historical Christocentric interest has sought an imaginative correlation between the Jesus account, on the one hand, and either human achievement or human crisis on the other. Loyalty to earth has been specified by seeing Jesus as genuinely within history's turbulence, truly "in the flesh." This immersion establishes his link with us, while on the other side he serves as cipher or metaphor for the work of God, or the movement of ultimacy on our behalf. In liberal terms, he may be the bearer of religious or moral values (Ritschl). In dialectical terms, his cross becomes paradigmatic of our crises, which also are found to contain within themselves the pattern of their own solution, just as his resurrection was implicit in his death (Tillich, Bultmann). Especially in the latter case, the overriding importance of poetic vision or metaphor is clear. The work of Christ enables one in moments of existential discontinuity (the ordinary incompatibility of the metaphor's two terms) nevertheless to find a surprising reconciliation (the final harmony or "fitness" of the metaphor). Crisis theology is the elaboration of an experiential, world-invoking image.

At this point, the harking back to Luther is clear. Therefore, in the work of Bultmann, the early Barth, Gogarten, Tillich, and Bonhoeffer, the "Word proclaimed" is central. This Word, the story of crucifixion, is not only a literary structure in itself, but is performative language; it tends to bring into being the reality it describes. Presumably, one who hears the Word truly will find himself/herself carried through authenticity, alienation, and finally to salvific recovery at a new level. A poetic crisis-and-renewal clearly operates. The recent concern with language therefore produced by the crisis or neo-orthodox movement in theology is no surprise. Heidegger's philosophy has nourished both existentialist and poetic elements of theology, raising questions of hermeneutic or principle of interpretation. From one standpoint, the entire question of hermeneutic has been a poetic question: how seemingly scandalous material—ancient documents, myth and mythology—without being overtly altered, can nevertheless come to "mean" in a contemporary manner.

Following Bultmann, the bearers of the "new hermeneutic" have increasingly emphasized the change in what we may call imaginative insight into a traditional set of documents: E. Fuchs has stressed the continuing tradition of language;[9] G. Ebeling has emphasized the secularity of ordinary words that may by a shift in insight become revelatory in a special way.[10] Even more than Bultmann, recent hermeneutic scholars have come to feel that all language is of a piece in its secular, historical origins (no language is set aside as closer to the divine); yet this ordinary language may become revelatory when the relationships it mediates profoundly change. From the biblical side, interest in the parables of Jesus has heightened, as in the work of James Robinson, Dan O. Via, Hendrikus Boers, Norman Perrin, and Leander Keck.[11]

Theological searching continues in the imaginative-literary documents Christianity has long honored. Ray Hart has combined this element with phenomenological study;[12] Robert Funk has pressed the nature of the parable.[13] A recent study by Sallie TeSelle, *Speaking in Parables*, comments constructively upon this development.[14] Thus theology continues to retain the secular, historical, "earthy" elements in Western experience, nevertheless finding in them an eschatological resolution, an end only to be gained by a strong imaginative and poetic focus.

At the literary level, the metaphoric approach to theology always appears to offer a certain freshness about it. Yet it is important to remember that even the latest preoccupations with the metaphoric foundations of theology only repeat insights common to the last two centuries and, behind them, the Reformation. Indeed, if one takes the long view of the Christian tradition, two salient facts emerge: (1) the metaphoric "engaging" side of Christian proclamation has remained essential throughout Christian history, though not uniformly either dominant or acknowledged; (2) the more descriptive, "objective" side of the Christian story, the "profile" of doctrine that has served to frame and exhibit the central images has consistently accompanied the metaphoric aspect, serving an equally essential role. Current research into theology and Christian origins is evidencing much concern with the first of these facts, the metaphoric roots of theology, following the philosophical clues offered by such analysts of metaphor and symbol as Paul Ricoeur.[15] In such a breakthrough of interest, it is of first importance that the liberal, apologetic cast of biblical and theological studies since the eighteenth century not simply be unwittingly—or even uncritically—repeated. Metaphor, as a function of the subjective idealist imagination, was hardly unknown to the major liberal Protestant theologians of the last two centuries.

As regards a rather "open-ended" confidence in metaphor, I do wish to distinguish what I am about in this study from TeSelle's position in her *Speaking in Parables,* referred to above. Although any such work is abundantly welcome for its resistance to reductionism in theology and culture, nevertheless the work appears to give almost a *carte blanche* to metaphoric insight as the single fundament of all that is good in theology. TeSelle's references to her work as "intermediary" theology do not relieve this implication. In only two instances, both in footnotes, does she make reference to objectively cited limits that have served the Christian tradition as criteria for the reading of metaphors and parables.[16] In other words, acknowledgment of the more descriptive, objective side of the Christian story is almost entirely lacking in her study. The consequent anthropocentric mood of her essay comes out in interesting ways, as for example in a reference to Augustine of Hippo as Christian convert:

> . . . For Augustine, then, the incarnation means something quite definite for the Christian: . . . that understanding certain things, things which bear upon his or her own existence, cannot be understood [sic] unless he or she is *prepared to embody them.* . . . What Augustine does in the *Confessions* is to show us the movement of that *process of insight and appropriation, of grace and of the struggle to incarnate it.*[17] (Italics ours.)

Surely grace and incarnation for Augustine meant that the struggle of becoming was worth it—and even possible—be-

14

cause in fact a particular event of incarnation had already occurred in Christ. That incarnation was for Augustine both an invitation to, *and a salutary limit upon,* one's own personal embodiment of religious meaning. Realization of human, metaphoric insight as personal incarnation found restraint in that remarkable intrusion, the incarnation in Christ—which was not only metaphor, but object. Metaphoric insight taken by itself can replace an objective, heteronomous "burden of the law" only with an equivalent, subjective burden.

Concern in this study with the poetic side of theology will involve not only metaphor, but the "discipline of metaphor," that is, the functions of style, form, and genre that effect a useful distance between reader and literary object, especially in the case of the central Christian story. The position adopted will be that both phases of literary reading, the metaphoric and the objective, in a certain rhythm, are essential for comprehending the imaginative foundations of Christian theology.

From Literature towards Theology

This brief survey of the literary and metaphoric side of theological work is really a sketch of how theology can be traced down to certain of its roots. Behind elaborate conceptualizing always lies the "vision" or proposal of a "world," with the concrete and the universal richly mingled, available for constructive "unpacking." Countless sorts of inquiries help to bring us to these roots when that move is called for: form criticism and literary structural criticism, genre studies, myth criticism, phenomenology of symbols—variously applied to biblical and historical-theological materials. Of special interest is the study of liturgy, the communal rehearsal of stories, beliefs, avowals and prayers, lyric poetry and song, indeed the store of poetic materials from which theology draws sustenance. Clearly, much can be gained from taking theological writings and rediscovering the artistic, literary moves that made them possible. For one thing, fresh theological possibilities may still emerge from these prime materials; they are not easily "used up."

But suppose the inquiry is made the other way about, from the opposite direction. Suppose traditional theology is not first considered, but the broad variety of literature as the modern West has known and produced it—and to say "modern" is to increase the variety of the literature and render the problematic for theology more severe. Much of classical Western literature was set within a Christian theological framework—as was the work of Dante, Milton, and Bunyan— but from *Madame Bovary* to *An American Tragedy* to *Krapp's Last Tape* the past century in particular has insisted on liberty from explicit Christian meaning. The question of theology "in" this literature has therefore been vexed and knotty. Yet the feeling has persisted that something genuine about ultimate relationships and human destiny, in Western terms, finds echo in this recent material. Can this echo be rendered more substantial? Perhaps in any case the resonance we hear is not theological but broadly humanistic, either "philosophical" or "religious."

The question becomes urgent for the purpose of this book, namely, to consider theology from its cultural side, as represented by literature. Perhaps there are simply no clear steps from the broad range of modern literature into theology. In that case, at least as regards literature, theology will have to exist isolated and self-contained, a demurring subculture of its own. Or it may be concluded that theology is no longer a feasible discipline of our civilization unless it drastically alters its norms, as in the movement of the new "polytheism."[18] The concern here is the true and appropriate "shape" of theology in contemporary culture. If in this case study the scope of modern literature dissolves the essential boundaries of theology, then one important negative vote will have been cast against rapprochement between theology and culture.

Much postponing and hedging about this question goes on in contemporary religious studies. Various students of biblical literature and biblical theology and hermeneutic take seriously the literary critical approach to their material. But

16

the full implications of this approach (likewise with the historical-critical method) are elusive. Thus there is considerable work on New Testament parables and narratives by such scholars as Funk, Via, and Perrin. Various canons of ordinary literary criticism, linguistic study, and hermeneutic of symbols are brought to bear. The parables of Jesus are thereby shown to function as parables will, granted individualistic features; the eschatological motifs play the role that eschatological motifs will play; the narratives behave as narratives. In sum, the studies are primarily formal. Now formal study is highly useful in relating unknown or little understood material to what is already known. The literature then presents itself to us in terms that are basically general, that are even familiar. The New Testament offers unique instances of the universal, or presents widely known themes specially developed.

Such an approach need not exclude confrontation with the *meaning* of the material. An "existential" meeting is possible, or an unexpected "address" of the reader by the biblical account, calling into question that reader's personal life-stance. Especially with the New Testament parables the inherent power of metaphoric engagement operates, opening doorways into new and threatening dimensions and shaking one's conventional security. Such engagement is no longer merely formal, but is *still universal*, since metaphors and parables in general may hold this capacity to "address," to "call into question." (Thus the existential phase of Bultmann's New Testament work is not equivalent to the unique kerygmatic phase.) Theology, to the contrary, has always grounded a major cornerstone of its effort upon the particular *content* (not of course actually separable from form) of the New Testament accounts. The explicit story of Jesus and not another like it, his particular parables and not similar ones, have claimed prime position in theology. Whether such "election" of documents is still defensible, regardless of their countless literary analogues, is precisely the question in hand. Funk, Via, Perrin, TeSelle and others occupy themselves at length with the biblical materials, so that it seems these command a unique status within literature. On the other hand, the definite impression emerges that the interest of these scholars is primarily historical and literary and their treatment of the New Testament is "accidental" to their universalizing concerns.

I intend no complaint against wide humanistic motives in study if only they are clear. If New Testament accounts are to be read in the same arena with literature generally—with any claim of unique status based on sheer literary merit or personal preference—then theology must surely inquire of general literature as its source. Indeed, there seems no question that the theological implications of the general body of Western literature must be pursued if we are to be fair to the humanistic and cultural side of our inquiry. One may caution that the results will vary widely from the explicit claims of the New Testament. No theological "results by association" should be allowed to occur because purely literary studies treat New Testament documents. Humanistic study requires free rein and may not "trade" theologically on Bible-oriented preferences.

The approach to theology through the breadth of literature has already claimed much discussion during the past thirty years. The matter can be considered from two sides: Does the general character of modern literature imply theological categories? What theological frame of reference is appropriate for a criticism of modern literature? The two questions merge into a single problem; nevertheless, the issue has predominantly been approached in this country through the second question rather than the first. Types of theological framework that are familiar to Christian tradition have been "tried" for their suitability in invoking literature's theological potential. As will be examined in detail later on, both a "confessional" approach and an "apologetic" approach have been attempted. The confessional approach undoes at the outset what we have conspired to accomplish, that is, to move from literature towards theology. Explicit confession of faith in Christ as a norm for literary criticism derogates any literature that does not honor that confession, no matter how aesthetically powerful the literature may be. Thus the confessional approach imposes itself upon literature. The theological potential of the literature *per se* is not free to find its own expression.

The apologetic approach turns out to serve no better. Here a certain overlap or common ground is discerned between the implications of a piece of literature and a portion of theology. Usually the human plight portrayed in literature is found to be in accord with the theological state of sin. In that case, the dilemma suggested by the literature looks toward a Gospel resolution or "answer." The theology of Tillich has long been associated with this approach. But again, the theological view is imposed on the literature in a manner scarcely less arbitrary than with the confessional. Indeed, the apologetic is perhaps the more throttling of the two because it seems more open, when in actual fact it is not. Literature is forced to serve certain prescribed theological ends and its variety is held captive to a single meaning.

Fortunately other possibilities exist for relating theology and literature than the confessional and the apologetic. Indeed, Parts I and II of this study are dedicated to the movement from literature towards theology. Part I will begin with a broad linguistic commentary and poetic in an effort to defend literary criticism that includes concern for communication of meaning. If criticism must limit itself to a formal analysis of a work's structure and components, then no progress is possible towards ethical and theological significance. On the other hand, if the work suggests an angle of vision on "how it is" in the world, then a theological statement of those conditions may be possible. Of high importance is just the manner by which artistic language has the power to present the world's affairs to us. The point is that if this power is carefully analyzed philosophically and linguistically, we shall find ourselves at the "brink of theology" without inappropriate strain. The question then becomes whether that implicit "theology" at the heart of the artistic function can be laid out in its categories without violating its own aesthetic ground.

Part II will be an attempt to cite the lines of this "theology" generally residual in all literature, and therefore to be offered as a theology *for* literature. In one manner of speaking, Part II will involve stating in other terms what has already been said aesthetically in Part I, with the conviction that the translation of terms will not in this case represent an essential translation of substance. If the point holds, there should emerge a "theological" manner of speaking about pieces of literature produced within a broadly Christian culture.

Still a most important matter remains. What is the status of this "theology" whose substance so closely inheres within functioning artistic language? The very fact of putting the term continually in quotation marks suggests that such theological material is distinct in some way from what I have already called theology proper. At this point, I shall want to show that the "theology" for literature, though rightly denominated a theology, nevertheless turns out to be ambiguous precisely at the point where theology *per se* must be decisive. Indeed, the ambiguity comes just at the point of theology's central affirmation. Nevertheless the link between these two theological levels, the one proper and the other broadly literary, is an important and intriguing one. The image I have chosen to specify that link or relation is "reflection." The theology found in literature is a reflected image of full-blown Christian theology, but for all that, is not without its precise significance, both for the theologian and for the critic of culture.

The distinction between these two levels of theology rests in what has been called theology's "central affirmation," and Part III will concern itself with outlining what that affirmation is and how it is arrived at. Again, the approach will be through literature but with a different program and emphasis from that of "reflected" theology. For now portions of New Testament material will be set aside from the general Western tradition in literature and a certain appraisal made of their theological force. The result of this examination will be an appeal to the strength of Christian theology as residual in *Christ*ology, suggesting that the requisite data of a fully specified Christology are found only in certain New Testament narrative documents. Nevertheless, it will be maintained that the theology implicit in Western literature generally has its peculiar claim upon our interest and credibility. What I shall have done by this point is to ask that two literary frames of reference be permitted, and finally be laid side by side: one, the general body of Western literature (including the Bible) with emphasis upon the modern; two, the general body of literature *excepting* certain biblical narratives distinguished from and set over against that general body. I shall have worked with both of these, the first in order to disclose a theology for literature, and the second in order to delineate theology proper. Reasons must then be given as to why one should be permitted two frames of reference and two theologies, the one a reflection of the other; and more importantly, the question must be raised as to whether the two referential frames and theologies can possibly relate to one another within a single arena of understanding. The attempt to respond to these questions will deal in its essence with the Christian view of revelation. The goal will be to disclose the rhythm of a functioning theology, a kind of theological "living breath" that in the end finds dogmatic theology and theology of culture not to be mutually exclusive. The sense of this study is that a catholic, inclusive integrity has always been the hallmark of the more enduring theological monuments in history, whether of Augustine or Aquinas, of Luther or Calvin, of Bultmann or Barth.

The problems of theology on the contemporary scene are severe and complex. It is hoped only that this study may lend some small assurance that the lines of traditional theology maintain a certain viability and constitute a worthwhile setting for life and for reflection.

NOTES

1. Dietrich Bonhoeffer, "Letters to a Friend," Advent II, 1943 in *Letters and Papers from Prison* (London: S.C.M. Press, 1953) 51.

2. Lou H. Silberman, "Apocalyptic Revisited: Reflections on the Thought of Albert Schweitzer," *Journal of the American Academy of Religion*, XLIV (1976) 492, 499. See also his "The Human Deed in a Time of Despair: The Ethics of Apocalyptic," in *Essays in Old Testament Ethics*, ed. J. L. Crenshaw and J. T. Willis (New York: KTAV Publishing House, 1974) 193-202.

3. See James Joyce, *A Portrait of the Artist as a Young Man* (New York: The Viking Press, 1964), ch. 3.

4. Phil. 2:7; Gal. 2:20; Romans 1:17; II Cor. 12:10; I Cor. 15:28.

5. *Confessions* X, 27, 38, tr. by A. C. Outler (Philadelphia: Westminster Press, 1955) 224. Concerning Augustine on words and the Word, see Kenneth Burke, *The Rhetoric of Religion—Studies in Logology* (Boston: Beacon Press, 1961), ch. 2.

6. Martin Luther, *Heidelberg Disputation* (Weimar Ausgabe, I, 350-365), theses 19-20. (Translation ours.)

7. See Charles A. M. Hall, *With the Spirit's Sword* (Richmond: John Knox Press, 1968) for the argument that the fundamental metaphor of Calvin's theology was that of military organization and campaign, or spiritual warfare.

8. See John Findlay, *Hegel—A Re-examination* (London: George Allen, 1958) 74.

9. For example, "The New Testament and the Hermeneutical Problem," in *The New Hermeneutic*, ed. J. M. Robinson and J. B. Cobb, Jr. (New York: Harper and Row, 1964) 111-145.

10. For example, in *God and Word*, trans. J. W. Leitch (Philadelphia: Fortress Press, 1967).

11. See examples in H. Koester and J. M. Robinson, *Trajectories Through Early Christianity* (Philadelphia: Fortress Press, 1971) 89-95, 112-113, 175-177 and *passim*; D. O. Via, Jr., *The Parables—Their Literary and Existential Dimension* (Philadelphia: Fortress Press, 1967), and *Kerygma and Come-*

dy in the New Testament: a Structuralist Approach to Hermeneutic* (Philadelphia: Fortress Press, 1975); H. Boers, *Theology Out of the Ghetto: a New Testament Exegetical Study Concerning Religious Exclusiveness* (Leiden: E. J. Brill, 1971) 9–25; N. Perrin, "Historical Criticism, Literary Criticism, and Hermeneutics: the Interpretation of the Parables of Jesus and the Gospel of Mark Today," *Journal of Religion*, LII (1972) 361–375; L. Keck, *A Future for the Historical Jesus: the Place of Jesus in Preaching and Theology* (Nashville: Abingdon Press, 1971) 243–249.

12. See Ray L. Hart, *Unfinished Man and the Imagination— Toward an Ontology and a Rhetoric of Revelation* (New York: Herder and Herder, 1968).

13. See Robert W. Funk, *Language, Hermeneutic, and Word of God* (New York: Harper and Row, 1966), and *Jesus as Precursor* (Philadelphia: Fortress Press, 1975) in *Semeia Supplements*, 2, of the Society of Biblical Literature.

14. Sallie TeSelle, *Speaking in Parables* (Philadelphia: Fortress Press, 1975).

15. For example, in New Testament studies, Norman Perrin, "Eschatology and Hermeneutics: Reflections on Method in the Interpretation of the New Testament," *Journal of Biblical Literature*, XCIII (1974) 3–14: also, *Jesus and the Language of the Kingdom* (Philadelphia: Fortress Press, 1975).

16. TeSelle, *Speaking*, 51, 81.

17. TeSelle, *Speaking*, 164–165.

18. David L. Miller, *The New Polytheism: Rebirth of the Gods and Goddesses* (New York: Harper and Row, 1974).

Part One
LANGUAGE AND LITERATURE

First- and
Second-Order Discourse   *I*

How is it possible to consider language and literature in such a way that they maintain a theological potential? The answer to such a question will clearly rest upon calling attention to certain powers and functions of language in general since it is obvious that all language and all literature do not refer to God by direct purpose or intent. Consequently, if any successful move from literature toward theology is to be made, it must be done formally, by calling attention to particular ways in which language is arranged and used. Those arrangements, it will be argued, are theological by implication, regardless of the content or outlook of the piece. In other words, a certain circumstance and rhythm in the function of language must be seen as invoking, pointing to, indeed presenting the true reality of things. If it appears that language is genuinely a medium by which reality comes to focus, then a theological dimension of this fact is at least open to inquiry. From such a point, appropriate theological matters may be pursued in their own terms, to see more carefully what sort of theology may find "reflection" in literature.

All the same, it is no small matter to propose that language truly invokes what is real. Is not language after all a mere tissue of convenience that human speech lays over brute reality, a fragile network that easily passes away? Interestingly, the twentieth century has shown itself more willing than some segments of the nineteenth to consider language as an actual bearer of reality. Perhaps Nietzsche in the late nineteenth century stands as an example of the ironic position that casts doubt on the nature and veracity of language. The separation of word-images from the "things themselves" seemed to him and others to undermine the validity of statements. Nietzsche's ironic preoccupation with the "lies" of language is cousin to others' concern for ideology—as with Marx—and to the desire to reduce varied patterns of language to simplified secondary schemes of interpretation. Such movements as phenomenology, expressionism, and language analysis have in the twentieth-century attempted to resist the distrust of the language spectrum, just as Owen Barfield's book, *Saving the Appearances*, has inveighed against a tendency since the middle ages to resolve sensuous representations into mere objective structures.[1] Perhaps indeed the true, if limited, presence of the real is qualitatively indistinguishable from the unique surfaces of our articulation—our living language. Thus Virgil C. Aldrich speaks of

> . . . this notion of language as a constitutive form, a form of life, modifying things even in the field of perception, not just conception. . . . [Thus] reality is realized in the forms of language-in-action, as character is in a face or in a pattern of human actions, of which language-using is the greatest and most refined.[2]

Has the theorist, then, long been probing for a substance beneath the appearance, while reality is articulate in the appearance itself? If so, the implication is to be more attentive to surfaces and less impatient with mysteries. The gift of clarity may thereby all the more readily surprise us.

The concern here, then, is to examine the patterns of linguistic movement that promise to disclose reality in some proper sense. The first step in such an examination is to consider the rhythm of language formation.

The Breadth and Richness of Language

The quality of language considered at its foundations may be designated by the word "richness." The roots of human language (certainly psychological, and perhaps historical) are far more dense and complex than the relatively abstract signs and signals that order our affairs in adult modern life. At these roots, the abstract and the concrete are very little sorted out; language at this level is therefore poetic, fulsome, "rich." Owen Barfield calls attention to the high degree of abstraction even in our simple, physical word "cut"; by contrast, an early human society may have employed a single concrete word to mean, "I cut this flesh with joy in order to sacrifice."[3] Regardless of the actual history of language, the point is clear: to invoke a complex and concrete situation requires the concrete density either of a word or a group of words.

Nevertheless, a sorting-out or secondary reflective process must take place as cultural occasions become more reductive and flexible. The adequacy of a "sorted out" language structure to articulate an immense variety of common situations is what I mean by "breadth." Consider our own written language: twenty-six simple letters can be arranged and rearranged to suit countless areas of common or specialized discourse. And notice that deciding upon the twenty-six basic letters themselves is a highly sophisticated refinement of thought and not at all "elemental." One problem, of course, with this breadth is that each specialized linguistic area tends to become reduced and monotonously self-enclosed. Or the opposite occurs; all situations begin to become alike. Then language yearns for richness once again. In the rhythm of breadth and richness and again breadth, like a powerful life-pulsation, the phenomenon of language articulates the history of a culture. This lively tension corresponds in its double-sidedness to two major, enduring interests: breadth indicates increased formal clarity, linguistic and conceptual analysis, publicability; richness suggests the recovery of primary communication, "understanding," total orientation and insight. Notice that the terms "objective" and "subjective" do not easily correlate with breadth and richness. Analytical breadth is object-oriented and therefore appears objective, but since grounded in human thought-forms and manipulability, may be highly subjective. Imaginative richness engages the subject's own existential concerns and would seem clearly subjective; but insight that includes "artistic distance" may recover a whole new clarity on the human being's real place in the world and therefore include a kind of "objectivity." The hope is that in finding the appropriate rhythm of breadth-richness the anguish of sheer objectivity or subjectivity is overcome.

At the risk of over-simplification, one may call the phase of richness first-order language and the phase of breadth second-order language. Second-order may also be called discursive, analytical, or steno-language. The gross difference between the two is easily illustrated. A first-order function of language evokes an extensive, concrete perspective on things in general, as in the lines:

> The sky seemed so small that winter day,
> A dirty light on a lifeless world,
> Contracted like a withered stick.[4]

A second-order response to the same setting that attracted the poet might be as follows: "The forecast for today is partly cloudy and cold with highs in the upper 30's." Also, each of the two orders is subject to further subdivision. For example, the language that itself reflects upon language is second-order, even if the language it reflects *upon* also is second-order. Nevertheless, the simpler division may be adequate for our purposes. Note also that neither of these phases exists without at least the implicit presence or potential of the other.

An important principle in searching out the nature of language is that the students of language are not permitted to lift themselves outside the historical rhythm of breadth-richness-breadth, as if one could be a pure spectator. Surely not, for language is the thinker's own natural element in which alone he or she both survives and reflects. Therefore, an "ideal" starting place, such as an actual historical beginning of language, or a beginning in subjective consciousness will not be sought. Indeed, Paul Ricoeur has been helpful in suggesting that reflection commences, not with Descartes' subjective "I," but with "situated" thinking, with the fullness of present written and spoken language in which we are immersed, asking that it be "recollected" so as to include its still present foundations.[5] Ricoeur proposes then to relate current speech to its "remembered" primary symbols. Some examples for him of such symbols are water (threat or renewal), deviation (sin), exile (alienation), stain (defilement).[6] Nevertheless, I shall risk another step deeper still, beyond primary symbols to a first "gesture" or emergence of reality in general. The caution needed in pursuing such "recollected" roots is that no such primal emergence of reality and language, investigated by philosophy, is ever actually a-historical, insulated from a stream of complex tradition.

Now if one is assuredly to think about language *from within* language, as our native element, then it appears that part of the approach must be to penetrate to a first-order level already presupposed in daily speech and even in our very language of inquiry. Not that first order is inherently superior to second, but that our ordinary means-ends existence "forgets" foundational language. Nor can the question of first-order language be asked apart from the question of reality. Though our distinctions here are not as complex as those of Robert Funk, nevertheless his point is appropriate:

> . . . a second-order linguistic activity does not have adequate resources to enable it to arbitrate over first-order linguistic activity . . . Philosophy must itself investigate the grounds of first-order language if it wishes to dispute language and/or reality.
> To put the matter abruptly, language and understanding have to be made to recoil upon the reality to which they allegedly refer.[7]

Such an approach to language thus clearly differs from "verification analysis" (the view that only those statements are meaningful which are subject to empirical, scientific verification) and from "functional analysis" (the external attempt to locate criteria of truth appropriate to the functioning of different realms of discourse).

If we thus commence not without, but within living language, are we then forever and inescapably immersed in passing appearances and phenomena? Is there no transcendence, no detached observer-point from which the truth-of-it-all comes clear? Assuredly there is a transcendence, though not the detached observer sort. The capacity for transcendence—for meaningful "openness," for "room" to live, and reflect, and have being—is one of the miracles of language itself, language that Martin Heidegger has called a "house of being." Transcendent "openness" appropriate to human beings is as natural as breathing except when we reflect upon it—just as breathing itself becomes deliberate only when we ponder it. Transcendence that attempts to get "behind" and "beyond" the crisp, self-forgetting articulations of our language is a flight into horror. By contrast, a life that knows both first- and second-order linguistic awareness in productive tension may open out upon the natural gift of freedom within our human setting. When language is functionally whole and well in its rhythm of breadth-richness, a person has a sense of energetic membership in a significant world. But one is also prepared for the fact that this sense of lively reality may move into crisis—as language itself is subject to crises—and much of one's learning is a learning to venture that risk.

First-Order Language and Primal Gesture

Our aim is to consider language in relation to reality, and our first step has been to note an important rhythm of language in its disclosure of the "real," a rhythm of richness and breadth, first and second order. For simple illustration, say that human well-being includes both heavily second-order statements like, "the descriptive terms are highly complex"; but also "gathered" first-order statements like, "Repent! for the kingdom of heaven is at hand," or, "Shall I compare thee

I

32

to a summer's day?" Let us ponder the first-order kind of language a bit further.

Language as it originates with and for the infant, what may be called the "primal gesture," is part of first-order manifestation. Here R. G. Collingwood helps by showing that original linguistic moments are not those of detached, "useful" concepts, but rather of a rich, dense joining of things. Indeed, he is generally against the notion that language is best understood as "used," like a separable tool.[8] The origin of language for Collingwood coincides with a rude, emerging self-and-world communication. Movements of the human being that are automatic and merely psychical (like a baby's first hunger cry) may be signals to an observer, yet they are not the infant's language; but the first flicker of truly conscious self-awareness is at once both conscious *and* linguistic, if only in the barest germinal mode. The automatic cry wondrously becomes the "angry" cry.[9] Collingwood sets his analysis within the framework of subjective idealism; he is inquiring psychologically concerning consciousness, whereas we have been inquiring directly of "reality," of which subjective consciousness is presumably one component. Nevertheless his point is a welcome one. Collingwood is saying that when a human being first expresses an "awakenedness" to things-'round-about, and to having a relation to those things both receptive and assertive—as a self—linguistic consciousness has appeared. Construe his point this way: linguistic reality emerges when the outline of a self-and-world relation emerges, of which language provides the structure. Thus the following may be proposed to serve as a working definition of language: *Gestures of community disclosing individuals and the world to one another.* We are still speaking, certainly, of "situated" communication. Therefore, insofar as language is not mere "chatter," then the *real world of our lives* finds both disclosure and articulation in language.

I have proposed that language is a gesture of community. Just what constitutes that "primal" gesture at the biographical onset of language, typical of the world of the infant, though resident through life? Even the infant's cry signals language by virtue of a certain quality within it. Perhaps one element of the primal gesture is the subtle act of "taking heed." To heed something means to move from blind participation under necessity into a state of being conscious: intending, evaluating, proposing. Yet taking heed is not the whole primal language gesture, but only one side of it, for considered alone, the phrase suggests that one's language and world are entirely produced by oneself. Taking heed is co-incident with the other side of this "gesture," which is the "presenting itself" of things in general. Consider the sentence: "The situation presented itself to me in a flash of realization." That statement, descriptive of some limited circumstance, recollects the much simpler case of every primal gesture. The awakening movement, *the presenting-itself to the taking-heed*, the coming-into-focus of things to the grasping of them, *is* the primal gesture, the germ of language.

Consider a play on the phrase, "to present itself." When a situation pre-*sents* itself to our taking heed, it also "*pres*-ents" itself, i.e., makes itself present. The structural gesture we are discussing, the taking-heed to the presenting-itself, is thus a *structure of presence*, which "presence" is in turn the quality of the real. The primal gesture, therefore, is a framework for the real, at the same time that it is made up of a reciprocal relation between two factors: the taking-heed and the presenting-itself. Thus, as stated of language, its gesture does originate in and disclose the real (i.e., "present-ness"); its primal moment is a fullness that tends to incorporate the richness of things into an extensive unity.

Language deeply "remembers" itself by strictly attending to the primal fullness of "presence" at its roots. What later will be sorted out as mind, body, and objects of attention began as a rich wholeness, all contained within a "packed" perspective for our sensing, touching, feeling, seeing, etc. Language refreshes itself by imaginatively re-opening that full perspective of "presence" and letting its total scene of reference be renewed. Now poetry (or literature generally) is just that formal mode of language which recalls "presence." Denise Levertov, for one, has been most helpful in noting that poetry need not always refer to concrete things, but must always provide "presentness."[10] Thus poetry, as first-order language, renews the primal gesture, a moment of wholeness in the rich "presence" of things.

At this point, a voice of objection is likely to be heard: what about the simple second-order function of naming objects?—an apple, a cloud, a symphony. Isn't this also a means of getting at what is "real"? The answer is yes, although the condition of reality is altered. Neither first nor second order holds an inherent superiority, the one over the other, for presenting and articulating reality. Either one can go wrong. The simple naming of objects can be narrow and blinding. But the first-order invoking of a whole field of "presence" can be imaginatively wandering and illusory. Only a certain rhythm between the two holds promise of success in the pursuit of reality. Yet the reason for emphasizing first-order, foundational language is that our century has given overwhelming prestige to second-order, analytical discourse. The poetic moments of "getting our bearings on things," inclusive of ourselves, have been largely left to informal chance. Yet the metaphoric and childlike moments of poetry, of foundational language, are equally essential to sanity as are the moments of analytical organization.

Reality as Present and Receding

Thus far, in the quest for "reality through language," priority has been given to first-order, foundational discourse, the impressive moment of refreshment when our total bearing within things is illumined by a dense, rich gesture. Many telling linguistic moments of foundational "presence" come to mind: "Know thyself"; "a certain man had two sons . . ."; "the heart has reasons that the reason does not know"; "workers of the world, unite . . ." Nevertheless, even in impressive first-order statements, an important qualification obtains that must be mentioned.

Presence, and therefore the real, stands forth in foundational language, yet simultaneously remains imperfect or one step removed from itself, as it does so. In other words, *lan-*

guage gestures arbitrarily limit "present-ness," or the real (giving it a distinct or particular shape before us) in the very act of allowing it to come to light. In this connection one must acknowledge the force of Martin Heidegger's work on language and Being, and the very important "difference" or "separation" that he affirms between Being and "things" (or "beings") around us.[11] The point of this difference is difficult in Heidegger and the attempt to understand it still goes on. Nevertheless, the core of the problem is simple enough. The reality or presence of beings, "things," suggests also the presence of Being as such, or causes one to wonder at the "reality" that provides beings their being. Says Heidegger:

> . . . Only man of all the beings experiences, when called upon by the voice of Being, *the wonder of all wonders: that* beings *are.*[12]

This single Heideggerian sentence nicely packages the entire experience to which I wish to call attention. A first-order language moment has an element of anxiety in it. The "things" that have been taken for granted are suddenly "heeded" in all their wonder—for they *are*, but surely they might not be. (Recall Miranda's "O brave new world, That has such people in't!" and Prospero's response, " 'Tis new to thee."[13]) That moment "to thee" is a marked signal of Heidegger's Being, the amazing *are*-ness of things. We at no time have a greater sense of the deeply real than in a moment of the fresh and striking, yet tenuous reality of things themselves. The characteristic, continuing tension of our existence is just this: the moments of widest consciousness and most inclusive "presence," of richest insight and disclosure, are the moments of deepest uneasiness, the hiddenness of the real as such. We are amazed at how things really present themselves to us; yet their presence also shows their deployment to be incomplete; their rich patterns devolve into something unclear, a presentness that is hidden and indirect.

A comment on this irony may refer again to the analysis of first-order language in the form of primal gesture. Without incipient language there can be no self-presentation of the

I

36

real. Yet this very linguistic structure must be a realization of self-amidst-things, which involves a certain division. There can be no community among self and things unless they are first distinguishable. That distinction, making way for the first linguistic structure or relation (and for articulate "presence"), is also a break or fissure in "presence." The real is somehow limited or marred by coming to articulation. Yet if we discard the limiting gesture and identify absolutely with pure "presence," the articulation of language vanishes and the wonder of the real is obliviated. In the same way, Heidegger comments on linguistic structure and this ironic "receding-disclosure" of the truly real in his treatment of the Heraclitean *Logos*. As W. J. Richardson comments, ". . . we are not allowed to forget that nonconcealment is permeated with negativity, for *lethe* (concealing) not only is prior to *a-letheia* (unconcealing) but remains intrinsic to it at all times."[14] Thus we as human beings stand "in-between," knowing the presence of ourselves and of real things about us, even as reality nevertheless recedes from its own structure of "presentation."

A good focus on this state of things occurs when Sophocles' Oedipus, having fatefully persisted in seeking his origins, stands at the brink of knowing from the shepherd the truth about himself. William Lynch has pointed to the lines:

Shepherd: My king,
    How shall I tell a story of such horror?
Oedipus: And how shall I hear it? . . .[15]

The real impinges terribly, just before language gives it the force of reality. Yet the words told and the deeds that follow, while they disclose "how things are," focus reality as particular moments: of a suicide, of self-blinding, of exile, while the *fullness* of the occasion has receded one step backward. The same situation obtains, though with reverse effect, in Sophocles' late drama, *Oedipus at Colonus*. Here the accursed figure of the wandering Oedipus becomes somehow a benign "presence," the veiled reality of love and favor from the gods. How this can be is not finally solved since the gestures of community limit as they disclose. Language must seek out its own roots in order to remember the fullness of reality, but it encounters something incommensurable, undisclosed in the very success of this undertaking.

I have alluded to Heidegger's pronouncements on this "disclosed-undisclosed" effect. At the risk of distortion, I have nevertheless not adopted his term "Being" because of its persistent English flavor of wide, generalized abstraction. Rather I wish to persist with the term "real" or "reality," even though it also presents problems. (Heidegger devotes an extended section to distinguishing "Being" from "Reality," the latter of which he associates with the error of subject-object realism in Western thought.[16]) Put in the terms used here, reality is present as things-in-general; yet these things, even in a gathered first-order account, do not fully disclose "the real." Yet the terminology is not as important as the demands made upon thought by the ironic circumstance. One movement of thought knows reality present as things; but another movement knows reality as *more than* those things that are here-and-now present. Walter J. Lowe sees Heidegger's thought as pursuing just such a forward-moving oscillation:

> . . . One can discern two moments of thought which remain characteristic of Heidegger throughout his career. There is on the one hand a relentless drive toward ever larger explanatory *contexts* . . . But accompanying this initial thrust of Heidegger's thought is another moment, an openness to *discontinuity*, which radically transmutes the first. . . . Thus while the first moment suggests ever-widening circles of context, eliciting a theme of continuity, this second cautions that such suggestions may be deceptive and that as one moves to fuller explanatory contexts there may be exacted the price of ontological discontinuity. This caution is of course the ontological difference—but now we have it not as a slogan to bludgeon all comers, but as one moment in the systole and diastole of living thought.[17]

Reflection that considers the rhythms of language and reality must allow for this movement of continuity-separation. First-order language brings reality to wondrous "gathered focus"; but even as it does so, the "looseness" of the reality of things means that second-order work will be done, that the definiteness of things as such will come to replace the power of their original togetherness. The inclusively real must then be hearkened for once again.

Horizon, Time, and World

No point in this chapter is more crucial to the effort of the study as a whole than the one just made concerning the articulate presentation, yet inherent separateness, of reality vis-à-vis our daily language. To consider reality is to consider the reality of *things*; yet things cannot finally "fix" reality's presence. Our search, then, to relate language to reality, having started out "situated" within our own language-world, has come upon both a yes and a no. The reason for the yes and the no may be clearer if we consider now the importance of "horizon" and "time."

The term "horizon" is of importance in giving the notion of foundational language its proper setting. In the first place, note that every conceivable utterance involves a certain perspective or background by which it is properly understood. To call attention to a box lying on the table assumes much, since the eye sees only three sides of the six-sided container. To say, "there is a box," includes a perspective that interprets the three sides actually visible—a rather safe perspective, in this case, and easily tested.[18] The intelligent perspective that knows a box out of only three sides may be called a horizon. Or, define the term this way: *Horizon means the framework of understanding and expectancy belonging to every linguistic moment.* I have spoken already of the primal gesture as a structure of presence. That structure of presentness is certainly a horizon. Nevertheless, the term horizon can apply to more than the primal gesture of things as they first present themselves. A horizon operates with so isolable a thing as the box on the table, or so deeply inclusive a thing as primal emergence. For that reason, a further distinction is needed in the discussion of horizon: when the horizon of an utterance is simply a context itself isolable for scrutiny, its limited nature may be identified by calling it a *contextual horizon*. For example, "There is a box" entails the contextual horizon of the other three sides, easily verified. But when the horizon of an utterance includes the speaker's own existence and its meaning, it may be called a *horizon proper*. For instance, if a person says, "I'm very tired," a contextual horizon would suggest simply a hard day's work or an overly busy week. But if a horizon proper is intended, the speaker is calling into question his ability to live on as such, with overtones of dread and potential death.

The discussion of linguistic richness requires some further dealing with its horizon. If the primal gesture, the awakening of what is real, includes a structural horizon for the "presence" of things generally, what is that horizon? Consider what has been said of things coming to present-ness in first-order language. The real discloses itself in the same instant that it slips back from direct fullness. Now direct, unqualified "presence" would dissolve all distinctions, including human awareness of it. Conversely, emerging reality (the ebbing of full "presence") *never* allows for the full resolution of all things, but maintains distinctions and antagonisms lest its own force be obliterated. Clearly, the horizon of "presence" that never permits a final resolution must be the time-space continuum, infinite by any rational standard, since we cannot conceptualize such a standard as outside of time and space. And since we are speaking here of horizon proper, the crucial factor in the continuum for human existence is time. Space opens apprehendably to human beings on all sides, but the fore-side of time, even the next moment, is uncertain. *The horizon of what is real, of things' presenting themselves, is time.* The framework by which we interpret, understand, and form expectations of things at large is the framework of temporality, the passing nature of anything that can be named. And this is the case, despite this horizon's provision of indirect, seemingly non-temporal "presence" or authenticity. Here another allusion to Heidegger may be helpful, namely, that time plays a highly important role in his thought pre-

cisely because of a problem with the notion of "presence."
For Heidegger, the presence of things' "presenting-themselves" led to the error (in Greek and Western metaphysics)
of preoccupation with *present* time. Metaphysics took up the
question of relating a present subject to a present object, and
thus statically conceived the problem of ontology.[19] To say
that the horizon of things' "presenting-themselves" is *time* is
immediately, and rightly, to complicate the meaning of "presence." Now perhaps it can be seen clearly why reality is
present in and through things, and yet is not fully so. As
present time is qualified by past and future, so "presence"
is qualified by the inevitable change that time implies. Reality is present in and through things, but its deeper "presence" must take account of time and change. Thus the presence of the real is true; yet that presence is also but a signal
of a deeper level of presence, one that embraces at their
source our past, present, and future.[20] The horizon of time
makes inevitable the continuing disclosure-undisclosure of
what is real. We are in the presence of reality, yet the tenuous quality of present time means that we have no immediate
access to the fullness of that presence.

Furthermore, since time is the horizon of "waking" reality,
such that the real itself is never manifest fully or wholly, then
clearly the world never manifests itself as quite the same from
time to time or from viewpoint to viewpoint. Foundational
language discloses the world, but limits its perfection in the
act of so-doing. By world here is meant *the totality of all
manifest things, strangely one in "presence," yet various and
unresolved in their interrelationships.* Since time is the horizon of the world, that world is necessarily unresolved, moving, changing, variously conceived. This is why it may be said
that a self-and-world relation is "of a distinct kind," or that
things come to be "in a certain way" in our human world.
The incompleteness of all language, no matter how primal in
authority, prevents full rest and satisfaction; but an advantage is the perspectival shape given to things that allows
analyses, sorting out, formulations, comparions, contrasts—
i.e., reasoned elaboration. The foundational gestures of lan-

guage offer us the world in time such that we are invited to sort out its meaning, even though a world within the time-horizon is not fully available. (The world is real, but not in a finished sense; it bespeaks "presence" without solving its nature.) Thus language can sort out the world up to certain limits despite the latter's moving, dense turbulence.

In addition, foundational language is *performative* language, bringing-to-be what it "says," since it constitutes the structural presence of what it articulates.[21] But if it is thus performative, such language must constitute an *event* rather than a fixed status. In so doing, it finds its functional identity vis-a-vis time: the "receding" character of language, its unique function of real disclosure always just incomplete, equals the essence of time, i.e., time's motion forward; there is always "more." So an event takes place *in* time. But an event does have its character and shape that can be reflected upon. Just so, foundational language envisions a kind of whole that diffuses time, that slows it down for us by allowing us to "get our bearings" within it, by providing a traceable perspective, a profile of meaning.

Second-Order Language: Literature

Thus far language and reality have been related by (1) dealing with our "situated," everyday language, (2) pointing out an essential first- and second-order rhythm within that language, (3) appealing to the particular "gathered" disclosure of reality through first-order language, in time, and (4) finding specific terms for that instance of first-order discourse called the primal gesture, or the "germ" of language: the taking-heed to the presenting-itself.

Clearly, something further needs to be said to relate (2) and (3) more fully. A general description of first-order language has been given, but what more exactly is its nature other than the quintessential "primal gesture"? In particular, how does second-order language play its part in the rhythm and make certain levels of first-order language possible? To pursue these matters will bring us into the arena of rhetoric and literature and to the ways in which reality is embodied in them.

Recall that first-order language presents us with what is richly suggestive though indefinite, while second-order language presents us with what is definite and therefore formal. Then to put the thesis of this section very simply: sophisticated first-order language (not the primal gesture) is actually a function of second-order language in special patterns—sometimes even in disarray.

What, then, is meant by second-order? If primal imaginative language is one kind of first-order expression, then second-order language has to do with the endless rational sorting-out and "unpacking" that human beings attempt within the world. The development of second-order language is characterized by two procedures: (1) a systematizing of abstract similarities out of the wide generality of things to produce ideas; (2) a proliferating of separate objects, each unique in its concreteness, to produce isolated things. Primal gestures that captured the near fullness of things are replaced by abstract symbols and public statements of fact. Do the generalizations and the facts emerge, present themselves as real, in the same way as the gathered primal situation? *In a sense* they do, in that they themselves were implicit in that first emergence. To that degree, second-order expression fits under our working definition of language, "gestures of community that disclose." Still, an additional move of "culling out" generalities, objects, and public states of affairs must take place as second-order language becomes explicit.

Considerable uncertainty haunts the question of how exhaustive our wider ranges of facts and ideas may be. How fully and well do they articulate the profound structures of presence that initially greet human beings? The weakness of countless linguistic systems in history (of philosophy and theology, of government, of economy) suggest how much of the primal potential must have been omitted in each of them, even more than what is incomplete in the primal gesture itself. Evidently, the ideas and facts proffered within the first-order potential have been biased time after time by humanity's peculiar interests. Explicating the real has not been a notoriously successful project in history.

But the concern here is to note that second-order language is inherently appropriate, even if subject to distortion (as indeed are both orders of language). The point is indeed to see how second-order is related to first-order. Poetry has been mentioned already as invoking present-ness and therefore as somehow constituting a first-order language, recalling the primal gesture. Now add the remark that poetry (and literature generally) does this by highly civilized means and by always adapting second-order discourse. Clearly, the dense primal gesture is only one part of first-order expression and is experienced largely by infants, while the usual adult world carries a vast complexity of secondary materials. Most first-order expression is thereby inevitably a function of second-order terms. For second-order discourse and experience have a capacity for "remembering"—calling up into present articulation—the perspective of their foundations. In any case, even the most sparse secondary data do not snap the threads that tie them to a first-order horizon. Statistics analyzing the infant mortality rate are far removed from the groans of a mother in labor. Yet the former does not entirely "forget" the latter. That link is a crucial one for first-order language and for literature.

The thrust of literary language is to adopt known words with countless secondary meanings and even detached "uses," and so employ them that the text as a whole "gathers" a wide presentness of things, implicating the primal gesture. Thus the language of literature sets out to arrange layer after layer of common meanings in such a way that, without being altered in themselves, their new order convokes the world to a condition nearer the state of its origins. In one sense, first-order language is second-order in an act of "return." Still, this is no simple return, since a definite "move" takes place from the primal gesture to the sophisticated *re-presentation* of it through unpretentious, even alien materials. This re-presentation through secondary materials marks a forward process away from elemental primacy, a movement that could not have occurred had not secondary discourse made its contribution. Again, everyday reality through time requires both

I

richness *and* breadth for its articulation. (Here, then, is a question for Heidegger, whose "glimpses" of Being, though in process, all seem on a par; whereas we may feel that with Homer, Virgil, Dante, something genuinely new opens up, even though "recalling" elemental foundations.) The important "plus" is that multifaceted, secondary language can retain what it has achieved and still recoil upon itself to the level of its forgotten roots.

Consider some first-order literary moments and their language:

> Cast aside dull books and thought;
> Sweet is folly, sweet is play . . .

> When I consider how my light is spent
> Ere half my days in this dark world and wide . . .

> Whose woods these are I think I know.
> His house is in the village, though . . .[22]

Though each poem should really be quoted in its entirety, the opening lines assist with the matter in hand. All the lines offer simple, universal words. The first is a carefree, reckless gesture; the second uses the known words in markedly figurative ways; but notice that the third is in one sense indistinguishable from a plain secondary statement of fact, yet surely begins to gather its "world." The third poem is likely not greater than the second, but for our purposes, the interest is in a second-order statement able to play a first-order role without shifting an iota of its secondary form. In this case, the incidence of rhyme and rhythmic regularity betrays what otherwise might be a simple statement of fact. Within a single sentence a significant world begins to cluster about these "woods" and the distant house and owner. In this connection notice that even a statement of everyday factual information can carry deep first-order impact, e.g., "The tumor is benign." Granted those four words assume much that is unspoken, they are nevertheless capable of summoning one's world into gathering and into new perspective. First- and second-order functions are all the more compelling when they coincide so exactly.

Perhaps it can now be said that first and second order are not pure, theoretical categories such that any statement belongs clearly to one or the other. They are rather tendencies both belonging to a greater or lesser degree to every utterance. A statement is first-order insofar as it tends toward *performative force in gathering and implicating the world,* is second order insofar as it tends toward *formal clarity about some part of the world.* Interest is heightened when both of these coincide in a single utterance. And as regards our everyday lives, an appropriate tension, rhythm, or co-inhering of both orders of expression is essential to well-being and to the clear persistence, yet veiled character, of reality.

I

NOTES

1. Owen Barfield, *Saving the Appearances* (New York: Harcourt, Brace and World, n.d.) e.g., 142–147.

2. Virgil C. Aldrich, "Self-Consciousness," in *Insight and Vision —Essays in Philosophy in Honor of Radoslav Andrea Tsanoff* (Rice University Studies, LI/4, 1965) 15.

3. In *Poetic Diction: A Study in Meaning*, third edition (Middletown: Wesleyan University Press, 1973) 79.

4. From Wallace Stevens, "Two Illustrations that the World is What You Make of It," in Rolfe Humphries, ed., *New Poems by American Poets* (New York: Ballantine Books, 1953) 153.

5. See Paul Ricoeur, *The Symbolism of Evil*, trans. E. Buchanan (Boston: Beacon Press, 1969) 348–349.

6. Ricoeur, *Symbolism*, 18.

7. Robert Funk, *Language, Hermeneutic, and Word of God* (New York: Harper and Row, 1966) 5.

8. R. G. Collingwood, *The Principles of Art* (Oxford: The Clarendon Press, 1938) ch. XI, secs. 1–3. See also I. A. Richards, *The Philosophy of Rhetoric* (New York: Oxford University Press, 1936) 31, 51–54.

9. Collingwood, *Principles*, 236–237.

10. In Tony Stoneburner, ed., *Parable, Myth, and Language* (Cambridge: The Church Society for College Work, Autumn, 1968) 20.

11. I am indebted to Walter J. Lowe, "Heidegger and the Theologians: Is there an Ontological Difference?" (an unpublished paper, Maryville, Tennessee, for the Society for Religion in Higher Education, 1974), for impressively and clearly showing Heidegger's relation to the point I am making.

12. From "What is Metaphysics," in Martin Heidegger, *Existence and Being*, trans. D. Scott *et al.* (London: Vision Press, 1949) 386. (*Was ist Metaphysik?* 8th ed. 46.) See J. Robinson, J. Cobb, eds., *The Later Heidegger and Theology* (New York: Harper and Row, 1963) 38. The translation of the above statement is Robinson's.

13. *The Tempest*, Act V, Sc. i, 183–185.

14. W. J. Richardson, *Heidegger—Through Phenomenology to Thought* (The Hague: Martinus Nijhoff, 1963) 492. See also comparable statements on p. 497. Heidegger's piece is "Logos (Heraklit, Fragment 50)," in *Vortraege und Aufsaetze* (Pfullingen: G. Neske, 1954) 207–229. See also E. Cassirer, *Language*, vol. I of *The Philosophy of Symbolic Forms*, trans. R. Manheim (New Haven: Yale University Press, 1953) 150, on the work of J. G. Hamann, who insisted that "reason is language," and yet found that "these depths are still shrouded in darkness."

15. *Oedipus the King*, trans. K. Cavander (San Francisco: Chandler, 1961) 36–37. Fr. Lynch's remark was in, as far as I know, an unpublished lecture, Emory University, 1967.

16. Martin Heidegger, *Being and Time*, trans. J. Macquarrie and E. Robinson (New York: Harper and Row, 1962) VI (43), 244–255.

17. Lowe, "Heidegger," 13–14.

18. See E. D. Hirsch, *Validity in Interpretation* (New Haven: Yale University Press, 1967) 221.

19. Heidegger, *Being and Time*, 47–48.

20. See Lowe, "Heidegger," p. 8: "In describing this extasis [of time] Heidegger retains the term 'presence,' but it is presence of a more fundamental sort. Thus there evolves a discrimination of levels . . ."

21. Funk, *Language*, 26–28.

22. Successively the opening lines from "Invitation to the Dance" (anon.) and John Milton, "On His Blindness," in G. B. Woods, *et al.*, *The Literature of England* (Chicago: Scott, Foresman and Company, 1941) I, 169, 647; and Robert Frost, "Stopping by Woods on a Snowy Evening," in *Selected Poems* (New York: Holt, Rinehart, and Winston, 1963) 140.

Metaphor, Symbol,
And Narrative

Several factors have been important in the discussion so far. The consideration of language has adopted a viewpoint "situated" within language as the structure of our everyday reality. From such a standpoint, a relation of some sort between language and reality is simply assumed, for it would be pointless to say that all our purposes, movements, decisions, projections are "unreal," or have no real consequences about them. Secondly, it has been noted that to adopt time as the arena of language means that the very reality we have thus grasped is imperfectly presented to us. Our very confidence in what we know, awakened in a moment of realization, triggers a "gap" of uneasiness about how things are truly real. Finally, it has been held that working to optimize this disclosing-concealing tension (an apparently inevitable accompaniment of a perceptive life) is the productive interplay between first- and second-order levels of language, nourishing and correcting one another. An example of excellent interplay is imaginative literature (second-order terms in first-order function); and not surprisingly, I wish to argue that successful literature does probe reality, that it is neither mere decoration, nor fancy, nor primarily "what-if." To approach literature in these terms suggests first a consideration of certain points in rhetoric.

Metaphor

> Besides the neutral expression that she wore when she was alone, Mrs. Freeman had two others, forward and reverse, that she used for all her human dealings . . .
>
> —Flannery O'Connor[1]
>
> . . . nothing in the world is as whole as a broken heart . . .
>
> —Elie Wiesel[2]
>
> Everything is grace . . .
>
> —Georges Bernanos[3]

According to the terminology already laid out, a metaphor is one of those instances of a secondary linguistic cluster that assumes a first-order function. Metaphor is thereby more than image, or more involved and complex than an image. An image *per se* may be self-contained: "light," "sea," "tower," "child." In the rhetoric of metaphor two images or references play on one another so as to suggest a third something that is more than either. Metaphoric function thus contains an element of mystery and surprise. Why does it "work"? In the first example above, how does coupling Mrs. Freeman's expression with the automotive "forward, neutral, and reverse" explore so quickly and deftly her identity?

One view of metaphor distinguishes two classes: the epiphor and the diaphor.[4] (The coupling of normally disparate factors in the metaphor is true in either case.) With the epiphor, a generally known "subject" has laid upon it (*epi-*) a striking "modifier," casting the subject into a new light. In the above example from O'Connor, the generally understood subject, "expression," is identified with automotive gears, thus focusing and intensifying Mrs. Freeman. (Some authorities use "tenor" for the subject and "vehicle" for the modifier.) In the diaphor, one element is not distinctively subject and the other, modifier; rather the two are simply juxtaposed and the subject of the metaphor is entertained by reading through (*dia-*) the unusual conjunction. A textbook example often cited is from Ezra Pound's "In a Station of the Metro":

> The apparition of these faces in the crowd;
> Petals on a wet, black bough.[5]

Probably the most helpful analysis is to think of metaphors as usually maintaining some of each operation, epiphor and diaphor, at different levels of the rhetorical figure. Consider this example:

> O Negro slaves, dark purple ripened plums,
> Squeezed, and bursting in the pine-wood air,
> Passing, before they stripped the old tree bare
> One plum was saved for me, one seed becomes
>
> An everlasting song, a singing tree,
> Caroling softly souls of slavery . . .[6]

In the case of "slaves" and "plums," the epiphorical impact on "slaves" is clear; yet an impact is made on "plums" as well. Indeed the poet regards the actual plum tree in a highly special way, until he sees in it also an epiphor, a "singing tree." The tree plus the remembered slaves foster between them a unique and suggestive reality—a world of sad, small deaths and pine-wood smell. More is offered than a rational similitude from plums to slaves. If, as Wheelwright says, epiphor hints at significance, while diaphor creates presence, then something of the latter's positive disclosure surely functions in Toomer's lines.[7]

The diaphoric element gets near to the heart of metaphor. To say that the diaphor "creates presence" quickly recalls the discussion in the previous chapter concerning language as the articulate structure of present-ness, more pointedly in its first-order function. Metaphor is therefore a rhetorical figure that peculiarly demonstrates foundational language, engaging us with an "angle" on things that challenges our life-orientation. A metaphor may therefore be distinguished from a simile by the quality of its performance; for a simile is a comparison that either is simply reasonable within secondary discourse, or is so open-ended as to "leave us cold." "What a tower of strength he has been!" has the syntax of a metaphor; but by constant use the quality has worn thin to the point of mere rational comparison of the "sturdy and comforting." On the other hand, the statement, "His brother meets you like a little mouse" (despite the linking word "like") has more rich metaphoric suggestion to it: a specific aura of the timid, the small, the supplicating. I. A. Richards points to surprising adjectival uses that open the metaphoric effect: giddy brink, jovial wine.[8] Such a phrase "gathers" a whole situation around us with its suggestive facets and levels.

Metaphor, and more especially diaphor, demonstrates a striking example of what we have analyzed as second-order terms functioning with first-order effect. A metaphor, then, is a certain rhetorical figure whose impact involves an entire arrangement of language, time, reality, and person. To involve four such large elements in the metaphoric structure does not mean, of course, that very many metaphors are earthshaking. A metaphor may do even considerable injustice to those four factors that it touches. Rather, to note this arrangement is simply to clarify the essence of what "metaphor" intends. The word itself etymologically means "carry over," and Daniel C. Noel nicely points out that moving vans in modern Athens carry the inscription *metaphora!*[9] Metaphors carry us across from one situation to another. The initial situation is that of the customary second-order experience, in which the two elements of the metaphor bear their usual, general meaning, like "slaves" and "plums." The second situation is the first-order experience of having the two elements "put" together, as in Jean Toomer's poem above. Notice that the first-order statement is no *logical* inference from the initial two elements. Indeed, a logical "gap" stands between second and first. There is, as it were, a certain movement in time from one moment to another, from the customary meaning over into the first-order disclosure.

Only the synthesizing imagination can accomplish that temporal movement "across the gap" into a newly gathered,

II

"charged" perspective. Indeed, imagination may be thought of as ordinarily an inclusive, synthesizing function, articulating a unity-in-tension along the line of time. ("Unity-in-tension," a term suggested by statements of Martin Foss, is to be distinguished from "formal unity," as of an object, which is quiescent in time.[10]) Thus metaphor seizes upon very ordinary materials with results both highly concrete and suggestive, opening out through time upon the fullness of things, or indeed, upon the world. The world itself, as we live in it, is not static but moves in temporal process. Now what structure of meaning is able to articulate a process in its mid-course without either containing it or halting it? Only an imaginative move of a metaphoric sort can do so, can "slow down" the process sufficiently to permit insight, yet allow the inferential gap of genuine unfolding. A penetrating metaphor glimpses the world "happening" and *lets* it happen in its own way.

Furthermore, we ourselves are part of the world in time. Therefore a deeply adequate and penetrating metaphor is a linguistic act that involves and "carries over" the lives of all those who realize its force. To know such a metaphor is to be "caught up" with an eye to the future and to one's crucial interests. Or, to use terms already appealed to, a serious metaphor opens us toward the present-ness of things gathered, yet not fully disclosed, in time. Only by such a first-order event can we get our foundational bearings.

Admittedly, I have moved all too quickly from a simple rhetorical figure to the most profound sort of metaphoric unveiling. A simple metaphor has no inherent magic in it; it may fail to "work," even as a figure of speech. Or a metaphor may invoke a "gathering" so specialized to our taste and fancy that it becomes lost in the myriad patterns of the larger, "real" world. My point has been rather to examine the essence of metaphoric process. Such a linguistic move may produce only superficial rhetoric, or on the other hand, may become profoundly involving of our reality. Whether it does the one or the other is primarily a question of the range, strength, and precision of the second-order awareness and terminology that goes into producing the metaphoric, first-order effect. Indeed, some particular attention should be given to this stabilizing strength that the second order contributes to metaphor.

Metaphor and Stability; Symbol

To speak of metaphor is but one step in relating literature and the "real" world. The metaphoric function itself emerges in many different forms, and its exact character is not agreed upon. A helpful exchange on the subject is that of Martin Foss and William Wimsatt, including the latter's review of Foss' book on metaphor.[11] A primary question in the discussion is the extent to which the two components in the metaphor retain their original (what we have called second-order) identity in the metaphoric tension, and the extent to which those identities are lost in the new metaphoric wholeness. Full emphasis upon time and process (typical of Foss' treatment) underscores the *new* situation, and consequently the dissolution of former identities. Foss comments thus on the metaphorical process:

> . . . here the known symbols [sc. second-order references] in their relation to each other are only material; they undergo *a complete change in losing their familiar meaning in each other* and give birth to an entirely new knowledge beyond their fixed and addible multitude. . . . "Creatio ex nihilo" means just this: That the parts are transformed to a "nothing" with regard to that which has become life.[12] (Italics ours.)

Insofar as the new issuance of the metaphor dominates the rhetorical function as a whole, the original components are "overcome" (another of Foss' terms), the passage through time is accomplished, and the quality of "necessity" in the result is heightened as things resolve into one another. Now recall that by general character a metaphor is highly concrete with rich universal implications, but is therefore, formally speaking, indefinite. Foss' approach heightens the rich results, but by virtue of acute indefiniteness. Wimsatt comments:

> . . . say that Foss' philosophy is a celebration of the
> bonfire to the ultimate negation of the fuel. The
> peacock flames of imagination leap up and up for-
> ever, the driftwood logs fall back and vanish. . . .
> [His view] enters the boundless gas.[13]

Sheer metaphor flames out and is over. If it is large enough,
it is the apocalypse—although even in the apocalypse an analogue has traditionally remained between the world that was
and the apocalyptic world that has come to be. The problem
with this unlimited or thorough-going metaphor is that the
"world" that is gathered and disclosed can hardly be spoken
of as a world, or as *the* world, since it is more like indefinite
extension. One feels suspicious that perhaps such a complete
imaginative resolution is a willful flight into subjectivity. On
the other hand, Wimsatt's determination that second-order
objects remain always the same, while metaphoric lights simply play about them, also fails to convince.

Surely it is the case that between the metaphoric components and their resolution *there remains a tension through
time*—not a static deadlock, but a relation that would find
now one in ascendancy, now the other. (Thus we have returned to the notion of a rhythm: breadth, richness, breadth.)
The only question is what linguistic evidence there is of such
a continuing tension—or of second-order objects retaining a
degree of their identity in the metaphoric process, which
means the same thing. Are there cross-sections of the first- and
second-order arrangement at different points on the time-line
that are distinct and yet analogous to one another?

Retaining the tension within a metaphor is in one way accomplished by symbol. In a symbol, the components of a metaphor are not dissolved, yet the power of the metaphor holds
good. A continuing, identifiable figure results. Paul Ricoeur
in his treatment of evil offers some good examples of metaphors that have become historically traditional as symbols.
Personal involvement in evil acts may be confessed or avowed
in a language of symbols that builds upon a metaphoric joining. Thus Ricoeur notes a confession of defilement that appeals to "stain," or "uncleanness"; a confession of sin in terms

of "missing the mark," "straying from the path"; an avowal of guilt as "weight" or "burden."[14] In any of these cases, the essence of evil-doing is, as always, difficult to specify. Against that hard mystery the confessor presses the everyday metaphor of "unclean," or of "going astray," or of "burden." The point here is that in moments of intense avowal the everyday meaning of "unclean" is virtually swallowed up in the anguish of remorse. On the other hand, that everyday meaning is not entirely lost, though it expands in the metaphoric context. The symbol has stabilized to a degree the metaphoric tension. Beyond Ricoeur's suggestions, numerous stabilized metaphors in religious and social life come to mind: "rest," "seek," "fall," "ascend," "rise up!" "press," etc. Such symbols as these persist, though their deployment varies with the individual occasion.

Attention should be called to a certain strategy of this entire study, illustrated by the move from metaphor to symbol. In the aim to see if literature does not present insight into real affairs, I have emphasized first-order (now clearly metaphoric) language as imaginatively presenting, through time, an arena of reality of which we ourselves as active, purposive beings are a part. One reason for an initial emphasis on first order is that foundational, metaphoric language has suffered loss of prestige in the analytically precise twentieth century. Metaphoric impact is easily relegated to "mere feeling," while actually it constitutes one whole side of our entry into language and reality. Nevertheless, the first-order emphasis needs quickly to acknowledge that only second-order terms are enablers for foundational utterance. A kind of sturdiness in second-order elements supplies bounds and measures within which metaphor serviceably functions. Indeed, the character and quality of second-order terms bear heavily on the aptness of the metaphor *per se*, as well as upon its historical continuance as symbol.

Certainly retention of its two components as entities means that a metaphor is "unfinished." (Recall the element of concealment in disclosure.) Yet the unfinished condition of metaphor holds a positive value: the very presence of secondary

II
——
56

language hindering full resolution helps preserve the meaning of historical process through recognizable secondary factors. Metaphoric speech as symbol, in other words, is not a simple, primal "return," nor does it embody the simply new, but is something of both. It is a *re-new-al* of presence, now somehow forever different—a *developmental repetition* of what is real made possible by the tension between first and second orders.

Consider for a moment Dante's symbol of "ascending the mount" as a metaphor of self-purification. The foundational impact is present of a primal intentionality "to try to . . .," or "to try to *be*," in the immediate image of one's climbing painfully upward. But because the second-order terms are not lost in the indefinite passion of striving, there remains the focused increment of historical loci: Ararat, Olympus, Sinai and Carmel, and the mount of Jesus' sermon, all influence Dante's medieval Mount of Purgation. The stability of the universal, "ascending the mount," has actually enriched the metaphor. At the same time, the terms of this secondary phrase ("ascend" and "mount") have shifted their meaning somewhat, even in general reference, because of the shift in their metaphoric setting. By Dante's 1300 A.D. the image of climbing to the peak has entered at least five different total metaphoric contexts. First and second order have enriched one another.

Symbol lives on the power of metaphor. But metaphor needs discipline, of which symbol is the prime example.

Metaphor and Narrative; Antimetaphor

The point continues to develop that the articulation of reality through language involves a productive tension between the two orders or tendencies of language. The disciplining of metaphor is one of those "productive tensions" and may profitably be pursued further.

Is it not the case that not only symbol, but any formal linguistic structure can contain metaphor to a degree and give it certain boundaries against which its power may be felt? A lyric poem, a drama, or a narrative may display metaphoric language, yet within a formal setting that is traditional and that provides a channel for metaphoric meaning. Probably the short lyric offers the best opportunity for witnessing a single, dominating metaphor within an appropriate frame. Take, for example, the couplet by Richard Wilbur:

EPISTEMOLOGY

II

We milk the cow of the world, and as we do
We whisper in her ear, "You are not true."[15]

Metaphor opens a perspective on the world; the metaphor in the first line above even has "the world" as one of its components, and the world turns out to be a cow. The perspective of ourselves and the world as milkers and milked "draws us in," as first-order will do; the deflating of our intellectual vanity in the second line adds a sting to the comic circumstance. The boundaries provided by the structure of the verse mean that the metaphor is contained; "the world" of the poem is not conclusively the world of reality. But the verse has contributed a teasing new angle on the myriad world, and our approach to epistemology will not be exactly the same after reading it.

A still wider frame for metaphor may occur in the form of a narrative. The chief characteristic of a narrative is that its *primary meaning is cumulative, unfolding in the terms or statements of the narrative itself.* Actually, Wilbur's little poem above is a very small narrative, if looked at from the point of view of that genre. Wilbur's "story" of ourselves and the cow unfolds part by part until the last line completes it. The very first meaning is the narrative meaning, followed quickly in this case by the referential meaning (to ourselves and to epistemology). A myth can offer another example of a narrative that offers a disciplined setting for a metaphor retained by tradition as a symbol. Consider the story of Saturn eating his own children lest one of them should grow up to overthrow him. Now a myth in general may be thought of as a narrative including the gods (or at least ultimate powers) serving to orient a people communally within the world.

Clearly, as the Bultmannian "demythologizing" controversy has well known, a myth employs numerous objectivizing elements in order to convey matters of wide orientation presumably not "objective." At the level of its objects (Saturn, his wife, his children), the meaning of the story is simply the story itself, told from beginning to end; the first meaning is simply the narrative meaning. But the story so obviously contains a powerful metaphoric act (the "eating") that very quickly the second-order terms cluster into first-order suggestiveness around that center. A primal sense opens of the titanic powers of the world giving forth creatively, and then destroying in death what they have given. The metaphor "catches us up," but does not engulf us because it is contained in symbol *and* narrative. The myth, centuries old, has traditionally come into play as occasion demands, casting its suggestive light on the world of affairs.

The two examples just given are both narratives with a dominating metaphor or symbol, but what of the nature of a narrative that contains few, if any, metaphors or symbols, and perhaps no dominant ones?

Reminiscent of a myth is a parable, though the parable is a narrative usually furnished with everyday characters and affairs, included in what we have called "second-order" items. (A myth also employs second-order terms, but their more fantastic quality keeps them closer to the foundational "aura" than are everyday things and notions.) Not only does a parable offer recognizable characters and circumstances, it need not "turn" on one central metaphor or symbol. Of course some parables do, as in the case of Jesus' New Testament parable of the "treasure" hidden in the field, or his parable of the "pearl," both direct metaphors of the Kingdom of God.[16] Of greater interest, however, are those parables in which the story itself, its action from beginning to end, constitutes the force of the parable. Any story has its turning points or surprises; yet the power of a story may be constituted by the action as a whole, rather than by some one dominant symbol. Many of the parables of Jesus evidence just such uniform, inclusive strength, for example, the parables of "the

great supper," "the prodigal son," and "the talents."[17] Robert
Funk's extended study of "the great supper" is helpful in
numerous ways, not least of which is his repeated notice that
the story is set within our everyday mundane reality.[18] This
bizarre tale of a householder whose invited guests oddly refuse to come, and who then collects—even by force—a sur-
prised and motley crowd to fill his banquet hall nevertheless
draws on no particulars not familiar in themselves. Our general second-order awareness enables us to know at once such
items as invitation, servant, guest, refusal, compulsion, etc.

The significance of the "uniform" parable is that the discipline of metaphor is thereby carried forward another step.
Not only do we have a literary structure, poem or narrative,
that sets a frame around an obvious metaphor. Notice that
now being discussed is the metaphoric impact of a parable in
which no actual, rhetorical metaphors need appear at all! In
fact, the "great supper" parable contains no trace of an actual
rhetorical metaphor. One finds, then, the sort of discipline of
metaphor in which at one level metaphor is banished, and
the familiar second-order account *as a whole* works metaphorically. The metaphor *is* the story. Consequently, the first-
order impact of a parable can be all the more telling, since
no obtrusive metaphor as rhetoric warns or raises suspicions
of imaginary fancy. One is "led down the path" of familiarity.
All the while, the tense and disturbing new situation is being
prepared; ordinary expectations are upset. One impulse of
the reader is simply to dismiss the puzzling story of the eccentric householder, the biased father, the revengeful business-
man. But the first-order engagement makes us feel that the
story is somehow about *us*; the account is alien and not sensible, yet it seems to recall something important, something
once known but now forgotten.

What is seen in the "simple" parable is what Beda Alleman
has referred to as an "antimetaphor"—a linguistic metaphor
in which no rhetorical metaphor appears. Indeed, his discussion takes its departure from certain impulses in the nineteenth and twentieth centuries to distrust metaphor and to
deal with it ambivalently.[19] Nietzsche, in one way, German

expressionism and the French *nouveau roman,* in another, all held the rhetorical metaphor as suspect in relation to reality (although Nietzsche preferred it to "scientific language"). One result has been the interest in certain quarters in a literary style that rejects the rhetoric of metaphor almost entirely, letting everything be called by its common name. Alleman's best example is Kafka, whose narratives indeed carry a first-order effect, and yet who deliberately avoided rhetorical metaphors, which he called a "seasickness on land."[20] Thus we have found the discipline of metaphor by second-order terms extended to the *exclusion* of metaphor (at the rhetorical level) only to discover that an everyday descriptive narrative can so "work within itself" that the foundational impact of the piece as a whole results. In such an instance, the relation between first and second orders is tightened, the tendency for one to displace the other in discourse grows less, and their cooperation in affording reality to us is well illustrated. The point made at the end of chapter one about the heightened interest of a poem ("Stopping by Woods") whose first-order force causes virtually no distortion in its second-order diction now can be reinforced. Such an instance is an anti-metaphor.

The conclusion is not that a poem or narrative using no rhetorical metaphors need be aesthetically finer than one that does. Rather, in consideration that language and literature can and do render reality for us, it is reassuring to know that the risk of rhetorical metaphor *can* be eliminated, that when called upon to do so, first and second order can nicely coinhere within a single text.

Antimetaphor and Absolute Metaphor

As well as the term "antimetaphor," Beda Alleman also speaks of "absolute metaphor," and he apparently considers the designations interchangeable.[21] His interest is not only in a text including no single rhetorical metaphors, but also in one that tends to become self-enclosed, severing itself from our ordinary arrangements of comparison. That is, a narrative may employ familiar objects and ideas, but the result of the story over-all is to leave us feeling that our familiar world has oddly changed. "The world" of the story seems a world to itself, an absolute.

Alleman's basic view may not be disturbed if a distinction is proposed between antimetaphor and absolute metaphor. For the character of containing no rhetorical metaphors and the character of being deeply self-contained in meaning need not necessarily entail one another. The notion of a literary piece that operates totally as metaphor with no metaphor present (the antimetaphor) is arresting in its own right, apart from absoluteness of meaning. Thus far the parable, the lyric poem, and by implication the novel and short story have been raised as possible candidates for antimetaphor. Drama is difficult, for the medium so lends itself to object symbolism that even a familiar, conventional setting may begin to bristle with metaphors, as for example in some of the noted realistic plays of Ibsen.

History and the history-like narrative may be seen as anti-metaphoric, even though history is not technically imaginative literature. Its difference from fiction is an ontological one, in that history's factual data are publicly "true," while the truth of fiction need not include this same factual level. At the same time, history is a literature that involves the imagination, even if a historical work is not "imaginative literature." Now quite possibly a historical narrative may fulfill the conditions of an antimetaphor. Obviously, history need not be expressed in ordinary metaphors and probably will not be. Is there any sense in which a historical narrative *as a whole* functions metaphorically? Certainly the imaginative work of the historian is a *sine qua non* for a proper narrative, though such work is unobtrusive and easily taken for granted. To compare a chronicle with a proper history quickly shows the difference: a chronicle is but a list of factual points set down; a historical narrative carefully weaves these, without violating them, into a meaningful narrative discourse of causes and effects. The chronicle is made up of stabilized, second-order items. What the historian adds are elements of discourse that *relate* these items to one another so that the metaphoric imagination opens, in and through the narrative, to inform us "how it was." Second order and first order stand in tension as in many of our examples of the language-reality relationship. J. H. Hexter's recent study of historical rhetoric is most instructive in showing how the imagination functions in choosing the significant "turning points" in the data of an event.[22] His thesis is akin to our own, that the narrative chosen by the historian does not simply reflect its "object" (past reality), but is actually the field in which that reality finds emergence.

Full comment on the "history-like" narrative will be reserved until later, a term that Hans W. Frei has recently indicated as of considerable currency in early modern European scholarship.[23] The interest concerns narratives that in every way behave as historical narratives except that the question of their detailed factuality remains open. In any case, the very tight relationship of first and second orders as an antimetaphor obviously holds, in a narrative that is "history-like."

A metaphor that is absolute is simply one that in its wholeness, if not in its members, stands apart from usual comparison to our second-order affairs. Alleman suggests that our contemporary situation is more given to expression in absolute metaphors than has been true in the past, possibly because of the cultural upheaval in the twentieth century. His suggestion is that the foundational impact of the absolute metaphor draws us into a world, or into a grasp of *the* world, that shocks and transmutes our usual expectations. An example of absolute metaphor that Alleman chooses from poetry is a bit of verse from Nelly Sachs:

> Wailing wall night!
> Carved in you are the psalms of silence.[24]

Alleman suggests that the two obvious metaphors in these lines are both absolute metaphors: "Wailing wall night," and "psalms of silence." His appeal is that the juxtaposition is so extreme in both cases that no "logical basis of resemblance" (his term) can easily be noted between the components of either metaphor. The extraordinary couplings "pull away" from the usual and carry us into a new vista of things. If this is what Alleman means by "absolute metaphor," then apparently it is identical with what Wheelwright and others have called a "diaphor," as we have already seen. Indeed, the diaphor "creates presence" in a new and stimulating manner; its juxtaposition overrides the less demanding epiphor, with its subject and modifier. Nevertheless, a diaphor is still a rhetorical metaphor and may be wanting in what we have tried to call "stability." In addition, we have noted that *any* rhetorical metaphor tends to have a diaphoric level of tension. "Absolute metaphor" seems less compelling as a term if it points only to a rhetorical diaphor.

Alleman's appeal once more to Kafka for instances of the absolute metaphor is more convincing. In Kafkian parables, paradoxes, and fiction, the narrative piece *as a whole* may serve not only as an antimetaphor, but as an absolute metaphor, giving expression to a world that is familiar to us on the one hand, yet shockingly disruptive of our conventional understanding of the world on the other. The effect in Kafka carries all the more weight because the pieces are also antimetaphors, drawing us into their scope and structure under the guise of plain narrative, an almost naturalistic style. Thus, for example, in *The Trial* Joseph K. experiences police, arrest, arraignment, lawyers, law-books, any one of which might be understandable within an ordinary setting. But when these and their eccentricities are related to one another in the particular manner chosen by the author, a world of numbing unease results, shaking our confidence in things, and threatening to displace life as we had thought of it. Another example of an absolute metaphor is again the "great supper" parable of Jesus, which uses our familiar world to shake loose the bland assumptions that belong to that very same world. Now an absolute metaphor need not be a strict antimetaphor, as in the case of *The Trial* and "The Great Supper"; but in both of these cases their strength seems enhanced by the absence of rhetorical metaphoric usage.

Inquiry into the power of metaphor, and the disciplining of metaphor, has suggested here an increasing preoccupation

II
___
64

with the antimetaphorical narrative, and with absolute metaphor as narrative. Recall that the aim of this chapter has been to pursue the problem of metaphor as "sheer" metaphor, that is, metaphor in its proper work of "carrying over," of resolving alien factors into a new finality. The completed metaphor is rich but indefinite. The exact problem with rhetorical metaphor, then, is that it leaves behind the "object" reality of its components (e.g., their simple names) in offering a new, imaginative realm. The strategy of this chapter has therefore been straightforward: to retain the power of metaphor while also retaining the integrity of the second-order "public" elements that either compose it or circumscribe it. In order to press toward this double-sided advantage (first and second order in balance), brief consideration has been given to symbol, lyric poem, and narrative. For our special purposes, the lyric is of particular interest when it contains no rhetorical metaphors at all. And to this possibility of being antimetaphoric, the narrative adds its peculiar "narrative meaning," the cumulative disclosure of the story *within* its own unfolding statement. (In one important respect, the story "means" what it "says.") The simple narrative thereby contributes twice over to the object-restraint of metaphor, while itself still powerful as a metaphor *of the whole.*

What, then, does the "absolute metaphor" add to the above summary? The absolute metaphor introduces us to our world, but "shaken" and transformed in its fundamental expectations. The element of *crisis*, implicit in every metaphoric "carrying-over," is heightened and broadened in the absolute metaphor. Now if the absolute metaphor happens also to be an antimetaphoric narrative, then a high degree of second-order "object" stability (on two counts) is added to a high degree of metaphoric transition. Kafka's *The Trial* and Jesus' "Great Supper" have been the two examples.

The purpose of this chapter's survey now needs to be recalled. The compelling transitional power of metaphor always combines with its indefinite richness as "flight"—which may turn out to be only a fanciful flight. This inquiry has been dedicated to demonstrating *one route* for harnessing metaphor, up to and including self-contained, cumulative, narrative meaning that effects an "absolute." I do not mean to suggest that this is the only or preferred route for first and second orders. The direction into anti- and absolute-metaphoric narrative may be serviceable for our day and age, or for religion and theology. But one must not infer that this route is privileged as regards literary excellence. The choice of right literary genre and diction lies with author and "muse," as always. Nevertheless, what has been done here is to observe one procedure for gaining maximum power and maximum discipline in the pursuit of metaphor.

One is reminded of Martin Luther's preoccupation with the Jesus story. As he sloughed away medieval theology's heavy layers of biblical allegory, the human realism of the Jesus account impressed and excited him.

> . . . And there was the maid of fifteen years bringing forth her first-born without water, fire, light, or pan, a sight for tears! What Mary and Joseph did next, nobody knows. The scholars say they adored. They must have marveled that this Child was the Son of God. He was also a real human being. Those who say that Mary was not a real mother lose all the joy. He was a true Baby, with flesh, blood, hands and legs. He slept, cried, and did everything else that a baby does only without sin. . . .
>
> Let us, then, meditate upon the Nativity just as we see it happening in our own babies. I would not have you contemplate the deity of Christ, the majesty of Christ, but rather his flesh.[25]

One may say that Luther delighted in being markedly anti-metaphoric. Insofar as the story was literature, it was plain-spoken and recognizable. Insofar as it was history, the interpretive narrative let the chronicled facts be themselves. At the same time, the very familiarity of the setting only accented the unique difference of this story, *as a whole*, from our familiar human expectations. (". . . everything . . . only without sin.") The everyday-ness, yet apart-ness, of the story gave it that lively tension of the two orders discussed above. The disciplined metaphor thus set forth became the appro-

II

priate arena in which Luther realized his own metaphoric (or dialectical) experience, "at once justified and sinner." That is, the plainspoken portrait of the divine-human Jesus served as grounds for a certain "hearing" of itself: Luther as individual worshiper seized the imaginative insight of being both damned, yet affirmed, by analogy to the human, yet divine character, of the Jesus figure. For all that, the story kept its own disciplined and self-contained integrity as a unique and unsubstitutable account. The story as balanced metaphor (or dialectic) was projected as address upon the reader, and was nevertheless preserved.

But one must not at this point be led into theology and away from the breadth of literature itself. Literature as an art must and will take many forms besides the narrative and the antimetaphor. Although the direction of this chapter and its results will hopefully serve us well later on, a broad range of questions and possibilities confront us if one calls to mind the wide scope of artistic, literary writing. For example, in the case of language functioning as a work of art, can we remain comfortable with that piece doing "first-order work" that clearly involves and engages us? How can art inaugurate changes in our existence, our world-orientation, without becoming ideology or worse? Must we not be committed to a much more cautious analysis of literature within its own structure so that its integrity will not suffer abuse? Such questions demand attention if literature is more than simply pleasing within its own aesthetic dimension, if it also plays a role in the linguistic presentation of everyday reality.

NOTES

1. Flannery O'Connor, *Three* (New York: Signet Books, 1964) 243.

2. Elie Wiesel, *The Town Beyond the Wall* (New York: Avon Books, 1969) 23.

3. Georges Bernanos, *Journal d'un curé de campagne* (Paris: Plon, 1936) 366. (Translation ours.)

4. Philip Wheelwright, *Metaphor and Reality* (Bloomington: Indiana University Press, 1962) 72–86. A helpful summary of approaches appears in M. C. Beardsley, *Aesthetics* (New York: Harcourt, Brace, and World, 1958) 134–147, 159–162.

5. E.g., in Wheelwright, *Metaphor*, 80. See Northrop Frye, *Anatomy of Criticism* (Princeton: The University Press, 1957) 123. See E. Pound, *Selected Poems* (New York: New Directions, 1957) 35.

6. Jean Toomer, "Song of the Son," in *Cane* (New York: Harper and Row, 1923, 1969) 21.

7. Wheelwright, *Metaphor*, 91.

8. Richards, *Rhetoric*, 106.

9. In "Metaphor," in D. C. Noel, ed., *Echoes of the Wordless "Word"* (Missoula: American Academy of Religion, 1973) 7.

10. See Martin Foss, *Symbol and Metaphor in Human Experience* (Lincoln: University of Nebraska Press, 1949, 1964) 61.

11. See William Wimsatt, "Symbol and Metaphor," in *The Verbal Icon—Studies in the Meaning of Poetry* (Lexington: University of Kentucky Press, 1954) 119–130.

12. Foss, *Symbol*, 61–62.

13. Wimsatt, *Icon*, 123.

14. Ricoeur, *Evil*, 9, 101, and *passim*.

15. From *The Poems of Richard Wilbur* (New York: Harcourt, Brace, and World, Inc., 1963) 121.

16. Matthew 13:44–46.

17. Matthew 22:2–10 (Luke 14:16–24); Luke 15:11–32; Matthew 25:14–30 (Luke 19:12–27).

18. Funk, *Language*, 194–195.

19. See Beda Alleman, "Metaphor and Antimetaphor" in S. R. Hopper and D. L. Miller, eds., *Interpretation: the Poetry of Meaning* (New York: Harcourt, Brace, and World, 1967) 105–110.

20. Alleman, "Metaphor," 111.

21. Alleman, "Metaphor," 113–114.

22. J. H. Hexter, *The History Primer* (New York: Basic Books, 1971).

23. In Hans W. Frei, *The Eclipse of Biblical Narrative—A Study in Eighteenth and Nineteenth Century Hermeneutics* (New Haven: Yale University Press, 1974) *passim*, e.g., 162, 187, 271.

24. Alleman, "Metaphor," 115. From Nelly Sachs, "Chor der Unsichtbaren Dinge," in *Fahrt ins Staublose; die Gedichte der Nelly Sachs* (Frankfurt: Suhrkamp Verlag, 1961) 62. (Translation Alleman's.)

25. *The Martin Luther Christmas Book*, trans. R. H. Bainton (Philadelphia: The Westminster Press, 1948) 39.

Language as
'Work of Art'   III

How can artistic language bring us to the "brink" of theology?

The parallel suggestion that language-in-general brings us to the "brink" of reality is by all odds a very closely related statement. In the pages that have preceded it has first of all been assumed that a purely theoretical stance towards reality and language is not productive, and further does not comport with the real situation out of which even theoretical questions arise. We as purposive, active beings know language as the "room" or medium in which we and the world become articulate to one another. To posit the unreality of this articulated relation in things would be to mock our situated condition, the vital agenda of life-problems that even the most skeptical among us never deny. The question is not so much *whether* language articulates reality, but *how* that service most adequately occurs.

The obvious delusions afforded by allowing either first- or second-order language to dominate us exclusively have demonstrated how important is the rhythmic tension between the two. The preceding chapter on metaphor attempted to outline one approach to a satisfactory handling of that tension. But to speak more broadly, it has been precisely the province of literature to exploit that tension to the best and fullest, and in a startling variety of ways. Literature, then, has especially functioned in and through a commonplace fact, that of our everyday language, but in uncommon and penetrating ways. It has been unceasingly varied in its hold on the two orders. Consequently, literature has invoked reality in countless versions and shapes.

Certainly it is no small matter to say that literature "invokes reality." Nevertheless, that will finally be my position here, recalling certain of Flannery O'Connor's comments:

> . . . The basis of art is truth, both in matter and in mode. The person who aims after art in his work aims after truth, in an imaginative sense, no more and no less. . . . I'm always highly irritated by people who imply that writing fiction is an escape from reality. It is a plunge into reality and it's very shocking to the system. . . . The type of mind that can understand good fiction is not necessarily the educated mind, but it is at all times the kind of mind that is willing to have its sense of mystery deepened by contact with reality, and its sense of reality deepened by contact with mystery.[1]

O'Connor's remarks seem sensible enough, although they leave any number of particular questions unanswered. The approach in this chapter will be to attempt to bring literature into line with what has been said broadly about language and reality. Yet a literary work is a special instance of language— language as a work of art. It will be useful, then, to approach literature and reality via comments on the nature of an artwork. The aim of this chapter will be to show that art in general can respond to our categories of first- and second-order articulation without losing its character as art. For literature, this means that we are ready to advocate a "full" reading. The experience of literature should include our availability *to* literature in its impact upon our world.

III

72

Admittedly, problems arise in what may appear as a subjective or "existentialist" view of response to literature (although by the end of the chapter it will not be so simply classified). A poem or novel can too easily become a "message," an ideology, or a victim of our own predispositions. A formalist level of criticism, letting the art object manifest itself in its own structure, is therefore of the highest importance in helping militate against such abuse. In the final analysis, however, a margin of imaginative judgment must be risked if the full scope of the literary piece and its meaning are to come into play. The nature of that "meaning," and the role of imaginative judgment in appraising it, now require further scrutiny on our part.

Artist and Audience: Illumination of the World

To clarify the discussion, comments on the interlocking trio of artist, audience, and world must precede consideration of the art object as such. Certainly the art object has its own integrity and at one level of conversation can most helpfully be distinguished from all else that gathers 'round it. Yet in the same way that first-order discourse is "foundational" in nature, so the full situation of art should be studied prior to the art object abstracted from it, as important as that object truly is. Therefore, without attempting a formal definition, I wish to propose a distinguishing characteristic of art as a *concrete transaction in time between artist and audience, evoking a certain outlook on the world.* Art occurs, in other words, within history, within the on-going sense that an articulate community has of itself through time. Regardless of how it expresses the "eternal," or the timeless, or alludes to "beginning" and "end," art is time-filled and perspectival. Were it not so, art would offer no convincing vehicle for the quality of timeless finality that does imbue it. As act, it lives within the time-space continuum.

Is it proper to say, then, that the relation among these three—artist, audience, and world—is "historical"? Such a statement could mean that this constellation speaks within a fixed pattern, a past event that is now only antiquarian. For example, Michelangelo's statement-in-stone to the people of Florence, his David statue, has become a customary relic within the Florentine memory and is thereby "historical." But this is not the full sense of the term "history" as I intend it here. Recall certain points already established that a first-order relation is necessary to realize full meaning in time and history, while a second-order status that is simply "past" makes its contribution, but is not of itself adequate. For the relation among artist, audience, and world to be fully historical means to constitute a "living" history currently taking place as the transaction proceeds. To draw further upon the example just cited: If I experience the David now, along with its remarkable past ties within Florence—and yet experience it as a transaction from the sculptor and his community to me, in my community; if, in addition to the monumental traits that cluster *int*ensively within the piece, I am drawn *ex*tensively to participate in the world in a fresh way—and I sense something of heroism, the end of simple happiness, the loneliness of power, so that the shape of the world is more vivid now for me; if I understand in this piece something of what the sculptor understood of existence; then art at that moment is truly historical. The David is renewed in time, and the world is renewed and illumined in our own time. The art is truly historical because in and through the act and response, history has moved, unfolded. The same is true of my response to a contemporary artist. "Historical" is not a matter of the past as such, although the past gives it wider perspective; it means reflective participation in the world's proper horizon, time. Fully historical means a second-order competence recovering the sense of our own first-order foundations, a shifting forward of the world and of us along with it.

Thus of the four factors typically available within literary critical theory—the artist, the world, the art object, and the audience—the approach being discussed sees a maximum unity of all four. The art object is the necessary focus, while the other three explore the boundaries of the artistic act in its full unity.[2] It is this "exploring of the boundaries" that occurs in time and history, providing a dynamic situation apart from which the isolated art object suffers a cramped significance. The unity of artist, audience, and world is therefore a dynamic unity, a *trans*-action, involving a shedding of new light upon the world. The art object, considered alone, locks in this potential within itself, to be realized whenever an alert response awakens to life once more the full transaction.

As regards this unity, Martin Foss' distinction between two kinds of unity comes once again to mind, one of which is intended here and the other not. Indeed, the distinction is one of the most important for the whole sweep of this discussion. There is a *unity of parts and whole* (the whole coinciding with the sum of parts) appropriate to second-order delineation within a contextual horizon. There is a *unity of process* (the "whole" process *qua* process not available by analysis into parts) appropriate to first-order recovery within the time horizon.[3] The first of these is formal; the second, metaphoric. The first of these implies timelessness. The second implies time and change, and an unfinished character. How can there be a unity that is unfinished? In the artistic transaction, a movement unveiling the world in a new way, there is a sense of having moved through the everyday ordinary-ness of things into a ritual merger and mingling of those things, between artist and audience. But since one's own selfhood is included in the movement, in the process, the unity cannot be examined directly as with parts-whole, any more than one can give a total accounting of oneself for all to see. The movement of first-order recovery is one in which my own being in its complex richness, intellect *and* will, finds itself moved to a perspective where certain affairs "fall into place." This insight is a unity of process, unfinished, having to be lived *through* (not contemplated), because it is in time. It is not the result of secondary delineation but the result of secondary rearrangement; it is also the *beginning* of secondary testing, analysis, sorting out. It is a disclosure, even if not complete. Thus the full scope of what happens in art engages the artist, the audience, and the world in a historical renewal of present-ness and point of view.

The nature of the artistic act-and-response, recovering wide "presence" must be of a peculiar sort in order to render its special disclosure. In the previous chapters, that peculiarity was touched on in discussing the first-order function of second-order terms—a movement "forward" that is nevertheless a movement of "recall," true of metaphoric language and thus of art. An additional feature of that peculiarity now will be added. The "communing" of artist and audience that gathers a "world" is characterized by a *significant concreteness* crucial to the function we have been discussing. That is, a work of art cannot be thoroughly abstract and thoroughly utilitarian at once. I mean, then, to part company with Eric Gill's view that "to make a drainpipe is as much the work of an artist as it is to make paintings and poems."[4] We may admire the fitting of a drainpipe, but as it exemplifies a precise typical model *and* a utilitarian means, I would hold it falls short of arresting uniqueness and thereby of art. The art work may be highly abstract, yet its lack of utility sets it apart. It may be utilitarian (a silver pitcher), but will not dissolve entirely into an abstract outline of the setting. It holds a certain element of the concrete that disallows its slipping away into the utility of things or the abstraction of mere order.

At the same time, there is no virtue in being concrete *per se*. Anything can be uniquely concrete without at all being artistic—unless a special kind of attention is called to it. Any combination of factors would be unique, but not interestingly unique; any grouping would be concrete, but not arrestingly so. The *significant* concreteness of a work of art is that which wins the gaze of our attention, steady and full. Note that concrete uniqueness at the center of interest has nothing to do with whether the artist is portraying a concrete physical thing (a particular man, or bowl of fruit, or human event), although some artists have on occasion theorized that using images of physical objects should be the way *par excellence* of bringing the work to its proper concrete nature.[5] Already cited was Denise Levertov's happy suggestion that this concrete quality rather be called "presentness."[6] A lyric poem, for example, may "say" a very general statement with minimal imagery, but it should evoke the present-ness of the speaker in the concrete situation of utterance. The more general the statement, the more difficult this becomes.

Why then is one drawn into one unique configuration and not into another? Is it because one simply "uses more" than the other?—as a landscape is transformed by a sunset, by turning up the "pyrotechnics"? Such elaboration can be disastrous in art, if not in nature. Rather the issue must turn on *how* the artist employs what he or she does employ. For example, Paul Klee's reassuring aim in his painting was, "to create much spiritually out of little."[7] Specifically, the artist offers us something quite concrete that manages to suggest its significance for much, much more—a hint of universality. Perhaps through the concrete unity can be traced the shadow of a general unity, suggesting that the painting or poem is a doorway into more and more of the same kind of thing. If Michelangelo's madonna and child has that noble, haunted look belonging to this statue alone, we nevertheless feel its exact quality is something we are remembering from our own past, that it reaches far abroad in human awareness. Thus the center of concrete interest invokes our gazing wonder because it suggests its own wider reality, its own extension, on and on, far past the limits of the given poem, or painting, or song, or novel. Thus J.-P. Sartre comments:

> . . . We follow the red path which is buried among the wheat much farther than Van Gogh has painted it, among other wheat fields, under other clouds, to the river which empties into the sea, and we extend to infinity, to the other end of the world, the deep finality which supports the existence of the field and the earth.[8]

The work of art has "intension" by its concrete focus; but the achievement of that focus coincides with the achievement of "extension," the sense that far more is unveiled than meets the eye.[9] We find ourselves presented with a work of special features and general overtones that merge so convincingly we could never reduce them to precise parts making up a precise whole. Thus "significant concreteness" returns us to our concern for a unity of process rather than a unity of parts-whole. The rich gesture of the artist focuses a recognizable, concrete level of affairs in such a way that through them we are moved in time to realize the world anew.

To sum up: considering art means considering the dynamic unity of artist, audience, and world through the historical focus of the art-work. This transaction so gathers known concretes that they illumine, in part, a world-unity; and the artistic act itself is a disclosure of insight in process, giving a shape to the past and intimations for the future.

Art as 'End,' as Gift and Demand

One problem with the above discussion is its tendency to imply that one does art work or responds to it with the aim of illumining the world. Perhaps in rare cases that has been a legitimate goal, but usually such illumining is "thrown into the bargain," a "shock-wave" expanding from a highly successful focus. Rather the approach of the artist is to be subject to the medium and its stubbornness, by the strictest of disciplines. The true craftsman is intrigued as to what sounds, or shapes, or colors, or words may disclose if one keeps experimenting with them. In that sense, "the play's the thing," and everyone knows how badly a piece turns out if prostituted to a "message." What has been discussed, therefore, as "illumining the world" is normally a powerful by-product of devotion to the rigors of the work itself. To balance the above section, then, the warning is appropriate: art renders up insight only if first it is given the mastery.

In an important sense, therefore, art is always an "end" and not a "means"—not in the sense of art for its own sake, since art is for *our* sake. Nor does it mean that art is an absolute end to replace all religion and worship by articulating the ultimate. Rather art is an "end" with respect to the level of our ordinary, relative "ways and means" of daily subsistence. Even Sartre, who has long been ready to "engage" literature in the cause of humanity, nevertheless insists that the work of art is not a means, nor does it *have* an end, but it *is* an end.[10]

In our anxious life-necessities of keeping on, art works are little vorteces that spiral to their own centers, while everything else links up as an endless network of preliminaries. The person with no art and nothing like art suffers endless bondage to affairs that are important only for something else up ahead. Contrary to such bondage, the art work must be a free act, a gift, both in execution and reception. A certain "generosity" of the artist offers an arresting poem, or painting, or sonata. Therefore the doing of it must be inherently free from ordinary types of utility: to make money, to manipulate feelings, to propagandize. The artist may hope for a living, but this aim must not dictate the "soul" of the work. A china plate will be made to be useful, but its impact as art will be something extra, "over and above." Thus at an important level, the art work is its own goal, as the free act of one who summons another into an equally free response. The question "what good is it?" suggests that whatever *extensive* good may at length unfold from it, this will emerge only by letting the work first draw us exclusively to itself. It stands liberated, as a gift always must.

Likewise, not only the giving, but the appreciation of a gift is free. So genuine response arises in a moment when average cares and concerns of busy-ness are let go, and a little gap of "risk" assumed; for appreciation requires enough personal security to let the day's machinery run itself for a time. Only by this free act can the work begin to "work," the object consummate itself in liveliness, indeed in *our* liveliness. At the same time, while art as "end" must be gift, it is also demand.[11] That is, since nothing less than a free act can offer and receive the work, then the artist and the audience can demand nothing less of one another. By implication, the author demands a disinterested reception—this, or nothing. One is free to leave the work alone; but involvement in it must be a free business also. To approach the work otherwise is to "type" it and classify it within the little arrangements one has for getting on with living. But the artist entrusts the work to a very busy world, in the reckless confidence that someone will meet its implicit demands for completion, will sense its peculiar individuality. Conversely, our requirements toward the artist are no less strict. We *demand* that the artistic act should be a free one; that the artist allow the right distance between self and materials so as to find their true potential; that the work not be abused by illicit aims and motives. We feel manipulated if our special readiness has been met only by a contrivance. Our demand is for the real thing, or at least an honest failure; otherwise, let us alone. A mutual generosity and a mutual demand lock together artist and audience, because of the work's nature as "end."

Some have likened the art work in its end-gift-demand aspects to a game, and therefore to "play."[12] The activity of art is play, at least in the sense that it does not participate in the usual "means" typical of daily work. It does not belong within the mesh of interlocking appointments each day requires. Art tends to subvert routine, the kind of routine that "playing a game" sets aside for the moment. In this sense the game is free, a gratuity, a gift. But once the choice to play is made, then the strictest demands and disciplines begin to develop. One must play by the rules; if not, one betrays oneself as insecure or "cheating," as not free, as introducing external motives (pride, greed, etc.); the game's not "the thing" anymore. Therefore, once the choice is made, the game itself is in deadly earnest. It is not a means to anything; it is "just a game;" but nothing limits the seriousness of the player, once that player has chosen to join. The "demand" to sustain the game —in its freedom from intrusion—becomes severe. Thus the "game" model does begin to illumine the end-gift-demand character of art.

Furthermore, the "game playing" approach to art illuminates another most important aspect of artistic function: psychic distance. The freedom of a game can be expressed as a certain withdrawal from life's ordinary pattern of demands. That withdrawal, or distance, also characterizes the artist beginning to assemble materials, thoughts, notations. The procedure then is to "play" with these to see what will emerge from them, what arrangements will suggest themselves. If the artist does not allow sufficient distance of the materials from his or her conscious intent, does not give them enough "play," their real potency will be suppressed from imagination. The first-order potential of second-order terms can never be realized, the metaphoric joining never sensed, apart from adequate play, the "gaming" experiment of seeing how things begin to fit together. Driving intent for "something big" must yield to the openness that allows rising, fresh possibilities. Yet once the "little game" has begun to sketch an elemental "world" (i.e., a pattern with implications for infinitely more of the same kind of thing), then the initial distance may give way to increasing participation and involvement.

In the same fashion with the audience, what started as a game may deepen into mortal seriousness, drawing the "players" powerfully to itself until even the world of ordinary duties we "withdrew" from is irrecoverably changed. The "demands" of the game once chosen—if the art is wide enough in scope—will press their "world" effect until the world of our lives is recalled, altered, illumined.

It is now possible to join this section on art as its own "end" with the previous section on art as illumination of the real world through the model of an increasingly serious game. Unless art is allowed its own sovereign domain, to make its "demands freely," it loses integrity. But once granted that integrity, its inner effect of "world" may so engage us as to draw the real world into its "looking glass"—with that world emerging not quite the same as before. Thus the "end" that art is is never a final end, since the world itself is never "finished"; rather art as "end" ultimately signifies insight, with overtones of finality. Nevertheless, if the intrinsic demands of a certain stubborn gamesmanship are not met, the wider experience of engagement will never come to pass. From all that has been said, perhaps a trial definition of art will help: art means *an arresting, independent arrangement of concretes, such that the factors present imply beyond themselves a "world" of their sort, on occasion illuminating the real world of becoming and the participant lives of artist and audience.*

The Art Object, Technique and Style

This rather broad discussion has thus far considered art as historical transaction, beginning in a stubbornly independent game and passing to an illumination of our existing world in time. Now that the art work has been seriously proposed as temporal exchange, it is appropriate to narrow the field and ponder that secondary abstraction called the "art object," or what has been termed the "game." What is it in particular about this artifact that enables it to suggest "world," and even to engage us afresh in real-world processes?

What is it, indeed, for which the artist must labor so long and hard in order to become effective? Why is the focus of concrete interest with its radiating implications so difficult to achieve? Part of the answer surely lies in the terms "style" and "technique"—seemingly small and precious matters for determining the depth of wonder or the sense of "world." Yet in a certain hairline finesse lies the touch that opens a work's entire potential. Technique as an ideal suggests the paradox of a relaxed control, a control of the medium so sure that full quality arises spontaneously without seeming forced. "She makes it seem easy." So a dancer may execute a series of kicks that a beginner would make exaggerated and heavy; but with an experienced performer, it looks like floating. Or a person uninitiated on a native drum may try with the flat of his hands for the sharp, ringing tone typical of a certain region of people. But he sounds only as if he were "slapping" the drum. He will have to begin with a mellow tone and practice narrowing it to ringing sharpness.[13] The person who lacks technique will give the impression of great energy and busyness brought to bear, but with cluttered, weak results. He will be "all over" his task, but without implicit definition. The person of skill gives the impression that his easy control is not so much producing as simply unveiling a region of rhythmic movement, a "body" of dynamic flow. Something strong in quality and motion was "there" all along; yet only skillful control (in dance, or poem, or painting) could reveal it. Good technique fades into the background as a wide-ranging arena of sensible form and movement is let open.

True style likewise retreats from all exaggerated "stylizing" and mannerisms and makes the very most out of the very least, as is true of technique. Indeed, recall the origin of the term "style" in the stylus, or precise writing instrument, leaving its angular characters on the tablet of wax. Style might be called the tight, strong economy of "surface" that any work of art presents to the world. If the texture of what is offered, the "grain" of the medium (words, pigment, stone) is handled with naturalness and consistency and yet with a winning variety of effects, then style can be said to have done its work. Style then somehow constitutes the integrity of the art object right at its surface. The art-work has been termed a "game"; one critic offers style as the "rules of the game"[14]—and, it might be added, how the rules are articulated in any one particular game. If so, then style emerges from the right "distance" as discussed above, the act of high freedom in which the artist withdraws ordinary motives and purposes and lets imagination and medium unite as "style." A certain independence and self-integrity thus emerges when stylistic strength *is* the life of the art-work. Only very unfortunately has style come to mean an outer decoration for some serious content of art. Susan Sontag helpfully quotes Cocteau: "Decorative style has never existed. Style is the soul . . ."[15] Therefore, if the details of texture allow the medium to be itself, and at the same time allow it to be supple and strong in doing its work, then the case is won, the work is alive. Success in style is "the soul" because it means overall success, considered from any angle.

A superscription for one of Miss Sontag's essays is taken from Oscar Wilde: "It is only shallow people who do not judge by appearances. The mystery of the world is the visible, not the invisible."[16] A summons to honor appearances is a refreshing one in a society so apt to reduce everything to one small set of conventional meanings. The staid doctrine, the grand interpretation, the stale romantic vista have plagued Western culture as increasingly dangerous resources of comfort. All these have been examples of hermeneutics or interpretive perspectives at their poorest. Thus a "bad" hermeneutic is one that clings arbitrarily to a ritual symbol ("my country right or wrong," or "history is bunk," etc.) and persistently reduces all experience to fit it. The dogmatic Freudian or Marxist errs equally with the inflexibly religious. One version of this problem is the everyday idealist pitfall that implies a private and ghostly self or "mind" within the physical body, separate from the physical, though in control of it.[17] Here another poor hermeneutic, or contextual horizon, is invoked to interpret our "threshold" experience in consciousness, the difficult gap between self-awareness and other-awareness. A realization of style helps with these poor quality reductions. For style is no physical lure for an abstruse spiritual content. Style means lively self-presentation at the level of concrete, surface detail—as with a mirror, whose rich depth is a function of how well its surface is ground and polished.

In discussing style as the soul, the relation between primary and secondary discourse, fundamental to the whole discussion, has been approached again. To say that the "soul" of an art work is a function of its surface detail, its visible appearance, is a corollary of my standing supposition: that second-order terms can, by their arrangement, invoke first-order discourse, yet without abandoning their recognizable second-order character. So the artist works with the "stylus" at the level of direct appearance; yet gestures, marks, fingerings are just so turned and ordered that a primal level of affairs emerges at the center of attention. In looking at style, we are inspecting the nerve-center where the miracle of first- and second-order concurrence takes place. Or, to change the figure, a sentence or a few brush strokes, betraying style, is like the living human cell, the nexus of vitality. The cell can be analyzed into certain chemicals, though their function as "life" is extraordinary; so examples of masterful style involve secondary terms, which nevertheless function in an awakening, primary manner. All this takes place *as* an articulation. And an articulation may be touched, seen, heard. There is no metaphysical "secret room" behind appearances; the secret and the wonder are *in* the appearance, the presentation itself, in the tension between primary and secondary forces. Nevertheless, the tension is unresolved, the articulation unfinished. To say no ghostly "stuff" stands behind the physical does not solve all our problems of understanding (though it does banish an illusory horizon). The real problem is not a mental-physical split, but a continuing dilemma as to how the human organism is rightly "disposed" in the world, how the tension between primary and secondary is to be readjusted continually. For all that, a major step forward has been made in grasping that the deepest matters function at the nearest level. The artist does not invoke the world afresh in any sense unless his or her humble "gamesmanship" at the surface locates a style in which the wonder of primary and secondary interaction takes place.

Style, 'Game,' and the Spectator-Player

Various items discussed to this point—artist, audience, illumination, game, style—need to be drawn together. Also, it may seem that such heavy attention to "style" does not do justice to the art object, which can be considered from other angles. For example, a literary object (poem, novel, short story) is open to intrinsic analysis regarding numerous formal elements besides style: point of view, character, plot, time, place, structure, mood, etc. Now there is no question but that careful formalist analysis of a literary work is an excellent beginning place for criticism. In the long run, formal analysis promises a more secure foundation for understanding the poem or novel than countless intuitive associations, which besiege the mind on a first reading. Formal study is a kind of "distancing" (parallel to the artist's original distancing) that paves the way for the work's full impact finally to be made. Also, when formal elements are examined, we find ourselves taking account of that second-order level in the work—the recognizable parts—already acknowledged as so crucial to a first-order function. According to its dynamic, the work must "dance"; but the nameable, second-order elements are the "dancers."

Nevertheless, style has received emphasis here because of its unique position relative to the total functioning of the piece. In a certain sense, style ranks as one of the "formal" elements for analysis in a literary work of art, along with such items as plot, mood, and point of view. But in another sense, style is a feature in which all fundamental components of the work meet and merge. For example, the meeting of first- and second-order functions of language has already been noted as occurring at the point of style. Also, what has been traditionally called "form and content" (and may more accurately be termed "form and matter") realize their merging point and unity within style. Indeed, to treat of style touches the literary work as a whole at both its primary and secondary levels. Hopefully, such an approach extends one's determination *not* to allow dismemberment of the work, or the abstract siphoning of it into one or another inadequate frame of reference.

Lest this last sentence be somewhat cryptic, let me expand on it by citing a move regarding art and literature typical of this study as a whole. Up to now, the terms "art object" and "game" have been employed interchangeably in referring to the work of art, or piece of literature. It is time, however, to draw a distinction between them and to observe how the model of an art-work as "game" is superior to the rather casual reference "art-object."

R. E. Palmer has rightly pointed out that to reflect upon an art-work as a "game" raises the question of who may be the "players" of the game.[18] If we attend a drama or a symphony, it seems obvious who the players are who present the work; the matter is not nearly so clear in the case of a work of literature. But even the drama or symphony leaves us with the question of whether we the audience are somehow "players" of this art-"game." Palmer cites approvingly the view of H. Gadamer that we are not, that we must strictly be counted as "spectators." In that case, the emphasis (especially in the non-performing arts) falls upon the integrity and independence of the game itself.

A good deal can be said for stressing the independent reality of a game in the "art-game" model. The point seems appropriate to the nature of an actual game, whose structure

III

86

and demands transcend the players themselves, and are a matter to which the players must and do submit. At the same time, the independent reality of a game presupposes the players' commitment to its structure. For a player to start thinking about the arbitrariness of the game and yield to caprice in the midst of the action is not to "play the game," but to destroy it. So long as commitment to the rules is assumed, then the force of the game in its own right holds good. From one viewpoint, the game is subjective (or more exactly, intersubjective) because grounded in conscious understanding and commitment. From another viewpoint, the game is objective because, once evolved and articulated, it becomes a public object transcending any set of players.

Suppose, however, that a game should become so far-reaching that it engages by its very nature one's vital commitments within the inescapable horizon of time. A pointed example is Hamlet's play before the king, his stepfather. Here an evening's diversion so directly evokes Claudius' true circumstances that the "conscience of the King," his biographical plight at that moment, is exposed. Hamlet's play is admittedly more of a device than a work of art; nevertheless, one can readily think of genuine works of art or literature in which the initial gaming model finally wields an impact equally as telling.

The point here is that *at the most significant level art and literature are neither subjective nor objective,* and the literary work is not best referred to as an "object." "Game" is a better notion than "object" precisely because "game" suggests both independent integrity *and* involvement. Art as "game" thus implies possible widening to first-order inclusiveness. The double situation of the players of a game also reminds us, in a preliminary way, of art: on the one hand, the players' conscious participation enables the game to exist; on the other, the players' behavior vitally responds to an order that is more than themselves. Now the thrust of Palmer's issue comes clear as to whether one reading, for example, a poem is a player-participant or strictly a spectator. If the reader is a player, "gaming" with the poet-author, then the work of art may consist of a mere subjective exchange of consciousness between artist and reader; the objective structure of the poem is lost. If the reader is a mere spectator at a poem-game "sponsored" by a poet, then the work becomes an interlocking set of formal components as "object"; the subjective communication of meaning is lost.

Perhaps the actual, ambivalent situation of a spectator at a game leads to a solution. A true spectator of a game is not technically "in" the game but deeply identifies with the action and may support one "side." Involvement may become as deep as that of the players themselves. Yet the game has its integrity over and beyond the spectator's personal intrusion. Now make parallel application to the reading of a poem or novel. The work has its articulate unity and integrity. The spectator-reader must be knowledgeable, even "scientific," about the work-as-structure if genuine appreciation is to result. Yet, to borrow the language of chapter one, the work may in time become "present" to the reader in a first-order perspective (the game involves the spectator). At that point, the reader identifies with a certain level of the work *as if a "player."* The problem with "presence," however, is that it may simply reduce the time-filled situation to one of present subjective awareness. We may find ourselves in the reflexive subject-object dilemma of "present" time. At this juncture, recall the views in chapter one: An occurrence of first-order "presence," though not illusory or irresponsible, may also constitute a clue or pointer to a deeper "presence," still embodied within the formal work. Reality gathers around in present-ness, yet in the same movement in time, takes one step back. The poem or novel discloses its "world," indeed its angle on *the* world; and if it is an important work, indicates *in that very act* the degree to which its "world" remains *undisclosed*, its present-ness more deeply hidden. Consequently, the work in its integrity as "game" (not as "object") still lies at hand to be fruitfully approached again and again.

Thus it is that we may be spectators at the literary-work "game," involved "as if" players, and yet beyond that, find the game in its integrity still at hand to invite us.[19]

In addition, the subject-object dilemma in literary criticism is transcended by recourse to the proper first-order horizon, time, in and through which the "presence" of reality is disclosed-undisclosed in a single movement. The poem or novel has opened an angle on reality; yet for just that reason the work itself remains pregnant with reality undisclosed. Hopefully, this discussion has shown that bringing the work of art into the arena of a two-order articulation of the real both respects the work in its integrity (the work as "object," its secondary components) and knows also its illuminating power (the work as "communion" of artist, audience, and world). The gaming model has seemed to serve well both sides of the artistic situation.

If so, does a literary work bring us to the "brink" of theology? One preliminary comment may be made at this time: it has already been suggested that a literary work participates in the same presentation of reality (on a two-order basis) as language generally, without negating its peculiar nature as a work of art. That a poem or novel both gives and withholds reality in a single "unveiling," while at the same time keeping its second-order integrity, offers a shadowy reminiscence of Western theology, in which the divine is realized as both present and distant, in and through everyday occasions. Of course, differences persist between literature and the data of theology, and the reminiscence is quite abstract. For one thing, the great variety of literary works demands consideration, as over against the single-mindedness of theology. Further, we have not even responded to all the particular questions on how literature presents reality. What about fiction, able to disregard matters of fact? What of differences in literary genre? in scope? in seriousness? Further analysis is necessary of what may be involved in a theological criticism of literature.

NOTES

1. In Flannery O'Connor, *Mystery and Manners; Occasional Prose,* ed. S. and R. Fitzgerald (New York: Farrar, Straus and Giroux, 1969) 65, 77–78, 79.

2. For a resumé of varying emphases among these four in the history of criticism, see M. H. Abrams, *The Mirror and the Lamp* (New York: The Norton Library, 1958) 6–29.

3. Foss, *Symbol,* 60. (See note 10, chapter II.)

4. Quoted in W. K. Wimsatt and C. Brooks, *Literary Criticism —A Short History* (New York: Vintage, 1957) 754.

5. See the comments on "physical poetry" by John Crowe Ransom in "Poetry: A Note in Ontology," *American Review* III (1934) 173–180.

6. See note 10, chapter I.

7. Norbert Lynton, *Klee* (London: Spring Books, 1964) 28.

8. J.-P. Sartre, *What is Literature?,* trans. B. Frechtman (New York: Harper and Row, 1949, 1956) 51.

9. See Ray Hart on "iconic penumbrity" in *Unfinished,* 254, 261–2.

10. Sartre, *Literature,* 42.

11. Sartre, *Literature,* 43–45.

12. See R. E. Palmer, *Hermeneutics—Interpretation Theory in Schleiermacher, Dilthey, Heidegger, and Gadamer* (Evanston: Northwestern University Press, 1969) 171–174.

13. I am indebted to Raymond McKeithen of New York for specifying such matters of technique, in an unpublished lecture.

14. Susan Sontag, *Against Interpretation* (New York: Dell Publishing Company, 1969) 41.

15. Sontag, *Against Interpretation,* 17. Original source not footnoted.

16. Sontag, *Against Interpretation,* 3. Fn. to Wilde "in a letter."

17. See the classic critique of this notion in Gilbert Ryle, *The*

Concept of Mind (New York: Barnes and Noble, 1949) 11–24, who labels it "the ghost in the machine."

18. Palmer, *Hermeneutics*, 173.

19. Compare the discussion in Palmer, *Hermeneutics*, 173–175.

Towards a Theological Criticism of Literature   IV

This pursuit of theology in literature has come to the point of assessing the theological potential, or dimension, within a literary work. Hopefully the topics dealt with thus far give some foundation for doing so. Dealings with language and reality, with metaphor, and with the work of art have pointed toward "world" moments within language. Thus, while the formal, definite specifications of language persist (second order), language has also the capacity to pose an indefinite, and therefore suggestive, extension of meaning (its first-order function). Both of these work together in a specific linguistic occasion to offer a "world," or a perspective on *the* world (though in this overt cooperation of the two orders, the primary or foundational tends more to command attention).

If language in general, if metaphor and symbol, if the literary work of art can to some degree illumine the world, then a theological suggestiveness is likely present. Theology is concerned to make some sense of the world vis-a-vis God, the world's foundation or creator. Very broadly speaking, literature effects a grasp of that world with implications for its ground and goal. That there would seem a theological dimension within literature is no surprise.)

Nevertheless, to indicate a widely general "dimension" in literature is but a bare beginning. How does this dimension relate to "fact," to "fiction," to interpretation? Why should it be called "theological," rather than philosophical, or religious, or even moral? Are we fair to the breadth of literature when we suggest that all serious forms of it maintain some level rightly called "theological"? Our first task should be to get some focus on these questions.

Fact, Fiction, and Interpretive Force

Much earlier in this study theology was referred to as the intellectual discipline of Christian faith. Such a working definition makes rather specific, traditional demands so that one can wonder whether the range of modern Western literature can and should accommodate them. There are questions of God as creator, immanent and transcendent, of revelation, of the person and work of Christ, and of the work of the Spirit in bringing all things to their appointed goal. But such precise matters hardly constitute the most favorable beginning point for comment on literature. A start can be made by pointing out very generally that theology concerns itself with statements both factual and evaluative. Theology builds upon the claims that certain factual events took place: the Israelite exodus from Egypt, the exiling of the Jews, the life of Jesus Christ, etc. Theology also adopts normative and evaluative statements of varying scope: God is love, creation is good, one ought not give false testimony.

Immediately one is into difficulty, since imaginative literature is not bound to present factual events. Fiction, for example, offers a foreground of hypothetical events not necessarily factual. The author does not speak directly to the reader, but presents the reader with a fictive "world" that stands between them. However, if literature seeks the truth and, insofar as successful, articulates reality, how is fiction's non-factual foreground reconciled with such claims? My position here, in part, is that the hypothetical character of fiction is a relatively superficial aspect of its nature. To look beyond the first level of fictive statement is to find fiction much concerned with the "truth," with "how things are."

Early in chapter three art was found to be "historical," not in the sense of presenting antiquarian fact, but in the sense of rendering a certain communication of reality within historical time. Yet at one level a real difference obviously obtains between literature and history—an ontological, factual difference. Perhaps there is one important clue to literary "truth": literature may not be factual, but it must somehow offer a serious and honest assessment of the author's experience. That assessment requires that the painful question of veracity pursue the serious writer. The fiction writer, for example, does not attempt to bring a "message," but to "tell a story." Yet the author must get the story "right"; the elements must fit together so as to comport with experienced reality. Thus the literary piece need not present what is factually true, but it must present the *type* of thing that is true, either *literally* or by *analogy*. A story may recount even the most unlikely kind of thing, to the point of the grotesque. Yet it may constitute an *explicit analogy* to the kind of thing that is *implicit* in the *real* world of affairs. Fiction does not offer prescriptive life-styles but touches by indirection levels of valid experience among us all. Admittedly, theology is more entangled than literature in certain factual claims, but literature must deal in a typology of real and true affairs.

Consider then the other theological "horn of the dilemma": the making of normative and evaluative statements. Clearly, when such statements are made in literature, they must initially be taken as merely hypothetical, parallel to the pseudo-factual statements of event. Northrop Frye is certainly right when he suggests that the ideas of literature are not real propositions, but *imitate* real propositions.[1] Thus a normative statement by a character in fiction or drama (e.g., "Neither borrower nor lender be . . .") is no message for our edification, but must first illumine the character who speaks it, and from there find its place in the imaginative structure of the work as a whole. Indeed, it is only by just such an approach to the work as a whole, initially by formal analysis, that one may begin to realize the horizon of the work's meaning. If, following such an appraisal, the thrust of that meaning does turn out to be in the mouth of one of the characters (e.g., "Hell is—other people!"[2]), only then are we prepared to affirm it for the entire piece.

It is better, in any case, not to speak of the work's "meaning," but of the horizon of its meaning. To stand vis-a-vis a work in a moment of its widest meaning is not to reduce it to a formula, but to share briefly in its "world," or horizon. In that sense, a work's meaning is *pre*-theological insofar as it is not stated directly, but rather expressed through its own first-order function. To stand, for example, within the horizon of *Mme. Bovary*, or its literary descendant, Sinclair Lewis' *Main Street*, is to realize a perspective on things through the "world" of a sensitive, frustrated woman and her small-town marriage. However, if the proper horizon of the world is time, as stated earlier, does standing within the horizon of a work simply mean standing vis-a-vis the work within time? Time may be considered the proper *formal* horizon of a work, but the proper *material* horizon must be a *particular* time. So the second-order limit or discipline of a particular occasion in time offers us a specific handle for grasping the work's wider suggestiveness.

Thus the particular "world" of a work, with its various characteristics, enables the work's illumination of reality. That illumination is implicitly evaluative, has the force of an interpretive judgment on human affairs, even though not directly stated. No literary work fails to engage the world normatively at an artistic level of full transaction. If the world is not in the least "summoned" in this way, then the arresting quality essential to art is absent. Every full reading of literature draws things to itself for a moment, and they are never just the same afterward. The world thus participates in the artistic act, though it is never "solved" by that act. The world itself is not separable from, though it is not reducible to, our continuing proposals of it.

Murray Krieger has suggested a poetic image of the relationship between the interpretive "world" of a literary piece and the "real" world, viz., the transformation of a mirror into a window. The literary work takes various materials from existence and mirrors these within itself as "world"; the mirror in turn then becomes a window offering a fresh perspective upon the real world.[3] When the literary work is considered as temporal transaction, the author communicates secondary matters such that they remember their foundations; the world is thereby illumined for a moment and shifts forward towards fuller articulation. The literary work not only looks out upon the real world, it penetrates it to a degree, to that same extent brings it to richer expression, and helps to complete it. Thus Giles Gunn, despite his position that a literary work is primarily a "hypothesis," calls attention at one point to the Aristotelian view that art helps to perfect nature.[4]

Surely enough has been said to indicate that a literary work does take a normatively perspectival view of the world's affairs, and even thereby actualizes elements of the world not realized before. By indirection, then, literature may include a theological level in its concern to be truthful about the world, and in its concern to realize that truth normatively through literary articulation. A question remains, however, as to why this level or dimension of literature should be called "theological." Why not philosophical, or "religious," or ethical? That a level of theological seriousness is being dealt with here, rather than some other kind, is of importance.

Religious Depth in Literature: the Usefulness of a Theological Field

It would seem that what I have proposed as a theological dimension in literature might more happily be termed "religious," thus allowing for the breadth and variety of literature while still acknowledging its involvement with questions of the world's unity and destiny. Indeed, the field that in this country arose under the name of "literature and theology" has increasingly emerged under the rubric of "literature and religion."[5] The term "religion" also holds some advantage over the designations "philosophy" and "ethics." Philosophy suggests definite rational conceptualizing, while literature's metaphoric and symbolic side offers as well a rich, indefinite field not subject simply to reduction. As regards the moral and ethical, a work of literature may indeed be considered an "ethical symbol" in that its "world" dimension offers a perspective on the moral, relational character of existence. The ethical nevertheless involves clues to an order within which moral relationships have their significance; "religion" can invoke that order while still comprehending the ethical-relational. Further, as Ralph Ellison has said concerning fiction, novels are essentially celebrative in nature; their aesthetic form recalls ritual and ritual practice, which may not initially yield to a moral agenda.[6] Maxims of behavior will have to be markedly derivative or only indirectly present within the art-work. Since religion indicates an ultimate, symbolic human awareness of a broad kind, the wider implications of literature for the nature of the world in which we live might best be termed "religious."

Nevertheless, "religion" as a designation does not satisfy for several reasons. For one thing, despite its wide current use, "religion" is a term of modern development now employed with a breadth that hardly recalls its roots in the Western monastic movement. The question then becomes what "religion" in contemporary usage actually stands for. Some attention has already been given "religion" in its general sense of human response to the sacred, however that sacred is understood. Certainly the word can be clarified in phenomenological and sociological discourse. Rather the question is whether its meaning is highly serviceable in literary-critical reflection.

Relative to literature, "religion" invariably tends to mean whatever the literary work offers at a level of serious depth about the human condition. Giles Gunn summarizes the matter nicely by asking:

> . . . how does one discuss the religious elements, mo-
> tifs, or characteristics of any given work of literature
> without either turning literature into a surrogate
> for philosophy or theology on the one hand, or re-
> ducing religion merely to any and every work's
> dimension of seriousness or depth on the other?[7]

For religion to mean any and every work's "dimension of
seriousness" comes very close to saying that it means nothing
in particular. Amorphous "religion," that boundless wager on
the "depth" of things, has no discipline or distinct articulation at all. Religion that wanders at will through a "secularized" culture is capable of serious monstrosities. Erich Heller
has unforgettably shown that an illegitimate "muddy poetry
of the depths" can erupt into a prosaic culture ostensibly
dedicated to rational criticism and technology.[8] Modern to-
talitarian ideology is the obvious case in point. What is bad
for the life of a culture is not healthy for literature and theology. To cite a vague dimension in literature significant for
the most compelling questions of destiny may delegate ill-
founded authority to literature and cast it in a role not meant
for it. With Gunn, we do not wish to turn literature "into a
surrogate for philosophy or theology," especially when no
specified tradition or disciplined articulation can render this
"religion" accountable. Clear lines of doctrine have historically been abused, but one of their merits is accountability in
the light of day. By the same token, if literature is to relate
either to religion or theology, some disciplined lines of statement are needed on the "religion" side that nevertheless do
not subvert aesthetic freedom on the literary side.

In this difficulty, the viewpoint I am offering favors acknowledgment of Western cultural roots as a continuing influence and therefore Western theology as the most accountable discipline vis-a-vis literature. Religion as a discipline
faces methodological complexities that are notorious. Furthermore, a Western oriented scholar pursues literature and
"religion" with certain presuppositions of that Western heritage undoubtedly still in force. It is better that they be acknowledged and open to scrutiny. I wish to emphasize that

the choice made here in no way identifies with a claim of Western cultural superiority. Rather, to acknowledge an identity of heritage is to deal more effectively with both its positives and its negatives. "Religion" in the West has pursued a recognizable form, with variations, of which theology has attempted to be both voice and critic. If this Western "religion" relates to Western literature, then theology and its long tradition may be the clearest, most distinctly accountable field to trace that relationship.

For reasons of clarity, accountability, and facing the difficulties "head-on," I have therefore elected to place literature by the side of theology, including the latter's doctrines of God as creator, of redemption as unique in Christ, and of a promised and worthy end or goal for the world. What pathway will then serve to cross from the one to the other, and how is that path to be negotiated? How can theology be a theology "for" literature and still justify its antique structure and affirmations?

The Idea of a Christian Aesthetic

Relating theology to literature has been under discussion in this country for some while. In the Introduction theological attempts of both a "confessional" and "apologetic" nature to bring to light the theological dimension of a literary piece were noted. Neither of these gave significant promise of good success. The confessional view recalls the injunction of T. S. Eliot:

> . . . Literary criticism should be completed by criticism from a definite ethical and theological standpoint. In so far as in any age there is common agreement on ethical and theological matters, so far can literary criticism be substantive. In ages like our own, in which there is no such common agreement, it is the more necessary for Christian readers to scrutinize their reading, especially of works of imagination, with explicit ethical and theological standards.[9]

Eliot's statement is logical enough. The question is simply to what end one employs the scrutiny he advocates. Much literature of aesthetic and humane power evidently fails to meet the standards indicated. Under such explicit scrutiny, how do Joyce, Hemingway, Faulkner, Beckett, Camus, Kafka, and Kazantzakis fare? If their works do not illumine the preferred theological view, are they not to be read? Are they to be read, but with caution? Surely their own integrity includes a theological potential that should be heard from before being judged so starkly.

A Christian apologetic approach to literature is even less convincing than the confessional. Undoubtedly the best-known theology brought into such harness with literary criticism in this country has been that of Paul Tillich, who proposed a correlation of culture with Christian belief as a correlation of question with answer. In that case, the "despair" portrayed in modern literature both raises the human, spiritual question and implies the answer of the New Being in Christ. The problem with this view is that in order to join literature with theology each of them is translated into the terms of a broad philosophy of Being. The "common ground" that constitutes the apologetic lets neither the literature retain its own form, nor the theology its own confessional identity.

Nor is it convincing to cite a kind of pilgrimage from the confessional to a newer and more radical form of the apologetic, as, for example, in the recent work of John Killinger.[10] In response to new insight, Killinger moves to disavow his earlier, more confessional stance on the "failure" of theology in literature. He now suggests that in its dread emptiness and negativity much of modern literature nevertheless invokes a sense of the numinous or of profound presence, bleak though that presence may be. There is something disturbing about this clear move from one thing to another by Killinger—as if he had forgotten his own injunction not "to think of a 'way' as a mere stretch with two fixed ends," inviting us to rush from one to the other.[11] As will be seen, there is something to be said for the "failure" of theology in literature; there is also something to be said for "presence" within even the most negative works. The appropriate "way" that Killinger seeks is toilsome precisely because it must ponder the claim of *both* these attitudes, not simply exchange the one for the other, as he has done.

The review of the more standard confessional and apologetic positions within theological criticism, as presented in Sallie TeSelle's *Literature and the Christian Life*, continues to be helpful.[12] Within the confessional view, which she calls "Christian Discrimination," TeSelle finds not only Eliot, but also T. E. Hulme, Randall Stewart, and Cleanth Brooks. Within the apologetic view, which she calls "Religious Amiability," TeSelle locates, along with Tillich, Amos Wilder and Nathan A. Scott, Jr. Of greater interest than either of these views, however, is the approach that TeSelle entitles "Christian Aesthetics." While she admits that a complete "Christian" aesthetic does not, and probably should not, exist, for it would tend to prescribe too closely what the artist should do, nevertheless she finds one particular insight or "Christian aesthetic" fragment highly attractive. The insight is grounded in work by Erich Auerbach and William Lynch: the Christ serves as a kind of model for the artistic imagination in that his glory was located in and through his full experience of everyday, finite affairs. In the same way, the artist assembles the actual materials of everyday and insightfully realizes through them a moment of the infinite, or of extensive vision. TeSelle quotes Lynch:

> . . . the Christic act, the act of athletic and confident penetration of limit, of the actual, and the human, can again become the model and energizer for the poetic imagination . . .[13]

Though one is not so sure about Christ as "athletic," the central point made by Lynch and TeSelle can be put in terms being used here: a certain view of the Incarnation ("God in the Flesh") is analogous to everyday, second-order terms metaphorically doing illuminating, first-order work. It is thus possible to note a resemblance between a successful artistic achievement and the central Christian affirmation of the Christ as fully entered into common, human affairs.

Only one significant objection arises to the work of Lynch

IV
—

and TeSelle in this matter. The point they have made linking Incarnation to a Christian aesthetic is excellent. One is not equally certain, however, about the *significance they attach to* this point, and the implications they apparently draw from it. With each of them the result of their insight is to set up a direct line of significance between Christology and art. Lynch is interested in what Christianity may do for the arts via its emphasis on Incarnation, suggesting to artists a set of assumptions that would, as TeSelle says, "give them confidence in and an image of man and the world which could help them to do their own job of celebrating finite reality . . ."[14] TeSelle also expresses some disappointment that Lynch does not see the contribution the other way about, as well—that literature which celebrates the finite may initiate and strengthen Christological thought. The suggestion of a direct connection between Incarnational doctrine and current imaginative literature is, in the terms I wish to use here, drawing too simple a line from reflected theology to theology proper. One draws back from urging the Christian doctrine of Incarnation upon an artist, while it is highly doubtful that reflection upon art that celebrates the finite has reason to arrive at an affirmation of God-in-Christ. The analogy does hold, as between Western Christian teaching and the process of artistic creation; but the significance of the analogy is much more subtle and indirect than Lynch's and TeSelle's straightforward joining of the two can allow.

For example, Erich Auerbach's work contributes more appropriately to this analogy by giving it setting and background through the history of Western letters. His monumental study, *Mimesis,* along with his work on Dante and the Western "figure" or "type,"[15] presents a remarkable case for the analogue between the Western grasp of reality through literature and the Western affirmation of the Christ story. The heart of Auerbach's contribution at this point lies in his work on "figure" (*figura*) and on the nature of the "mixed style." By "mixed style" Auerbach refers to the emergence during the Christian era of a style of literature in which matters of high seriousness are nevertheless treated in everyday language dealing with ordinary, or lowly, situations.[16] By "figure" or "type" (as opposed to allegory) Auerbach means a historical situation or event that bears within itself a larger reality of which it is the "type," *yet with no loss of its own, particular historical actuality.*[17] (Thus the Exodus can be a "figure" of Christ's resurrection with no loss of its own concrete historicity.) Both of these formal emphases, "mixed style" and "figure," offer the coincidence of a highly serious, universal reality with the concrete, everyday components that surprisingly present that reality. They are formally reminiscent of metaphor, and materially reminiscent of God-in-the-flesh. Furthermore, Auerbach's work on biblical style with its abrupt, incomplete nature suggests that style's emotional engagement of the reader in a universal process of historical "becoming."[18] Recall in this connection what has already been said concerning metaphoric, first-order functions *in time* with their giving-and-withholding of reality. Note that in each of these emphases, Auerbach is working with either biblical documents or with early Christian biblical commentary. Then the Bible, which offered the Christ-story and that story's peculiar literary form, became the dominant influence over Western literature generally. Little wonder that an analogue emerged between Western literary art and the account of the Incarnation.

In a most illuminating study of Auerbach, Arthur R. Evans, Jr., notes that in numerous of his works ". . . the story of Christ, in all its ramifications, will serve as a chief point of reference in Auerbach's search for the distinctive character of European history."[19] And Auerbach himself states explicitly at one point:

> . . . In the life story of Christ and the typological interpretation of history based on it Christianity possessed a universally appealing view of earthly events, in which human destinies are dramatized, [and thus] succeeded in imbuing men with its substance . . . By lending the feelings of men a new depth the Christian dialectic of suffering and passion laid the groundwork for what is most significant and characteristic in the poetry of modern times;

IV

and the confrontation between ancient thought and the paradoxes of the Christian faith was the school that made European philosophy what it is.[20]

Surely the notion of even a partial "Christian aesthetic" grounds itself in the peculiar aesthetic character of the Christ-story, form *and* matter, and the influence as model that story had over the Western literature that followed upon it.

Thus even modern Western literature may lead to the "brink" of theology insofar as it takes the actualities of earth seriously, but casts them into a dynamic, metaphoric tension that moves to penetrate and renew the world. Literature and theology have a formal link in and through the Christ story, which heavily influenced the shape and substance of them both. Within the Western arena, there may yet be a theology "for" literature.

The Continuing Problematic of Literature and Theology

It has been a long road towards a literary expression of theology and, in turn, a theological criticism. The discussion of the two orders of language has defined a dimension in literature evidently theological in potential in the following manner: what we have discerned, through first-order language, as the present reality of things "gathered" can serve as analogue to the order of God expressed in and through the world. The "slipping back" of reality coincident with its self-presentation finds analogue in the transcendence-immanence of God, the hidden and revealed. The metaphor (ordinary, second-order components in a first-order function) is analogue of the "enfleshed" Word, God-in-Christ. The metaphoric transition through time, with nevertheless a certain second-order stability, suggests the work of the Spirit through history, yet with retention of certain recognizable, "figural," intersecting points. Second-order crises or disarray that nevertheless effect metaphoric transition (diaphor, or absolute metaphor) are analogue of the irony of the cross, the crown in suffering, life in death. The "move" of the world toward renewal in the aesthetic act is analogue of Christ's resurrection and the end-to-come, glory following upon upheaval. The list could be extended. The original grounding of Western life in the biblical narrative virtually guaranteed that what Auerbach called Western literature's "representation of reality" (the sub-title of *Mimesis*) would bear analogy to theology's confession of faith.

Yet many knots remain untied. For example, the very work of Auerbach himself shows that a gulf persists between literature and theology. Auerbach's work is monumental, but it is not a theological affirmation, nor was it meant to be. His vast review of the parallel between the biblical story and the shape of reality through styles of Western literature remains theologically ambiguous. Indeed, Auerbach himself considered remarkable the various intentions ascribed to him by readers of his work,[21] none of which matched his own purpose. The conflation between the account of Jesus' life and the modes of Western literary expression by no means implies for him a confession of faith. Auerbach's study discloses a certain clue to the nature of Western reflection and traces types of historical dependence. But if his work holds any theological or "metaphysical" purpose, it is rather a broad one of finding some general, ontological foundation across the whole span of Western culture. Evans rightly says of him:

> . . . A metaphysical, quasi-religious need to comprehend the human condition of Western man in its varied historical manifestations and in its total destiny, and then, beyond this, to determine in the unfolding of history a *logos* or principle of order— these are the driving passions animating the articles and books which trace with exact philological skill and a humanist's intense commitment the entire course of European literary history.[22]

The quest for a historical *logos* may find a useful paradigm and traditional clue in the biblical narrative of Christ. But it would be entirely inappropriate to infer from this that Auerbach, a committed humanist of Jewish background, wove himself into a Christian confession of faith through scholarship. The humanist who finds broad philosophical clues to culture through literary study may well separate himself from the people that originally lived by that literature. In an interesting and rare kind of passage in *Mimesis*, Auerbach notes concerning the biblical stories:

> . . . their religious intent involves an absolute claim to historical truth. The story of Abraham and Isaac is not better established than the story of Odysseus, Penelope, and Euryclea; both are legendary. But the Biblical narrator, the Elohist, had to believe in the objective truth of the story of Abraham's sacrifice— the existence of the sacred ordinances of life rested upon the truth of this and similar stories. He had to believe in it passionately; or else . . . he had to be a conscious liar—no harmless liar like Homer, who lied to give pleasure, but a political liar with a definite end in view, lying in the interest of a claim to absolute authority. . . . without believing in Abraham's sacrifice, it is impossible to put the narrative of it to the use for which it was written. Indeed, we must go even further. The Bible's claim to truth is not only far more urgent than Homer's, it is tyrannical—it excludes all other claims. The world of Scripture stories is not satisfied with claiming to be a historically true reality—it insists that it is the only real world, is destined for autocracy. All other scenes, issues, and ordinances have no right to appear independently of it, and it is promised that all of them, the history of all mankind, will be given their due place within its frame, will be subordinated to it.[23]

I have quoted the passage at length because it is easily overlooked in the general zeal for Auerbach's work. First, Auerbach clearly did not accept the biblical authority he so forcefully describes. He probably thought contemporary acceptance impossible. (". . . through the awakening of a critical consciousness, . . . the Biblical claim to absolute authority is jeopardized; . . . the Biblical stories become ancient legends . . .[24]") Secondly, the worrisome business of theology's claim to certain essential, *factual* truths—not simply metaphors, paradigms or concrete symbols—starkly urges a difference between theology and literature.

Literature's relative freedom from biblical theology's strictures, described above by Auerbach, finds expression also in the wide number of genres open to literature and the wide variety of examples within each genre. What single theological frame of reference can serve a lyric by Dylan Thomas, a novel by Theodore Dreiser, a drama by Samuel Beckett?

Actually, if clues to the theological dimension are primarily formal, aesthetic ones (two orders of linguistic function, metaphor, symbol, "game," style, world-horizon, "present-ness," "hidden-ness," etc.), these are able to cut across different genres and pieces within genres in a way that particular content emphases could not. Presumably any Western literary piece can be *formally* reminiscent of the Word-made-flesh in rather special ways, as summarized at the beginning of this section. At the point, however, of the particular "world" of a literary work, the angle or illumination on things in the work's first-order effect, real differences emerge among works and types of works. For example, a work may be very much spoken in the author's "voice," as in a lyric, giving the outlook a highly personal slant. Or the work may be far more objective insofar as many-sided and reflecting, like a polished stone, a variety of possible viewpoints. A tragedy like *King Lear* is an example. Whether by virtue of genre or of the author's "slant" or scope of genius, the "world" of a literary work has virtually endless possibilities for the "shape" it sees in disclosed-undisclosed reality.

One approach to theology through the variety of literature is via ancient polytheism, realizing in the "world" of a literary work one of earth's "gods."[25] Indeed, Vincent Vycinas has spoken of a "god" as interchangeable with the notion of a "world."

> . . . Gods as worlds never merely dominate or support a section of reality; they dominate everything whatsoever. However, everything is shown and seen in a different light by a different god and therefore is different.[26]

At the same time, ancient Greeks living in awareness of the gods, granted that each one did constitute an entire world, nevertheless did not lack the sense that there is finally one world. Vycinas concludes that "gods" as "worlds" must final-ly constitute modes of *the* world.[27] Or, as we have suggested here, the "world" of an art-work offers a particular illumina-tion of the real world. Polytheism, therefore, does not neces-sarily deny a single, over-arching unity, though pluralistic in its presentation. And the world of a god may suggest that sin-gle unity in its character as world-mode. Zeus, as ruler of the gods, provided the order to which the several "worlds" be-longed. No less in Augustine of Hippo do we find gods uni-fied under the Christian God, though further classified with him into "good angels" and "bad angels."[28] The point here is that the variety of Western literature, especially modern, may nevertheless probe the kind of ultimate unity that theology must be concerned with; the "gods" and their "worlds" final-ly bespeak the real world and its principle of order. Never-theless, literature's indicators of that principle are indirect and manifold and bear great variety of witness. The theologi-cal dimension of literature hardly promises clear and un-equivocal invocation of that order's character and nature.

The Scope of Theology in Literature

From the affirmatives and negatives noted thus far concern-ing literature's theological dimension, the time has come to draw conclusions as to the nature and scope of that potential. This study has indicated that literature probes the truth of the world, and moves to interpret the world, and that its very aesthetic form in the West remembers its foundations in the Christian story, formal and material. At the same time, it has become clear that the wide variety of literature cannot be ex-pected to meet the peculiar demands of a clearly specified Christian faith as regards theological perspective. Were lit-erature measured by such demands, much that is of real aesthetic power and penetration would be counted unworthy. On the other hand, if theology were altered or "stretched" so as to include the breadth of literary perspectives, then the-ology would lose its disciplined accountability and literature would be pushed towards the role of a theology-substitute.

As anticipated in the Introduction and in the title of this

study, the position taken here will be that theology is significantly "reflected" in Western literature but that literature need not, and indeed usually does not, embody in its own medium the essential outlook of that theology. The reflection of theology in literature does provide literature a theological dimension that can be appropriately commented upon. But that dimension need not imply a confession of Christian faith, and even when it does, the literary work cannot directly pronounce that confession, but must let its own fictive world speak for itself.

Inquiry to this point has made it clear that the surest approach to theology in literature lies with certain formal, generalized traits of the literary work which recall the theological roots of Western culture generally. On the one hand, literature must be true to earth and to our knowledge and experience of earth. Only so can the sensuous actualities be assembled that are necessary to art. On the other hand, literature sees its things of earth "together" in a fresh way so that earth is realized as "world." Things are not forced out of their true character; yet they offer a new prospect not present before. These formal characteristics of any literary work recall the Christian story, as we have noted in greater detail above. John Crowe Ransom has referred to these same artistic functions as the "inexhaustible play" between the "moral universal" and the "concrete of nature" within a literary work.[29] Nature proffers us "things," particulars, which in their second-order fashion maintain a steadiness, serene and available. But a certain gathering of these particulars suggests something universal in character, including the quality of human beings' relation to their world. This "universal" is "moral" not by way of injunction, but by way of freshly illuminating the significance of the human role within the world's affairs. What Ransom calls the "inexhaustible play" we have dealt with here as the continuing tension between the two orders of language, unfinished through time. The literary work offers renewal and a certain fruitful increase of the world, but the inexhaustible play goes on. The gathered vision is not complete; finality is hinted at, but not realized.

In keeping with these formal characteristics, a certain content will be proposed that can be assigned to the "reflected" theology found in literature. To that end, recall an essential clue adapted from Heidegger's philosophy in chapter one. In Heidegger's terms, beings do "present" Being within the realm opened up by language. Yet, in the very same move, Being is also hidden beyond beings and present time, so that the "presence" of beings turns out to be an analogical indicator of Being's "full" presence—so near, yet so far. Using the terms adopted in this study, the first- and second-order interplay of language does present reality, which nevertheless "sinks back" even at the point of the richest first-order tension. The subject-object dilemma of present time is thereby sidestepped in the double movement of reality, "presenting" itself coincident with "sinking back." We are "as-if" players in the first-order game (subjective); yet we are spectators of that which still holds certain secrets of reality (objective).

It has already been suggested that the view of a two-order linguistic function is a certain "reflection" of Christian theology, borrowing on the notion of a fragmentary "Christian aesthetic." In this connection it is most serviceable to notice that Heidegger's philosophical position, of significant import in this study, has also been declared as bearing a kind of analogy to classical lines of Christian doctrine. Indeed, this analogue was at least at one point acknowledged by Heidegger himself. In the period following World War II, continental theologians increasingly concerned themselves with the possible theological implications of the "later Heidegger." At a certain meeting of theologians in 1960, featuring an attempt by the theologian, Heinrich Ott, to correlate his work with Heidegger's, the philosopher himself was present. Heidegger at that time proposed an *analogia proportionalitatis* between theology and his own philosophy: A is to B as C is to D. James Robinson summarizes the point in this way:

> . . . As philosophical thinking is related to being, when being speaks to thinking, so faith's thinking is related to God, when God is revealed in his word. . . . Thus theology in its speaking of God is not re-

quired to choose whether God is in Heideggerian terms a being, or nothing, or being itself, or that which is implicit in the awesome awareness of the being of beings. God would not "fit into" the Heideggerian system, but *the whole of theology,* operating within its own language, *would have a structural correspondence to philosophy* of the Heideggerian kind.[30] (Italics ours.)

While most theologians' interest in this "structural correspondence" turned toward seeking a philosophical ground for doing theology, my interest here is just the reverse. The speculation I wish to offer (though hardly new) is that Heidegger's position, for all its rootage in the Greeks, broadly reflects the presuppositions of a Christian theological culture. The relation of Being to beings in time offers a structural analogy to the relation of the Christian God to creatures in time. Theology is "reflected" in Heidegger's philosophy. I suspect, therefore, that theology lends Heidegger's philosophy its deepest significance, rather than the other way about.

In just the same way, theology is "reflected" in literature, whose nature I have discussed in terms parallel to Heidegger's. Reality, offered and yet hidden within the tension of the two linguistic orders, glimpsed through our situation in time as moving and eventful, constitutes a shadowy image of the Christian God. If "reality" thus offers an analogue to the Christian God, then presumably there are in the artistic function of language rough analogues to the doctrines of grace, of Christ as God the Son, of salvation and the atoning work, of the Spirit in the community, of the sacraments, and of the end-to-come. These analogues may occur through literature in a most heavily ironic form, so that the substantive result of their impact is quite the opposite to the original intent of Christian theology. For example, the "grace" of the "reflected" God—what a literary work finds as the spontaneously "given" at the core of a situation—may turn out as inexplicable mystery or as forgetful indifference. Literature is not limited in what substantive perspective it adopts toward the world. At the same time, the structural framework of that substantive view can, and to some degree always does, reflect the structure of Western Christian theology.

Earlier in this chapter I suggested that theology would serve better than philosophy as a discipline in tandem with literature. Yet the "theology" proposed here as implicit in literature has turned out to be an adaptation of Martin Heidegger's philosophy. Does this turn away from a commitment to the theological field? To the contrary. Rather, I am willing to argue that Heidegger's work is one of those exceptions to the rule of philosophy's exclusion, and for the reason already given: Heidegger's philosophy is itself highly reminiscent of the Western theology that gave it birth—perhaps even more so, for example, than Hegel's heavily immanentalist position. This is not to say that his work does not constitute a valid philosophical option; it can represent a chapter in the history of philosophy as well as in the broader history of theology. Yet Heidegger's very determination to rethink the entire philosophical tradition since Plato is instructive. To rethink it by what standard, or in what terms? I believe his central criticism of the Greeks, that the "presence" of things they inquired into rendered the Greeks too intent only upon "present" time, is a crypto-Christian remark. Thus to adapt certain of Heidegger's essential points in our work here is not to stray from the wider sphere of theology.

Another question may emerge: the theological dimension within literature has been consistently noted as an imaged reflection of Christian theology. What of Jewish theology, also of such essential importance in the West? Admittedly, while the difference between Jewish and Christian theologies "proper" is of the highest significance and must not be slurred over, at the level of "reflected" theology in Western literature many of the same structural analogues apply. The framework of history, of covenant, of creation and promise are broadly the same in the two traditions. Consequently, at the level of theological implications within literature, comment is often possible that is suggestive for either tradition. When a literary work obviously takes its signals from one or the other heritage (as with Elie Wiesel's Jewish background, or Camus' Catholic background), appropriate adjustment of the theological analogues can be made. The substantive openness of the "reflected" framework permits it.

The philosophizing kind of theology reflected in literature, while making few concrete, doctrinal demands, nevertheless has sufficient "shape" and structure to permit a degree of explication. It also has a history in the unfolding of Western thought. In other words, the fact that modern literature (if not modern culture generally) evidences a "reflected" theology rather than a theology proper (contrast Dante and Milton) has a story behind it. In part two of this study, "a theology 'for' literature," an attempt will be made to follow something of that story by way of elucidating reflected theology's structure and meaning.

The aim, then, of part two will be to trace the parameters of that theology suggested largely by the aesthetic form and force of Western literary works, keeping in mind as guidance the loci of Christian theology proper. To put it another way, I shall try to give significant form to the theological "dimension" that presumably appears in all Western literary works, simply by virtue of their character as works of art, and do this in a manner combining history with analysis. Finally, one or two illustrative examples will be offered, showing how the theological schema proposed finds specific content or viewpoint in being correlated with a given literary work. If these efforts are fruitful, a kind of theological criticism should begin to come into view.

NOTES

1. Frye, *Anatomy*, 84–85, 113. Yet we do not have to agree with Frye to the point of remaining always at a hypothetical level in reading a work of literature.

2. Stated by Garcin in J.-P. Sartre, *No Exit* (New York: Vintage Books, 1949) 47.

3. Murray Krieger, *A Window to Criticism* (Princeton: Princeton University Press, 1964) 33–37. Dan O. Via has a helpful review of this whole issue with comments on Krieger in his *The Parables—Their Literary and Existential Dimension* (Fortress Press, 1967) 70–88.

4. Giles Gunn, ed., *Literature and Religion* (New York: Harper and Row, 1971). From the editor's Introduction, p. 6.

5. E.g., Gunn, *Literature and Religion*.

6. Ralph Ellison, *Shadow and Act* (New York: Signet Books, 1966) 121.

7. Gunn, *Literature and Religion*, 12.

8. Erich Heller, *The Disinherited Mind* (Cleveland: The World Publishing Co., 1959) 93.

9. T. S. Eliot, "Religion and Literature," reprinted in *The New Orpheus: Essays Toward A Christian Poetic*, ed. Nathan A. Scott, Jr. (New York: Sheed and Ward, 1964) 223.

10. John Killinger, *The Fragile Presence: Transcendence in Modern Literature* (Philadelphia: Fortress Press, 1973) 1–10.

11. Killinger, *Fragile*, 7.

12. Sallie TeSelle, *Literature and the Christian Life* (New Haven: Yale University Press, 1966) 8–59.

13. TeSelle, *Literature*, 41. The quotation is from W. Lynch, "Theology and the Imagination II: The Evocative Symbol," *Thought*, 29 (1954–55) 547.

14. TeSelle, *Literature*, 43.

15. See Erich Auerbach, *Mimesis—The Representation of Reality in Western Literature*, trans. W. R. Trask (Princeton: The University Press, 1953). Also, *Dante—Poet of the Secular World*, trans. R. Manheim (Chicago: The University Press, 1929) and "Figura" in *Scenes from the Drama of European*

Literature—Six Essays, various translators (New York: Meridian Books, 1959) 11–76.

16. For example, Auerbach, *Mimesis,* 40–48.

17. For example, "Figura," 29.

18. Auerbach, *Mimesis,* 7–23.

19. Arthur R. Evans, Jr., "Erich Auerbach as European Critic," *Romance Philology,* XXV, 2 (November, 1971) 208.

20. Erich Auerbach, *Literary Language and its Public in Late Antiquity and in the Middle Ages,* trans. Ralph Manheim (New York: Pantheon Books, 1965) 337–338.

21. Evans, "Auerbach," 215, esp. fn. 31.

22. Evans, "Auerbach," 198.

23. Auerbach, *Mimesis,* 14–15.

24. Auerbach, *Mimesis,* 15–16.

25. I am indebted to Dr. Jerry W. Cullum for calling my attention to this possibility in an unpublished dissertation, "The Edenic Imagination: Studies in the Sacramental Reconciliation of Self and World" (Emory University, 1975) 10–26.

26. Vincent Vycinas, *Earth and Gods: an Introduction to the Philosophy of Martin Heidegger* (The Hague: Martinus Nijhoff, 1961) 188. See also Cullum, "Imagination," 16–17.

27. Vycinas, *Earth,* 189.

28. *City of God* IX, 18–23.

29. John Crowe Ransom, "The Concrete Universal: Observations on the Understanding of Poetry II," *Kenyon Review,* XVII, 3 (Summer, 1955) 394; also, 397–403. I am indebted to Mr. James Tichenor for bringing these points to my attention.

30. J. M. Robinson and J. B. Cobb, Jr., eds., *The Later Heidegger and Theology* (New York: Harper and Row, 1963) 43.

Part Two
A THEOLOGY FOR LITERATURE

Theology and the Western
Way of 'Knowing'

In order to pursue a "reflected" theology, two matters will be considered. First, it will be important to note something of how the classical lines of theology have dissolved in much of the history of the modern West. Secondly, one will want to discover whether the influence and effect of those lines nevertheless remain in certain phases of culture not usually or necessarily thought of as theological.

The decline of theology from its position as "queen of the sciences" is a many-sided phenomenon in Western history. Social, political, and intellectual issues all combined to cast great suspicion upon theology as the synthesizing field to which all other disciplines were, by implication, subservient. For purposes of analysis, I will take a commonplace intellectual problem, "the subject-object dilemma," and briefly treat its emergence as a particular example of the intricate developments that removed theology from its place of prominence. To a degree, the subject-object problem has already been addressed in Part I, and in the long run the treatment here will be a continuation of what has been said earlier. But for the moment, the structure of the subject-object question may be used in focusing attention on what has happened to Western theology in the post-medieval centuries.

Very simply, subject-object is an obvious scheme for analyzing our general knowledge of things—a scheme that in its application nevertheless eventually renders knowledge uncertain. In any case of clear and certain knowledge, there would seem to be an object "known" (what we have called a second-order linguistic item) and a subject, or "knower." Yet subject and object are of different orders or classes, so that reliable community between them (and therefore reliable knowledge) becomes intensely difficult to specify and defend. Either the objects are defined by concepts or categories the subject brings to them, in which case reality appears as expanded subjectivity ("nothing but ourselves"); or, by the same token, the objects as they "really" are elude our categories, in which case the subject, "I," is adrift amongst a flood of unmanageable particulars. Either way, the apparently obvious and reassuring subject-object relation is collapsed into a continuum of disorder and alienation.

The subject-object problem has intellectually intruded itself into all attempts to validate knowledge; and from one point of view, it was this dilemma that broke theology's hegemony in the West. As the medieval period became increasingly elaborate in the twelfth and thirteenth centuries, a greater variety of individual particulars emerged—of individual human beings, of individuality in artistic representation, of individual lines and instruments in music, of individual forms in philosophic reflection (Aristotelianism). A sharp question arose as to whether the increased variety of particular objects in experience any longer found a rational unity within the massive Western Christian world-view. For example, Shakespeare's Globe Theater was a model of the world as viewed by the Christian middle ages; but the impact of plays like *Hamlet* and *King Lear* threw their own setting in that model into question. Dante's immense success in portraying the medieval Christian world in his *Comedy* was at one level that world's undoing. As Auerbach comments:

> . . . the principle, rooted in the divine order, of the indestructibility of the whole historical and individual man turns *against* that order, makes it subservient to its own purposes, and obscures it. The image of man eclipses the image of God. Dante's work made man's Christian-figural being a reality, and destroyed it in the very process of realizing it. The tremendous pattern was broken by the overwhelming power of the images it had to contain. . . .
>
> . . . even in Hell there are great souls, and certain souls in Purgatory can for a moment forget the path of purification for the sweetness of a poem, the work of human frailty.[1]

Thus the individualized object, the mysterious concrete, was coming into its own, threatening the subject-knower with uncertainty and exceeding the lines of classical theology's doctrine of creation with its aesthetic wholeness of all things (Augustinianism). The birth of modernity appeared to coincide with the emergence of a spectrum of autonomous ideas, objects, and situations, challenging theology's right to render them within its structures. For the post-medieval West, the subject-object uncertainty seemed preferable to an evidently outmoded authoritarianism of theology and church.

At the same time, it is easy to exaggerate theology's decline. Obviously, theology continued as a recognized discipline following the medieval and Reformation periods. But large numbers of the culturally enlightened refused to follow it. Schleiermacher's work *On Religion: Speeches to Its Cultured Despisers* betokens a mood and a tension that speaks for the modern West. True to the subject-object problem urgently posed, theology had begun to appear as a projection of certain subjective preferences. With its historical and metaphysical objective references thrown into confusion by critical thought, theology found itself yielding to the exact sciences much of its former ground. Let science master the world, and let theology and religion reflect upon "moral values." Faced with the immense achievements of exact science and technology, theology appeared to be indulging either in archaic dogmatism or in private moral whim. The subject-object "split" had divided theology's unified world-view into two equally untenable options.

The Subject-Object Dilemma: Its Medieval Forerunner

This entire picture, theology's world-unity versus the modern subject-object separation, certainly holds true at one level of analysis. A movement of secularized autonomy *has* penetrated and organized the "objective" world in such a way as to make theology's ancient world-embracing schemes seem fanciful and "mythic,"—childish at worst, symbolic of isolated subjectivity at best.

Nevertheless the simple oppositions of medieval versus modern, and theology versus modern "objectivity," should be thought through again within a more inclusive and conceptually flexible framework. Is there no commonality between the medieval and the modern West? If such a reality as historic Western culture has actually existed, are there no common traits that join together even its most diverse periods? The point that we shall try to explore is the fact that the modern subject-object problem had its medieval counterpart; and that when both versions of the problem, modern *and* medieval, are considered, a common version of the dilemma emerges. Furthermore, discussing that "common version" will necessitate a historical frame of reference, a specific mode of reflection, which can make its own contribution to our pursuit of cultural theology.

In fact, medieval catholic thought did experience its own subject-object problem, an analogue and forerunner of the post-Cartesian situation. For medieval thinkers, the subject-object "split" was a crevice, not between the individual knower and the known, but between the world and God. And the split was precisely located in the "creation out of nothing," attested by church dogma. The notion of a single, qualitative "gulf" across which God had acted to create was really an idea of a subject-object division. In this case, the object was not an item within the world, but God himself,

V
―
122

who was the "object" of love, fear, and intellectual reflection; and whose nature as object was attested by the "objective," publicly available sacraments of the church—to say nothing of concrete, miraculous evidences of the supernatural. The subject, then, was the world, inclusive of everything in it, which was understood to be "subject" to God in his providential rulership. The marked difference in this use of the subject-object notion from its modern meaning should not turn us away from the possibility of finding a link between the two.

The "gulf" of creation played an essential role in medieval theology in that it acknowledged God to be independent of any structures of necessity in the world. God was not to be "subject" to the ambiguities of world affairs, but quite the other way around. At the same time, the gulf must not be so sharply divisive that the world finds its favored status as "creation" undermined and its destiny cast in negative, Manichaean terms. To see God as free of the world and yet responsible for maintaining its rational, beneficent structures of order was to see him under categories of both "will" and "reason," and to ponder the tension of these two elements in him. God as sheer will would be arbitrary; God as sheer reason would be enclosed within rational necessity.

Situated at the cornerstone of medieval thought, Augustine of Hippo had affirmed in a dialectical manner both God's free initiative and his rational responsibility. It is notable to see Augustine in his intricate scriptural commentaries locating entities of mediation between Creator and creation so as to preserve the delicate tension between freedom and order. One such mediator, according to Augustine, was the "heaven of heavens" named in Psalm 113:16 (Vulgate). This phrase—actually a simple Hebrew superlative—Augustine understood in Latin as referring to a prime intellectual creature, a "dwelling place" for the Divine.

> And therefore the Spirit, the Teacher of thy servant, when he mentions that "in the beginning thou madest heaven and earth," says nothing about times and is silent as to the days. For, clearly, that heaven

> of heavens which thou didst create in the beginning
> is in some way an intellectual creature, although in
> no way coeternal with thee, O Trinity. Yet it is
> nonetheless a partaker in thy eternity. Because of
> the sweetness of its most happy contemplation of
> thee, it is greatly restrained in its own mutability
> and cleaves to thee without any lapse from the time
> in which it was created, surpassing all the rolling
> change of time.[2]

A mutable creature that nevertheless serenely reflects eternity
is for Augustine a fit prolegomenon to God himself. The
"heaven of heavens" thereby becomes an image that approaches "bridging the gap," reminding us that the intellectual order of the world is fulfilled in God, though he is
coincidentally free in his own inner counsels and purposes.
Augustine thus bequeathed the notion of God as both formal
and final cause to the medieval thinkers that followed him. A
bridge between free, transcendent divinity and the formal
order of the world was implicated in the standard medieval
view.

Yet the bridge was liable to philosophical criticism because
it effected an elusive meeting between freedom and rational
accountability, between a formal and a rather open-ended
final cause. No one simple model could set forth the merger
of the two causes in God and therefore specify with public
clarity the nature of God's relation to the world. Thus the
historically inevitable occurred: when the formal uncertainty
of that relation was joined to the late medieval corruption of
the Western church, which avowed the relation, then rationally and philosophically the relation became problematic.
Certainly the Christian movement did not abandon its view
that God both freely and, in the final accounting, rationally
governed his "subject" world. But now that view was affirmed
much more fideistically in and through the unique mediator,
Christ. Little of the former Augustinian confidence remained
of rationally and philosophically clarifying the relation of
God to the world. Ontologizing reason no longer followed so
easily upon faith.

Consequently, many Western individuals turned away

V

from the disappointing "fall" of the medieval sacramental order to find God through their own personal subjectivity (i.e., forms of Protestantism), or to allow their subjectivity to assume some of God's old tasks, e.g., controlling the natural environment as in Cartesian rationalism. But they could not finally escape the original dilemma. In assuming either a greater private intimacy with God, or something of a personal God-like role, thoughtful persons now found the troublesome gap not between God and creation, but between *themselves* and creation. It would be tempting to say that whereas God had been the supreme "object," to which we were "subject," the modern period inaugurated a period in which the world became "object," "subject" to us. But the terminology should not be strained to that degree. Rather, one may say that the world-order grounded in a knowledge of God began to deteriorate because of doubt cast upon that knowledge, setting the stage for the modern subject-object dilemma. An important analogy does stand between the uneasiness of medieval knowledge of the "object" God and modern uneasiness concerning knowledge of an object in the world. Either way, the adequacy of the "forms" of things, *as* we perceive those forms, is at issue—in one case, adequacy to present to us the divine ideas, in the other, adequacy to present to us the things in the world for which the forms stand. In Western history, disarray in the first instance (loss of medieval order) contributed to disarray in the second. Thus the modern subject-object problem finds its historical setting in an earlier phase of the culture that gave rise to it. The anticipation of contemporary object-alienation lies well within medieval thought. Is there not some continuing aspect of Western culture that illumines this sequence of intellectual dilemmas?

The Moral-Theological Setting of Western Knowledge

The point has been reached to lay out a framework for cultural or "reflected" theology in the West, one that acknowledges both the medieval and modern periods. Furthermore, continued use will be made of the particular entrance-way through the subject-object problem, with hopes of formulating the knowledge question more comprehensively. At the foundations of Western culture, theology set the organizing principles of knowledge, their nature and their modes. Indeed, theology laid the basis for the intellectual problems of the culture generally. The aim here is then to trace the lines that theology gave to inquiry, holding that these retain their force, even today.

Certain steps will be followed in this section: (1) designating the positive role that knowledge of the world and of things in the world has played in Western theology; (2) noting the accepted nature of that knowledge beyond the simple subject-object relation; (3) considering the frame of reference involved in "knowing the world," which is also the frame of reference for theology.

First, then, it is important that in its theology, Western Christianity did not look for the dissolution of the world, but rather expected the world to be finally and evidently affirmed, in and through the perfecting of its nature. In some theologies, this notion of a positive destiny for the world led to something like a view of historical progress (Origen, Erasmus). In others, history was seen in episodic stages with progress-regress undetermined until the precipitate end (Augustine). Either way, Catholic expectation held that the world to be transformed and affirmed is the world we now know, and that its present state somehow anticipates and prefigures its final happy and ageless condition. The present world (including our earthly selves) holds a level of significance, even in ultimate perspective, and must be so considered.

This Western view of the world recalls Auerbach's analysis of "figural" interpretation already discussed (see above, p. 104). An earthly event is properly both itself *and* a figure or type of fulfilment-to-come, which will "catch up" and preserve the figuring event that foretold it. Without question, Western religion committed itself to affirm the reality of the world, even eschatologically, and therefore sought to *know* the world and its affairs, whether by revelation or reason. Very early at the birth of the West, Charlemagne so con-

V

strued Augustine's City of God on earth that he proposed to actualize it in his empire. Much social and political tension that has marked Western life is traceable to this sense that the world already manifests (or should) a part of its own better future state.

To know and deal seriously with the world requires the right setting for that knowing and dealing. In a figure of speech, those who would achieve knowledge must locate the optimum "distance" from the world and the things in it, in order to make knowledge viable. To seek out via the Greek tradition the "forms" of things evidently locates that ideal "distancing." By contrast, to attempt to know the world universally and immediately through "vision" is to lose both it and oneself; while to attempt to know the particular concrete thing in its absolute concreteness means entry into the abyss of the concrete. "Forms," by contrast, yield things to us, yet keep them at a manageable distance.

In effect, the West made a choice to include within its affirmations an element of the material and sensational. The material world known through its "forms" is neither evil nor does it lack a transfigured destiny in the divine *eschaton*. The difficulty is that once the importance and significance of worldly knowledge is granted, its imperfections also rise to plague us. The availability of the world through what we have called second-order discourse knows the tension between "presence" and "absence" inherent in the first-order foundations. Indeed, the more that second-order world is sorted out, the more urgent that tension becomes. At a point that must remain unclear, the very "distance" that initially makes the world available for knowing and dealing threatens to become a distance that loses essential communication. Or put the matter in other terms, the part-for-whole symbolic form, the abstract universal that makes things manageable ("apple," "table," "justice," "H_2O") omits much of the concrete situation it refers to in order to do its work. Yet that omission also finally threatens its adequacy. One need not follow all of Claude Levi-Strauss' views and methods to appreciate his comment on the disturbing gap in the very act of knowing:

. . . When we make an effort to understand, we destroy the object of our attachment, substituting another whose nature is quite different. That other object requires of us another effort, which in its turn destroys the second object and substitutes a third—and so on until we reach the only enduring Presence, which is that in which all distinction between meaning and the absence of meaning disappears: and it is from that Presence that we started in the first place. It is now two thousand five hundred years since men discovered and formulated these truths. Since then we have discovered nothing new—unless it be that whenever we investigated what seemed to be a way out, we met with further proof of the conclusions from which we had tried to escape.[3]

An example of Levi-Strauss' "effort to understand" can just as easily be a formula in physics or a proposition in medieval Latin theology, either of which illustrates the multi-levelled second-order efforts to gain clarity by introducing systems of part-for-whole abstractions. Recall, for example, the horror with which the Eastern Orthodox Church during the middle ages viewed the Western communion's tendency to scholasticize by philosophical concepts certain essential doctrines of the Catholic faith.[4] For the Easterners, essentials could never thus be rationalized; yet their own doctrines represented ancient second-order commentary on the original Christ narrative, which itself included second-order components!

Quite clearly, theology that incorporates knowledge of the world as more than a mere shadow of reality must assume a posture that permits an element of incompleteness. The West, medieval or modern, has perennially done so. Knowledge may be valid within a given scope and nevertheless require a stance that obscures the whole to which the known parts belong. It is this particular stance or disposition toward things that the West has traditionally chosen, again and again. Yet the attempt has remained to achieve the vision of a whole order without loss of its articulate parts. That has been a Western striving—to know parts *and* whole—whether in relation to God, or to the world, or to things in the world.

And in return for what has been disclosed, the price of the "undisclosed" has been exacted. Dealing with reality in this manner has produced a certain eccentricity or "distancing" that has qualified the very results that demanded such a posture.

If, then, we are true to the story of Western culture, this certain eccentricity in our ways of knowing and dealing should not be called simply a matter of individual "subjectivity" or the problem of an unknown "object." Unfortunately, the modern trend has been to do so. One of the standard conceptual tools in the West is that of a separable, interior self ("soul," "mind," "subject") that mysteriously pushes the fleshly body about or retires into its own sanctuary to "reflect." That this "ghost in the machine" is a poor chart or diagram of ourselves should be clear after a little thought.[5] All of our acts are in some sense mental, and the circus acrobat should not be thought of as less mental than the philosopher just because his work is more physically direct than symbolic. The middle ages have received much blame for this mechanical and wooden "soul" concept (though Augustine and other thinkers were hardly so crude). Furthermore, medieval life held a notion of the rational shape of the world as a whole and thus of reason as not limited to the human, mental interior.

To be fair to both medieval and modern instances, the problem and possibility of knowledge should be seen as one of "disposition," or how humankind is disposed in the setting of existence, whether *individually or corporately.* Alienation is not then viewed as the isolation of an interior, individual mentality—from the body, from others, from nature and God. Rather, *the mental acts of humanity, whether private in the imagination, or individual bodily, or corporate (e.g., government), are seen as eccentrically disposed in their setting,* as not finding the complete rational response desired from that setting. And lest this statement sound derogatory of the situation, let us surely add that this eccentricity in the setting not only renders our knowing and dealing incomplete, but also makes them possible in the first place. Analysis of the situation can stand without prejudice as to "good" or "evil" consequences. This "eccentric disposition" of Western humanity in its setting can thus be seen as the "common version" throughout our history of what has only been partly known as the subject-object dilemma. More particularly, there is not some mental substance within us that is metaphysically abhorrent to a physical substance without, as oil is to water. Rather we should speak of a persistent eccentricity, individual and corporate, in how we as Westerners deploy our mental acts.

Furthermore, as proposed above, if a common Western version of the so-called subject-object question emerged, then a specific mode of reflection, a historical frame of reference, would render that version. Is that the case with Western humanity as "disposed eccentrically" within its setting? Indeed it is. Affirmative knowledge of the world in religious or theological perspective cannot be limited to knowledge of particulars *within* the world, but must also involve knowledge of the world as a whole. By their very nature, religion and theology cannot eliminate the level of wholeness from their consideration of the world's character. Religious commitment necessarily selects some key or clue that serves as a link to the world's general meaning, inclusive of ourselves within the world. Theology necessarily asks about the world *qua* world because it asks about the world's relation to God, its source and ground.

Yet to ask about the world as a whole, including ourselves, is to ask about it *in time*, for one has no general, direct sense of reality except in time and process. To speak of Western culture, therefore, and its sense of the world is to make a statement of historical communication within the temporal flow. That communication in its own terms cannot be final and complete because of time's movement. Yet this incompleteness or unfinished quality is precisely the affirmative state of affairs to which we wish to call attention by speaking of the "eccentrically disposed." The eccentricity itself grants us the "room" or perspective to make any sort of statement, including a statement on our fundamental disposition in

V

130

things. The eccentricity coincidentally calls our attention to the unfinished quality of our knowing.

Speaking, then, of a common condition across Western culture's way of knowing and dealing is speaking "situated," as noted in chapter one. We do not understand our medieval forebears fully for just this reason; yet we understand them very well at the point of their struggling with the eccentricity of their knowing, since we do the same, even in our historical communication with them. Therefore both a content (eccentricity of disposition) and a frame of reference (the temporal process) have been located for speaking about the presuppositions of Western epistemology. The modern subject-object problem is but a refined, second-order reminiscence of a more truly foundational state. Those who would affirm the world theologically enter at once into both knowing and unknowing, a happy condition of eccentricity, in which things are appropriately known and handled, but always in an anticipatory, unfinished manner. Moral and theological thought, reflection upon the very broadly pragmatic realities within which all are willy-nilly participant, deals with the hardiest and yet most mysterious level of presence. Reality is close and clear; yet its manifestation in time decrees that it not be final.

The Full Scope of 'Knowing' as Morally Situated; the Role of Christ

To summarize what has been said: Western theology determined that to know the world, yet to know it in the ultimate perspective of God, required a certain "posture" or position vis-a-vis both God and world. I have called that position the human stance of being "eccentrically disposed" toward reality within the process of time and history. The human assessment of things is "situated" within the imperatives of time and of our own vital interests; that assessment is also at a sufficient "distance" (the ec-centric standpoint) to permit knowledge through forms, a distance which nevertheless must render incomplete the knowledge it provides. Our knowledge of God through things (natural or revealed) is not direct or full; our knowledge of things vis-a-vis God is not final. Both statements are true because of the factor of time.)

For theology thus to have set the stage for "knowing" means that a framework and set of suppositions analogous to theology have characterized Western knowledge generally, regardless of whether dedicated to theological ends. Thus, let the term "reality" stand cipher for God, or for the elusive harmony between God and the world. Then one can say that from a gathered, first-order standpoint, human beings know reality; yet the presentation involves coincidentally a "sinking back" of that reality. From a second-order standpoint, the observer knows an object under its idea or form; yet an uncertainty opens between the form and the object because of the original gap in first-order foundations. Western knowledge is grounded in a time-filled eccentricity of disposition that recalls the interests of its theological roots.

Once the actual hegemony of medieval theology was gone, the possibilities and problems of knowledge became secularized so that the Western version of the subject-object problem was born. Under the impact of secular reason, God as an object of thought became much like any other object within the world. Little wonder that the subject-object question tended most of all to disrupt theology; for if all objects became uncertain within "pure" scientific reason, how much more the object "God," for whom there is no tangible, agreed-upon evidence. Under the impact of pure subject-object thinking, the "eccentric distance" that had made knowledge possible became intensified to the point of alienation because of the pressure of science to push knowledge to perfection. The early modern goal of establishing philosophic and scientific certainty (vs. acknowledgment of the unfinished character of all knowing) ran afoul of incompleteness by presuming to overcome it. In Hegel, for example, the anticipation of victory is astonishing. Heidegger thus quotes from Hegel's lectures on the history of modern philosophy:

> . . . With [Descartes], we in fact enter into an independent philosophy which knows that it is the independent product of reason, and that the conscious-

ness of self, self-consciousness, is an essential moment
of truth. Here, we may say, we are at home; here,
like the sailor at the end of his long voyage on the
stormy seas, we may cry 'Land'! . . . In this new
period the principle is thinking, thinking proceeding from itself. . . .'[6]

Heidegger interprets Hegel's position in the following comment:

Thinking seeks its *fundamentum absolutum* in
its own unshakable certainty of what it has thought.
The land in which philosophy has since then made
itself at home is the unconditional self-certainty of
knowledge; and it is conquered and fully surveyed
only step by step. The land is fully taken over when
the *fundamentum absolutum* is thought of as the
Absolute itself. The Absolute, for Hegel, is Spirit:
that which is present and by itself in the certainty
of unconditional self-knowledge. *Real knowledge of
beings as beings now means the absolute knowledge
of the Absolute in its absoluteness.*[7] (Latter italics
ours.)

The subject-object view could therefore make heavy-hand-
ed, autonomous claims because one "side" of knowledge, the
knowing subject, seemed handily in control of a baseline of
certainty, viz., its own self-assurance. Descartes established
the incontrovertibility of his own existence by the simple act
of wondering about it: if I am thinking, I must be. His "I
think, therefore I am" has often been paralleled to Augustine's meaning (if not his words): "God thinks, therefore I
am." In the parallel lies more than a simple inversion. The
Augustinian position built upon a full moral and historical
grasp of human "knowing," which included, but was not limited to, precise second-order perception such as sense data.
To say "God thinks, therefore I am" is to indicate a fully
"situated" range of possibilities *and* limits for human knowledge, including "hard" scientific analysis, yet all set within
the movement of time and moral choice. By contrast, to say
"*I* think, therefore I am" is to reduce the character of knowledge to what can be "fixed" in relation to a static and autonomous knowing subject. The modern West seized upon what

was a happy feature of its heritage—the eccentric "room" that rendered appropriate human knowledge possible—and transformed it into an alienation. This was done by attempting to protect and indeed aggrandize that phase of knowing for which the fact of eccentric "distance" is the most awkward: analytically precise objective knowledge. Modernity has denied the implications of distance most heavily in the area of objective technical control; yet to resist the consequences of eccentricity at their most stubborn frontier is only to enhance them. No cure is possible except through re-evaluating the full scope of knowledge in Western heritage, inclusive of its "situated" moral circumstance.

Much of modern theology since the enlightenment has attempted to acknowledge and to recover what I wish to call the "full scope" of the Western approach to knowing. That is to say, theologians like Schleiermacher, Kierkegaard, and Ritschl, in quite various ways, deserted the "metaphysical objectivity" of theology (a position most vulnerable to the new "critical" objectivity) and appealed either to a base of "religion" or "existence" or "history" from which alone theological meaning could be unfolded. From one point of view, the entire movement of Protestant liberalism was an attempt to remember and renew the fundaments of Western knowledge and their theological dimension. That is, liberalism saw knowledge of God and the world as pragmatically "situated" within the stream of time and moral values. Liberalism discerned that the cultural achievements of the West had presupposed an affirmation of world and God together in a certain linkage, and aimed to preserve that affirmation. Furthermore, the liberals shared a kind of Augustinian confidence channeled through the middle ages that Christian belief comports with the deeper rationality of the created order, and is not essentially inimical to reason's proper functions.

A descendant of liberalism, "crisis" theology of the twentieth century in its own way pressed for recovery of the original Western arena of knowing. If representatives such as Bultmann and Tillich are considered, everyday knowledge and the functions of reason are linked to knowledge of God via a

V

134

"crisis" or collapse of ordinary objectivity such as modernity has stressed. That is, the inquirer emphasizing analytical, scientific knowledge will come to a point where the larger questions of God and world either must be dismissed or else acceded to as challenging the narrow subject-object base of the inquiry itself. Granted that for crisis theology everyday second-order knowing and foundational knowing are linked only by hostility, yet a kind of logic informs that hostility—a dialectical logic, in which the crisis of modern investigation heralds and even "invites" a profound new grasp of what it is to "know." The evidences of dealing with the situated condition are more personal and private in crisis thought than in liberalism; nevertheless, encounter with the divine challenge produces a transformed orientation towards second-order knowing and dealing. The "fullness" of knowing is reaffirmed.

Do liberal and crisis views therefore constitute examples of what we have sought as cultural or "reflected" theology? Surely both have adopted clues from the broader cultural situation while maintaining a version of the West's antique theological frame. Nevertheless, neither of these traditions matches the character of reflected theology for one most important reason: both approaches set out not merely to reflect Christ within cultural analogues, but *to perpetuate essential Christology* as handed down from the New Testament until today. As liberalism in America has been a recasting of Calvinist confessionalism, so crisis theology has been a recasting of Luther. Both have been attempts in light of modernity to find an essence of Christianity or of the Christ-event that will allow for modern erosion of creedalism, while continuing to persist in Christian faith. For that reason, they have let Christ stand as cipher for some form of human, historical transaction —either a renewed ethical dynamism, or a dialectic of trust and self-acceptance, as the case may be. In one respect, both these movements have built upon the imaginative insight of metaphor and story, calling into play both first and second orders of language and finding Christ to be "real" through a "revelation in history." That revelation has further been conceived as a dynamic Christological work that attaches to one's personal affairs by incarnating a spirit of universal love or a spirit of gracious acceptance. The problem is that the Christ *becomes exhausted in* the lively metaphor of one's affairs or the metaphoric appropriation of his story. Morally and historically oriented theologies grounded in metaphor can only interpret the Christ, not confess him; so it was with liberal or crisis theologies based essentially on metaphor, so it is with such theologies today.

In an odd sort of way, modern Protestant theology aimed both at retaining the Christ and affirming the fundamental elements of a broad secular humanism, but fell between the two tasks. Indeed, the procedure for pursuing the former task doomed the latter, for there was neither a decisive retention nor dismissal of the Christ. Either way would have provided a better chance to transcend the subject-object split, but Christological hesitation left both liberal and crisis theologians open to charges of subjectivity in an objective world. In brief, Protestant theology exhausted knowledge of the Christ in moral or religious or existential "insight." Cognitive historical work on the life of Jesus was declared free to pursue its course. The results would either pave the way for true Christological "value" to appear (the liberal "quest" for the historical Jesus), or would not prejudice one way or the other the kerygmatic preaching of the crucified and risen One (crisis theology's kerygmatic Christ). In neither case would cognitive historical work on the life of Jesus count *against* Christology or revelation "in history." Nor would any level of historical factuality count against the "religious" or the "kerygmatic" power of the Jesus story. In other words, Protestant theology determined to retain the Christ, but with all elements removed from the Christ-account that might resemble, or come into conflict with, modern objective factual claims. As a simple example, a miracle of Jesus would be seen as legendary or as invoking a profound natural law (liberal) or as presupposing in its account the church's proclamation of the risen Lord (crisis).

This general Protestant strategy was "hesitant" in that it

permitted the modern subject-object frame of knowledge to do the initial map-work of theology. That is, theology permitted elements in the Christ account to be designated as "objective-factual" in a modern sense and to be theologically excised on that account. Then by having admitted the modern epistemological standards and surrendering what those standards registered as "objective," Protestant theology invited upon itself the mantle of "subjective." The realm of "nature" was given over to science and technology and theology contented itself with matters of the will—either moral vision or identity crisis and recovery. Meantime, the good opportunity to develop the "full scope" of Western knowledge —inclusive of natural scientific claims—was given up because of the compromising intent to retain some version of Christ as theological cornerstone. Christology was retained by appeal to a subjective "internal miracle" in place of former external miracles that offended objective inquiry. Hans Frei has noted, however, that this subjective Christological "retreat" was actually no more secure under the pressure of scientific method than the older claims to validating miracles:

> [There has been an] appeal to a miracle of direct or special intervention by God in man's inner, spiritual life through the events connected with Jesus and the founding of the Church. For historical method such claims for inner miracle are not one whit better than were the claims for external, natural miracle in the face of the earlier growth of natural science. Yet it is precisely on such claims to internal miracle and its foundation in the special, direct presence of God through a *noncognitive source of practical knowledge* that dogmatic theology has been based since the days of Schleiermacher.[8] (Italics ours.)

Modern Christological appeals based on general insights via metaphor, symbol, or paradigm invariably evoke the embarrassing question, "Why Jesus?" In all such cases, Christ has been embraced because he fulfills personal standards implicitly prior to, or independent of, serious Christological proclamation. Better that serious Christology be either logically prior or be dismissed altogether in order to avoid the hesitation that loses the struggle on two fronts.

To summarize: modern Protestant theology responded rightly to the challenges of analytical science insofar as it recognized that the grounds of Western knowledge were originally theological, and that the retention of something like that original theological base is essential to retain the full human meaning of knowledge. Protestant theology failed, however, to distinguish what we have called here cultural or "reflected" theology from theology proper, but rather blurred the two at the point of Christology.

Perhaps it will be useful to recall the two aims set up in the first paragraph of this chapter—to note the dissolution of theology in the modern West, and to discern what sorts of cultural influences nevertheless continue to flow from theological origins. By way of response, I have attempted to find a certain framework for general knowledge presupposed across Western history, whether medieval or modern—thereby constituting a continuing "cultural influence" of theology. That framework has been termed a certain "eccentricity of disposition in time" on the part of Western peoples, a posture aiming toward knowledge of the world both in its parts and as a whole (i.e., as related to God). The eccentricity rendering knowledge possible has also entailed its incompleteness, but that has not in itself been inappropriate or evil.

At the same time, the medieval period has been distinguished from the modern by the foundational theological claims of the former vs. the secularized theological "traces" of the latter. The middle ages knew the full moral *and* theoretical scope of knowledge as explicitly including, indeed presupposing, the presence of God-in-Christ. The modern age has urged the predominance of the theoretical alone (critical, analytical, scientific knowledge), thus dissolving the old doctrinal lines that held to theology as queen. Modernity can be

V

recalled to affirming the full moral and theoretical scope of knowledge and therefore the eccentric "posture"; this chapter has pressed for that "recalling." But when modernity so affirms (if it does), the explicit acknowledgment of the Christian Incarnation is no longer included because no factual level of that event is presumably available. Reminiscences of theology persist: reality, like God, is present, yet "hidden," through time; we know "in part." But this situation is not explicitly linked to knowledge through Christ.

The initial point here is to let what has been so acutely divided remain divided. Either Christ is an *a priori* reality setting the shape of culture, or he is merely a paradigm of culture, produced and governed by it. The subjective Christ of liberal and crisis positions is neither fish nor fowl. He is an interpretation of the Jesus story that proposes to continue the essence of Christian faith; yet he draws his substance *from* the experience of culture rather than setting its terms. The religious and cultural situation today therefore requires that we begin with the divided circumstances that are given us. On the one hand is Christ, the imperious ruler. On the other is the "situated" state of modern culture, moving along lines strongly reminiscent of its theological foundations, but no longer affirming the Christ. Yet even the reminiscence is intriguing, for modern culture has produced many excellent works. "Reflected" theology can assuredly hold our attention at an important level.

Accepting modernity's terms, then, yet remembering its theological heritage, I now wish to turn to the actual delineation of "reflected" theological elements, holding that they will provide a certain mirror, a reflected theology that is a theology "for" modern literature.

V

NOTES

1. Auerbach, *Mimesis*, 202.

2. *Confessions* XII, 9, 9, trans. Outler, 275–276.

3. In Claude Levi-Strauss, *A World on the Wane*, trans. John Russell (New York: Criterion Books, 1961) 394–395.

4. See George Every, *Misunderstandings between East and West* (Richmond: John Knox Press, 1966) 42.

5. Gilbert Ryle, *The Concept of Mind* (New York: Barnes and Noble, Inc., 1949).

6. G. W. F. Hegel, *Sämtliche Werke*, XV, 328, von H. Glockner (Stuttgart: Frommanns Verlag, 1959) v. 19, p. 328. Quoted by Heidegger in his *Hegel's Concept of Experience* (New York: Harper & Row, 1970) 27. Translation not credited.

7. Heidegger, *Hegel*, 28.

8. Hans Frei, "Niebuhr's Theological Background," in *Faith and Ethics: The Theology of H. Richard Niebuhr*, ed. Paul Ramsey (New York: Harper and Row, 1957) 56.

Theological Reading of
Literature: Theory VI

Part I of this study set out to consider how language and literature function so as to present everyday reality. The notion of linguistic "presence" as both giving and withholding "the real" recalled Martin Heidegger's treatment of the presence of Being. So long as we are concretely in time, the two orders of language disclose reality to us, though in an unfinished way, just as Heidegger's Being is present in and through beings, and yet coincidentally differentiates itself from them. The two chapters immediately preceding have gone on to argue that such a modern discussion of language and reality searches out important theological roots in Western history. Modernity has kept its age-long Western aims of knowing the world, and affairs *in* the world, in both limited and ultimate perspectives. Thus modernity maintains a quasi-theological structure for knowledge in those moments when it seeks out the fullest and widest sense of "knowing."

The present task, then, is to apply these generalizations about knowledge to the particular case of knowing reality in and through literature. If a certain modern approach to knowledge still operates within a horizon abstracted from theology, then a grasp of reality through literature likewise follows a scheme of theological origin—though without the fullness of a theological confession being present. In the context of what has been said about the two orders of language, as well as about metaphor, symbol, narrative, and work-of-art, one may consider how analogues of theological concepts such as God, revelation, sin, and redemption may be suggested through the materials of imaginative literature. At the same time, note that these are "reflected" theological concepts— analogues of Christian doctrine that hardly require the concrete strictures associated with specific revelation in Christ. Indeed, their ironic use may even oppose and invert traditional theological meaning. Such "openness" of intent is a mark of the same modern pluralism that produced the literature these concepts may hopefully illumine.

The approach to locating the theological analogues in literature will be first to recall certain traditional Christian doctrines and their intent, thereby setting criteria for their analogues or "reflections." In particular, the doctrines of God and of the Incarnation in Christ will be discussed.

Christian Origins and the Doctrine of God

The Western view of God within Christianity received its most characteristic features during the Hellenistic period of the ancient world, that late antique time that produced the Roman empire, the New Testament, and the work of the Church fathers. It was fateful that the Christian formulation of belief occurred at a historical moment when the most compelling trait of any acknowledged deity or ultimacy was that of transcendence. In the work of Jesus, as best as it is historically known, God's kingdom promised an astonishing apocalyptic reversal of the accepted order of things. Paul of Tarsus, in his letters, saw the order of the cosmos as the Greeks had conceived it, broken by the intrusion of demonic agencies; only the insertion into history of a transcendent order could recover and renew the original orderly character of the world.

In analogous fashion, gnostic systems proposed saviors from "beyond," and mystery religions took sacred figures once identified with stable communities and presented them within private, "initiated" circumstances. The order that no longer appeared inherent within the world seemed necessarily to come from a transcendent realm quite beyond earth.

The new style of "savior" could not be available as a local public or political deity identified with an organized community, as had the deities of the Greek city-states. Since outward communal forms were breaking down, the new transcendent reality—however named—worked its effect upon the worshipper not from the vantage of a political order (excepting, of course, "divine" Rome), but personally, from within. Thus Paul could exhort his readers: ". . . be not conformed to this age, but be transformed by the renewing of the mind . . ." (Romans 12:2). Deities were no longer localized but "adapted themselves" to more individual needs found increasingly everywhere. As Moses Hadas has noted:

> . . . In the Sarapis example, for instance, the worshiper bred to the Egyptian tradition would find enough that was familiar to satisfy the conservative propensity of religious observance, and so be able to assimilate the Greek elements easily, and the Greek could similarly assimilate the Egyptian. And the resulting amalgam could in turn assimilate still other elements more easily, and, more important, new and spiritualized interpretations of the old. The general tendency of such a process is in the direction of monotheism.[1]

If the tendency was toward monotheism, then it was toward a transcendent universalism, however variously appropriated.

Many contemporary thinkers today throw up their hands at the unfortunate transcendence of the deity that the Hellenistic period foisted upon later Western culture. Excessive emphasis upon transcendence is said to be inimical to human life and reason, leading to self-contradictory and unfruitful epithets for God, such as Augustine's "Infinite Being." Nevertheless, coincident with the universal transcendence of the deity, certain slender influences of a counter sort were at work in the Christian movement. From its Jewish origins Christianity held a certain earthy realism all too quickly overlooked in its later "spiritualized" centuries. For example, in its Jewish-like apocalypticism Christianity did not abandon real goods and hopes of earth, but projected them "upon the clouds" (see the introductory comment above, page 6). Studies of the historical Jesus vary greatly, but there is wide agreement that his activity arose primarily in light of the reality of the apocalyptic kingdom.[2] Whether he perceived that kingdom as primarily present or future in its consummate power, there is much to argue that he found the clues to the kingdom within the common affairs and relationships of his people, rather than through other-worldly asceticism, esoteric knowledge, or privileged rites.[3] The transcendent power ready to abolish history had a way of relating to ordinary affairs and "turning" them so as to disclose images of itself in the commonplace. Transcendence was both communicated and qualified by an unusual presentation of the familiar (see comments above, pp. 59–60, on New Testament parables).

Paul's letters constitute a similar vision of the transcendent as coincident with the common lot of humanity, though in a mood much different from that of the Gospel accounts of Jesus. Paul's irony about himself as Apostle (e.g., II Corinthians 11–12) parallels his paradoxes of the Christian life: "I have been crucified with Christ; I live no more, but Christ lives in me . . ." (Galatians 2:20). Such a style of existence finds its origin only in Christ himself, the bearer of genuine divine authority, who nevertheless

> . . . emptied himself, taking the form of a slave, and being made in the likeness of men; and being found in fashion as a man, he humbled himself, becoming obedient until death . . . (Phil. 2:7–8).

The follower of Jesus as Lord finds the nearest point of contact with deity, not in a circle of secure religious privilege, but through "taking life in its stride," including the ironies of suffering and death. Now unquestionably, Paul shared the concern of his contemporaries for a transcendent, divine order. The notion of an inherent principle of order *within* the world had broken down in the face of intruding chaos; if order was being restored, then the source of it necessarily lay beyond the creation and was entering human and natural affairs from *outside* the world. Yet for all this emphasis upon transcendence, Paul found the actual availability of the new order coincident with the temporal, moving figure of the human Jesus. That is, Jesus was *Christos* (Messiah) and *Kyrios* (Lord); at the same time, he lived his humanity through to its full conclusion (". . . obedient unto death . . ."). Only by living one's given humanity through to its full conclusion, in direct personal attachment to *kyrios* Jesus, could one claim membership in the new emerging order. Paul thus struck a blow at those various "super-apostles," his competition in Corinth and elsewhere, who supported their Gospel pronouncements by certain "glimmerings" of divinity in their own works and affairs. These men let fall impressions of heavenly power-at-hand through their polished rhetoric, their personal mystical visions, and their miracles of healing—to each of which Paul declared his ironic preference for the everyday ambiguities of existence as clues to apostleship (II Corinthians 11:6; 12:2,5; 12:7–9). It was clear enough that the self-generated "lights" of the super-apostles had nothing in common with the divinity-humanity of Christ, the source and standard of the faith exercised in his name.

Jesus and Paul, each in a different fashion, were extraordinary figures in at once urging the transcendent exclusivism of God, and at the same time insisting upon direct, divine action coincident with human affairs. The point is that in their views a reference point for God exists beyond the world of things, and a reference point for God exists *within* the world of things, and the two reference points are found to coincide. Nevertheless, the coincidence does not preclude speaking of the two points separately. I wish to argue that this arrangement or framework for speaking of God wielded a significant influence over the formal, and in some respects substantive character of the Western literature that followed it. It must be clear that in the "reflected" theology present in modern literature the particular constriction of the historic

Christ upon the God-reality has dissolved. Yet his place is taken by thousands of other "incarnations," which offer at once the reality of things both given and withheld.

But before the transcendent and immanent "God" of literature is further pursued, other matters concerning the traditional Christian view of God need to be addressed.

God as Process through Time, as 'Everlasting'

Another way of speaking of the two reference points for God is to speak of God as "everlasting," yet as process in time. Of chief importance in the above section is the coincidence of the divine with the contingent, the human, the time-filled. That is, the stream of tradition from Jesus and Paul maintained a dynamic element that would not allow a fixed appropriable structure for the actual presence of the earthly divinity-in-humanity. Rather, the very assertion of the concrete and everyday as a crucible of deity instantly locates the divine-human exchange within the stream of time.

Indeed, to attend to concrete affairs and their suggestive aura means to attend to things as they move temporally. Reflective thought is often misled at this point. One may think of a nameable, concrete object as if it were simply a fixed, static example of some abstraction. But to conceive of a concrete thing statically is to pursue an abstraction still. Unless one were to attempt reflection on a concrete in its *absolute* concreteness (which is inconceivable), then pondering concrete affairs may not "freeze" them, i.e., actually separate them from the time flow in which they are bound. Just so, the location of a transcendent God at a point coincident with certain human affairs means that the location must be in some sense flowing with time. God must be in process. Now this is not to say that, in the Christian tradition, the story of Jesus may not be circumscribed and looked at as a "literary object." The story as a structure of language can be objectively examined like any literary piece. Rather it is to say that what the story tells is a transaction through time in which God is somehow revealed. It is, of course, a particular transaction. But if the particularity is given up, and the formal character

VI

146

retained, as in a "reflected" theology, then the "God" who is indicated cannot be known except through certain broadly concrete, moving circumstances.

Thus literature reminiscent in various ways of the Christ story may well recall the reference-frame of a moving divine "presence" articulate within dynamic, concrete affairs. Again Auerbach is most helpful with his comments upon Hebraic style and "mixed" style. In Hebraic expression, especially certain parts of the Old Testament, Auerbach finds the rude syntax and the unfinished character of the linguistic surface lend themselves directly to a sense of participation in historical time.[4] The accounts offer not careful, illuminated detail, but the force of suggestion and intimation. God's sudden entry upon the scene makes him immediate to the characters involved (e.g., his speaking to Abraham); yet the instant of his self-declaration is likewise the instant when he is realized as shrouded in mystery. Much of that mysterious quality lies in the nature of the Hebraic god as working out specific purposes for all of history, through the events of the story being told. Accounts of Abraham, Moses, and David presume to gather to themselves all world-events from creation until the promised Day, as if to an interpretive key. Consequently, the manifesting of God is present and nevertheless is future-oriented. Knowing God's self-disclosure means that the events of his appearance are at once realized as unfinished; they are in time and of a particular time; they stand firm in their meaning, but they must pass away in order finally to be caught up and consummated in God's ultimate, universal goal. Thus, when Auerbach speaks of the Hebraic accounts as being "fraught with background,"[5] one thing meant is that the temporal, moving nature of the theophanies leaves much that will become articulate only in some final time.

If Auerbach is correct, then the Hebraic style provides a literature that means to engage and incorporate within its own telling the movement of universal history, with both the decisiveness, yet incompleteness belonging to temporal reality. In a similar fashion, Auerbach treats that "mixed" style that he finds emerging with the spread of early Christian literature, and to which we have already made reference (see above, pp. 103–104).

> The story of Christ . . . transcended the limits of ancient mimetic aesthetics . . . The distinction between the lofty and the vulgar style exists no longer. In the Gospels, as in ancient comedy, real persons of all classes make their appearance: fisherman and kings, high priests, publicans, and harlots participate in the action; and neither do those of exalted rank act in the style of classical tragedy, nor do the lowly behave as in a farce . . .[6]

Auerbach's point is that a common figure like Peter the fisherman may now be cast in a role of high seriousness. The significance of human affairs is not cast within a fixed social hierarchy; the most penetrating of occurrences may take place through restless movements that cut across class structures. In other words, the mixed style signals historic movement from below, whose goals and purposes move beyond a classically stable social order. For Auerbach, the Hebraic style and the "mixed" style are related to one another in their grappling with historical time and with the range of divine providence through time.[7]

It should be clear by this point that an analogue to the Christian God within a theological theory of literature must be in some way "transcendent," must express itself through what is commonly human, and must locate in the concrete stream of time. Ultimacy coincides in some manner with what is contingent and moving, if the framework of Western theology persists. Such a formula may appear tendentious or surprising in light of the Christian God's reputation for serene, metaphysical aloofness—at least God the Father. Doubtless many moments in Christian history appealing to the names of Augustine, Aquinas, and Calvin (if not with full justice to their positions) have proposed such a Godhead, or at least an image of God as the distant and lordly General of his forces. It has been easy enough for the theological tradition by the very loci of its agenda to begin attributing to God a static transcendence, rather than a transcendence intimately related

VI

to the temporal and concrete. What I have presented in this section and the last assuredly represents a normative judgment of my own within the plethora of materials afforded by historical theology. Nevertheless, that judgment means to appeal to the vital roots of the tradition (in Jesus and Paul) and to de-emphasize the strands of thought that in "all too human" a fashion reified or fixed the transcendence of God in a separate, metaphysical realm.

Avoidance of reified metaphysics does not, on the other hand, require abolishing the notion of God's transcendence *per se*. It may be useful in such regard to consider the term "everlasting" as applied to God. The word implies some form of continuity in the midst of change, more so than "eternal," which suggests something out of time altogether. Unfortunately, in common parlance, "everlasting" has assumed the static quality often associated with the eternal, as if the nature of God were an immobile endurance, immune to every challenge. If, however, time and process and their all-encompassing character are first acknowledged, and the thought of an "immobile endurance" not permitted, then "everlasting" points to the continual "there-ness" of God on a wide variety of different occasions. Times and circumstances change and perhaps change radically. Yet the God of Western Christianity has had the characteristic of coinciding with a variety of events, while nevertheless presuming to retain a constancy or integrity never fully comprehended. That is to say, God's transcendence has been claimed as articulate in and through different situations (e.g., Exodus 33:23 is one of the surprising ones, as Moses sees the "backsides" of God from a cleft in the rock); yet the transcendence manifest in events has never been, in this tradition, a transcendence exhausted. Presumably, the line of time *as a whole*, in the Christian tradition, bears the reality of God and of providence without any one segment or manifestation clarifying in explicit fashion all of who, or how, God is. Thus even the self-declaration of God in Christ Jesus, as the act of salvation, is normative and final precisely through this: that the revealing of God in the flesh involved an element of God's continuing concealment entailed in his very manifestation as human. Eric Auerbach's allusion to the Christian historical use of "figure" or typology suggests this approach to time and transcendence. Events manifesting God are real and not simply to be dissolved in favor of a supernature to which they point. At the same time, they are "types" of a present fullness only to be clearly seen at a later time.

Formal Elements of Reflected Theology

Suppose one gleans from the items concerning God within the particularity of the Christian tradition, as discussed above, certain formal characteristics, with much of the historical content laid aside. What emerges is a series of eventful or illuminating moments along the line of time, analogous to one another as if suggesting a common substance, yet sufficiently various that their plurality remains. One suspects that the series simply recalls the general process of time itself, whose meaning (if it has one) is inherent within time's full extent; yet there are manifestations of that meaning under different versions on different occasions. In this situation, what is it that is "real"? And obviously here the term "real" carries a certain freight not incorporated within many contemporary references to realism. What may be termed inclusively real is indeed the process of time itself, in which all things nameable are contained. Nevertheless the process of time is recognizable only in and through things, whose integrity, or whose "gathering" into suggestive forms, "slows down" change and flux and makes us aware of time by resisting it. Thus the temporal process is manifest through all things ("God" in the flesh, first-order linguistic moments) at the same time that temporal process transcends any of its articulations (the flesh disguises "God," first-order language is mysterious).

With restricted historical names and occasions sponged away, God becomes the temporal process of things itself, including the meaning of that process. And, although the process of time is constant, certain particular events gather in which time's "transcendence" seems slowed and penetrated.

Such a manifestation is never complete, however, for the meaning of time is larger than any linguistic disclosures can contain. Thus second-order attempts to organize and regularize first-order vision gain in clarity but lose in penetration.

This study has often spoken of everyday "reality" and the presentation of it through language. Time has also been proposed as the meaning-horizon of the world. It is but one more inevitable step to suggest that reality is the temporal process, with its peculiar mode of including and yet transcending all things. The implication is, of course, that the concrete flow of time invites inquiry and penetration of its meaning—indeed, surprisingly "gives" the components of vision by which the meaning of things is glimpsed. In a "reflected" theology, such reality is "God," both including and yet mysteriously "stepping back from" all things; "God" is thereby the temporal process. Time and history suggest a meaning so that "God" does not seem fully impenetrable; at the same time, no configuration of first- and second-order languages is able to capture "God's" significance in a finished manner.

Therefore, in a theological reading of literature "God" is the inclusive reality of time and process *as* illumined through an artistic play of first and second orders within language. Reality in the literary piece is illumined, yet not fully; it is at once given and withheld. It may then be asked how the general process of things in time is significantly illumined through the forms of language. The answer lies in what has already been considered of the metaphoric power of language at its first-order level: that only an imaginative linguistic move of a metaphoric sort is able to articulate a process in its mid-course without either containing it or halting it; and that metaphoric language can "slow down" a process sufficiently to permit insight, yet allow an inferential gap in genuine disclosure (see above, p. 53). Metaphor is often taken as a weak recourse, wanting in solidity and actualizing power. Thus we have already discussed at some length the question of "disciplining" metaphor in order to resist mere flights of fancy. Certainly the rhetorical metaphor *per se* is subject to a disconcerting range of use and abuse. The point remains that one whole side of language and its presentation of reality is metaphoric in character, if that designation is carefully understood. Only by a move that is broadly metaphoric can language "assemble" the parameters of reality and provide an over-all orientation to the world.

Works of literary imagination are metaphors of the process of things, a process caught and illumined in a certain segment of itself by the "gathering" power of words. Therefore, within a "reflected" theology, works of literature are metaphors of "God," moments of celebration and insight into temporal process, moments that both capture reality and intimate its mysterious depth. Thus we may say that "God" is present as the reality of things-in-general, though all things are a metaphor of temporal process, and thereby of "God." If such statements appear too highly monotheistic for the pluralism of literature, then consider again that a work of literature invokes a "world," which is really a version of *the* world, and may present a "god," rather than the single "God." Nevertheless, we have previously noted that an awareness of "the gods" need not contradict the sense that there is finally one world pp. 108–109). Even though each "god" is in a sense an entire "world," sensibility can allow for a world of such "worlds." Or we may say that a piece of literature may read "God" from a peculiar perspective without losing the intimation of a final unity. If it is objected that in our discussion the term "process," offered as if a definite indicator, is itself a metaphor, then this is to be admitted. The terms "process" and "metaphor" are closely linked; indeed "process" could be called an abstracted outline of any and all metaphors. The circularity of "reflected" theology is thereby indicated, but such a point does not devaluate its substance.

Only one further matter requires attention in this section: the question of a "reflected" Christology. In effect, the topic has already been discussed since no attention has been given to the doctrine of God and its analogue in and for literature apart from giving attention to God's incarnation. The view of this study is that whether in reflected theology or in theology proper no talk of God is possible apart from a specific, con-

VI

crete manifestation. Thus this chapter began with a brief survey of key elements from the earliest Christian tradition on locating God as inherently God-for-us within common, human affairs. In other words, the model for reflecting upon God has been the apocalyptic "Kingdom-in-commonality" teaching of Jesus and the "Christ Jesus" teaching of Paul. Thus incarnation in some sense must render God present, and indeed as early Christianity stated, must be an incarnation of "the Word," or else language concerning God becomes vapid. "God" as "present" yet "withdrawn" in and through rich first-order language; "God" as articulate in metaphors of process—these are reflections of the Christian Incarnation, God-with-us, and therefore of Christology. It must surely be clear how appropriate and important such thinking is in relation to a work of art. Notice as well the attempt to avoid the pitfall with respect to Christological thought as found in the liberal and crisis traditions of theology described above in chapter V (pp. 134–139). No attempt is being made here to derive a full Christology from general materials of culture, artistic or otherwise, or to imply such a connection. The Chistology of theology proper is well outlined and confessional. A reflected Christology within general materials of the culture is not an actual Christology, but deploys its substantive viewpoint through a framework theologically inherited from the past.

If all language that presents God is Christological, directly or indirectly, should that second-order level of reflection be discounted that has produced well-known philosophical arguments for God, such as the ontological and the cosmological? An initial response to this question would be to place such arguments within the first- and second-order rhythm of language and note that they must presuppose a first-order "vision" or standpoint in order to make their analysis. Then after such a second-order abstraction is produced, it may stand as outline for other first-order moments that fulfill its conditions. Take the ontological argument as example (although basic analyses that are widely available will not be rehearsed here).[8] The nerve-center of this argument is that necessity-contingency is a polar relationship; one cannot be thought without the other. If one is willing to generalize about the world at all, then the obvious component of contingency in reality is reckoned only by contrast with a component of necessity always present to thought. If the contingent is admitted, then unity-necessity must also be real, and "God" is the name of this necessary factor. Taken in its bare bones, this argument may show that anyone venturing to reflect on the world in general necessarily affirms God, but only as an empty principle of necessity. In order to give that principle force in life, worshippers and thinkers invariably select some concrete situation to serve as "link" or clue to the significance of the Necessary Being in daily affairs. This may be a totem, a loved person, or a cultic figure such as Jesus. It may be a style of life grounded remotely in experience. In any case, the first-order gathering must lie at least somewhere in the background, if not dominate the foreground. Apart from some selected incarnation, such arguments are finally inconclusive.

With the designation, then, of "God" as process, metaphorically incarnate in works of the imagination, the analogues to God and Christ offered in a "reflected" theology for literature have been covered. If it seems that more discussion is needed on how literature responds to such critical concepts, the matter will nevertheless be postponed until specific cases arise. Meanwhile, since the term "process" has been chosen for God, it may be useful to comment on the distinction between what is being done here and what is well known as "process theology," developed out of Alfred North Whitehead's work.

God and Process in the School of Whitehead

The position taken in this study should be distinguished from the currently much discussed Anglo-American "process philosophy" (or theology) grounded in Whitehead's work and developed in this country by Charles Hartshorne, Schubert M. Ogden, and John B. Cobb, Jr. True, there are aims in common between what I have attempted to say here and, on the other hand, the work of the above men: temporality and process are honored; the notion is affirmed that abstract or "eternal" forms do not identify some realm inherently superior to the fluid and concrete. Furthermore, I find the phenomenological side of Whitehead's work attractive, with its commitment to the full actuality of experience (vs. conventions of reduction) and its openness to the aesthetic. Nevertheless, the differences between my views here and those of the process theologians are essential and finally determinative.

For example, the natural scientific and cosmological foundations of process thought represent a choice at variance with my own. For in addition to his phenomenological interests, Whitehead emphasizes even more the natural scientific side of his work. So, among present-day process theologians, fundamental confidence resides in beginning with "hard," abstract metaphysical concepts; the hope apparently is to provide a solid intellectual base (reminiscent of scientific method) for speaking about God, the world, ethics, art. All readers in this area are familiar with Whitehead's initial conceptualizing: "actual entities" or "actual occasions," "occasions of experience," "prehensions," "eternal objects," "physical and mental poles," "principle of concretion," etc. Whitehead was (in the careful, modern sense of the word) a realist, not an idealist. His choice was to begin with actual objects that can be rigorously conceptualized, even if they are not the traditional "substances" or "monads," but rather Whitehead's philosophically unusual entities of "experience." In other words, he takes as fundamental the subject-object relation. As Victor Lowe very helpfully cites Whitehead's view:

> . . . instead of describing, in Kantian fashion, how subjective data pass into the appearance of an objective world, he describes how subjective experience emerges from an objective world.[9]

Though I confess myself disturbed with the phrasing above that cites the "Kantian fashion," I also readily admit that the forebears of the view being offered here are nineteenth-century philosophical idealists, not scientific empiricists. In that case, I would see the process theologians' view, not as a "hard" foundational conceptualizing of the real cosmos, but as a fascinating analytical explication—a secondary rehearsal —of one historically relative poetic vision. The very highly specialized language in process thought therefore serves a very different function in that system from what the adherents of that school apparently see it as serving. Since I am oriented to history and crisis rather than to cosmos and system, it is natural that I would look upon the remarkable, yet awkward Whiteheadian prose as of less interest than the grand metaphor standing behind it. Is it not astonishing that a scientifically oriented empiricist would suppose every, single cosmic event to be somehow the "experience" of a "subject"? Yet this is but one more historical attempt to recover first-order linguisticality; and I would think the solution of our problems does not lie primarily, or even significantly, in the painstaking second-order elaboration of that intriguing metaphor—as worthwhile a task as that may be. Not in rationalist metaphysics, but in historic symbols of religion, freshly engaged, lies the clue to process. Yet the Whiteheadians would persistently remind us of a universe of measurable entities that must be given its due, and I have attempted to recognize that simple, everyday fact throughout these pages.

Besides the sharp difference in orientation to language, there clearly follows a marked substantive difference between mine and the Whiteheadians' views on the nature of "God." Space does not permit elaborating here. Suffice it to say that God as a principle of determination or harmony is far more specialized—and rationalist—a view than my own. God is not the missing item that completes an otherwise viable metaphysical view of things so much as he threatens through real crises to be alien from our rational standards and subtleties. Thus he includes that deeper, hidden level of "presence" that marks even our wider and more penetrating moments of vision as "unfinished." Thus, what Whitehead means by "substantial activity" is very close to what I have proposed here as "process," so that my outlook favors the link Whitehead had to Spinoza and Spinoza's disposal of the term "God."

VI

Crisis and Recovery

Following the terms employed thus far in this study, consider a work of literature read theologically as offering a first-order insight into the process of time, or a first-order disclosure of a "god," or of *the* "God." With whatever particular meaning, a literary work that draws common elements into a fresh configuration alludes at some level to the world's destiny. If such an allusion hardly restricts itself to some confessional theological tradition, nevertheless the standpoint that is "fleshed out" can speak through a broadened or reflected theology. The particular nature of "God," incarnate in and through the literary piece, depends upon the specific materials used and the artist's own angle of vision.

To enlarge further upon the theory of reflected theology, one needs to consider the "gap" that exists in all metaphoric, first-order discourse: the "gap" between the terms as second-order references and their gathered function in first-order richness. The model here is the rhetorical metaphor. Consider the difference between the metaphor's two components taken separately in ordinary discourse and, on the other hand, taken together in a striking newness. As considered in chapter two, the synthesizing imagination is able to "see together" in a suggestive unity items whose everyday inferences would not entail each other at all: "giddy brink," "psalms of silence," "slaves . . . plums." Since no logical inference exists from one item of the set to the other, the concrete unity that they effect arises on the other side of a "jump" in meaning. Metaphor necessarily entails the uniting *de novo* of normally different or antagonistic items. The issue of how "new" may be the newness in a metaphoric linguistic act has already been discussed (pp. 54–55). Certainly, the "gap" in logical inference will vary greatly depending upon how normally antagonistic are the items that compose the metaphor. The epiphor, for example, usually does not produce the strikingly new act of the diaphor, which does more apparent violence to second-order systems. In any event, two facts emerge to be dealt with in relation to a reflected theology: one, that an inferential gap does open in the move to a first-order linguistic function; and second, that the gap may be more or less severe, i.e., the "new" meaning born in the metaphor may more easily be accommodated to the old situation, or it may represent a more severe departure from the old.

Suppose the gap in transition from second to first order is designated as a "crisis" in meaning, a point where old meanings are modified, if not lost, and where a decisive introduction of new meanings takes place. From the model of the simple rhetorical metaphor, the notion of a crisis in meaning between second order and first order may then apply to any imaginative work of literature in the large. That is, a novel or a poem represents a creation composed of materials that have experienced a crisis in their usual, second-order meaning. If a work of literature invokes a "world," and indeed illumines the real world from a certain center of vision, then it is clear that a significant act has occurred in arranging the materials of the piece so that this powerful suggestion emerges. Words, sentences, and paragraphs play upon one another in and through the style of the piece so that new shades of meaning come to birth within a first-order horizon. The disruption of former meanings and the birth of new ones within a suggestive unity indicate a transition through crisis.

"Gaming" through the work of literature, as described in chapter three, will lead the reader to know the real world differently, as a result of having experienced the work of art. The point is that in a full reading of a literary piece one's own "world" is subject to crisis. Importantly, this crisis entails an unexpected passage in time, a passage along which metaphor bears one into the future, yet without solving the nature of the temporal process in precise public terms. The reader must enter the new, with the risk such entry involves. The crisis itself may be a gentle transition or a most drastic one. Indeed, for some literary works the term "crisis" is really an exaggeration, while with others it is highly appropriate. Jane Austen's *Pride and Prejudice*, for example, not so much sets a world into crisis as it "surprises" us into experiencing a

world believable but unobtrusive before. Camus' *The Plague,*
on the other hand, offers the paradigm of a world thrown into
shock, with events that disrupt what convention assumed to
be permanent.

A reflected theology finds the "gap" or crisis in the aesthetic, literary act to be typical of Western religious concerns
expressed in the Christ narrative. The account of cross and
resurrection, that is, concerns itself with "mixed," recognizable human affairs that enter into crisis and thereby surprisingly into renewal. The same structure occurs in Jesus' own
parables of the Kingdom, and in Paul's celebration of the
Christ self-emptied and "seeing his humanity through" to his
own peculiar glory (Philippians 2:5–11). Likewise the Jesus
narrative of the Gospels drives towards a crisis in common
human affairs, out of which the resurrection of the dead One,
as an astonishing result, takes place. These various testimo-
nies to the Christ share a structure and theme suggestive of,
and unquestionably influential upon, the aesthetic mode of
Western literature that followed in their train.

Now the principle of cross-resurrection as a principle of
"crisis and recovery" in aesthetic work may seem to be so
elastic and to include such a wide range of literary forms and
effects that its significance is lost. A principle that can apply
either to *Pride and Prejudice* or to *The Plague* may seem of
little helpfulness simply by embracing too much. Actually, a
measure of that breadth and scope already appears in the
theological presentation of the same theme. For Christian
theology in its varied history has interpreted and related the
cross and resurrection of Jesus in different ways. Generally in
catholic tradition, the cross is primarily an important transition point in a continuum of God's forward-moving work
with his people. In core-Reformation tradition (Luther and
his interpretation of Paul), the cross is a severe and ironic
break in religious continuity, reminiscent of the cataclysms
announced by the Old Testament prophets to the nation Israel. That in such a rupture of religious confidence and practice there should be hidden the substance of renewal and recovery is heavily paradoxical indeed. (Thus, for Rudolph

Bultmann the resurrection is already implicit in the crucifixion, for those who have insight to see it).[10] Thus the Christian heritage of theology varies its own substance as between
continuity and paradoxical disruption, with differing positions possible in relation to these two. Therefore, a reflected
theology already knows and can acknowledge wide variations
in the handling of "crisis" and "recovery" as a theological or
aesthetic act.

Furthermore, there is certainly no disposition to argue that
literature in the scope of its works represents any conscious
dependence on the part of all authors upon the Christian
story. If Auerbach is right, then the story of the Christ appears to have made itself felt culturally so as to give an initial
orientation for the Western experience of reality. In any case,
the delineation of a reflected theology is interested in no
more than this: that certain prominent theological motifs
find strong analogues within the act and the results of literary
creation. As the "crisis" factor in the Christian story offers an
ironic and astonishing approach to renewal, so the metaphoric transition in literature embraces a "jump" in meaning that makes the creation possible. The more disruptive of
tradition that "jump" has been (as in the modern West particularly), the more the analogue of the cross informs the
conditions of creativity and renewal effected by the artist.
One has only to think of the intense alienation expressed in
contemporary literature and drama to realize the analogue or
theological "reflection." Elements that theology has spoken
of as "sin," "atonement," "redemption," and "salvation," as
stilted as they often have become, know a distant resonance
in the work of the individualistic or even alienated artist. No
direct conclusions may be drawn from that resonance except
that a vocabulary of theological criticism is possible, if nevertheless highly abstracted, vis-a-vis Christian theology *per se.*

The task above has been to draw some specific elements
from the theological tradition into certain abstracted con-

cepts that may serve the interests of theological criticism. In discerning reflected theology's "God" as the general process of things in time, given "incarnation" in the first-order metaphoric structure of a literary work, the basic terms of theological-critical theory have been set. By noting that a certain crisis in continuity distinguishes both the basic theological narrative in Christianity and the imaginative act of literary creation, I mean further to qualify the manner in which reflected theology appropriates itself to artistic creation.

Clearly, the application of this theory to literature itself alone can indicate its limits, its success, or its want of usefulness. A select experiment in the theological reading of literature should therefore be the next concern of this inquiry.

NOTES

1. Moses Hadas, *Hellenistic Culture—Fusion and Diffusion* (New York: Columbia University Press, 1959) 191.

2. See, e.g., Norman Perrin, *The Kingdom of God in the Teaching of Jesus* (Philadelphia: The Westminster Press, 1963) esp. Chapter III.

3. E.g., Boers, *Ghetto*, 26–56.

4. Auerbach, *Mimesis*, 16–17.

5. Auerbach, *Mimesis*, 12.

6. Auerbach, *Dante*, 14.

7. Auerbach, *Mimesis*, 22, suggests the kinship of the Old Testament and the later "mixed" style.

8. See, e.g., Charles Hartshorne, *The Logic of Perfection* (La-Salle: Open Court Publishing Company, 1962).

9. "Whitehead's Metaphysical System," in D. Brown *et al.*, eds., *Process Philosophy and Christian Thought* (Indianapolis: Bobbs-Merrill, 1971) 7.

10. See "New Testament and Mythology" in *Kerygma and Myth*, ed. H. W. Bartsch (New York: Harper Torchbooks, 1961) 41.

Faulkner's The Sound
And The Fury   *VII*

The assertion in this study has been that language, in its tension and play between first and second orders—as in literature—does present everyday, working reality. This reality can further be thought of as the nature and meaning of the temporal process, equivalent in reflected theology to "God." Thus "God" is present as all things; yet all things are a metaphor of process, or of "God." First-order language instruments the metaphoric or imaginative "jump" to offer a grasp of the process of things, even as process simultaneously transcends ("sinks beneath") any presentation of itself. The jump itself means a greater or lesser crisis in the known circumstances that have preceded it, depending upon the difficulty of keeping pace imaginatively with the turn of process involved. The theological reading of literature, therefore, must concern itself with insight into the general process of things afforded by the literary work as metaphoric act. Realizing a version or view of "God" can be the result of "gaming" with a literary work, if theological subject matter is of interest to the reader. The intensity of the crisis that stands between the old second-order and the fresh first-order configurations marks the intensity of the crisis that history and "God" undergo in the renewal of meaning on the other side of that "jump."

It remains to be seen whether such theological reading of literature is serviceable. In this chapter and the following, the plan is to see what results obtain from applying the proposed theory of theological reading to two literary works, both novels. The choice of works is arbitrary; yet the two selected here can be said to offer challenge to any ordinary effort at theological reading, and thereby to constitute a significant test of the approach. The novel to be considered in this chapter is William Faulkner's *The Sound and the Fury*.[1] The following chapter will deal with Franz Kafka's *The Trial*.

The Story; Themes of Time and Order

Faulkner's novel is a technical masterpiece that includes both events and allusions of a Christian guise. For all that, the question of its theological import is a complex one and can hardly be settled by noting that Faulkner's imagination flourished in a Protestant culture, or that he drew significantly upon Christian themes and symbols. Indeed, as the title of the story suggests, the chaos and sterility portrayed give the sense of no order or meaning at all, except for that insisted upon by a childish idiot.

> . . . The broken flower drooped over Ben's fist and his eyes were empty and blue and serene again as cornice and façade flowed smoothly once more from left to right; post and tree, window and doorway, and signboard, each in its ordered place (p. 336).

Thus in the novel the idiot-character Ben concentrates in his cramped and limited person vestiges of love and order that the articulate figures of the story have allowed to erode.

The account itself tells a story of aristocratic degeneracy in the South, the demise of an old Mississippi family, and the disaster of its failing code of honor. The Compsons of the mid-nineteenth century had given a Governor to the state and a Brigadier-General to the Confederacy. By 1910, through mortgages and sales, most of their solid square-mile of land was gone, and the head-of-house, Jason Compson III, had only the faltering real estate, an alcoholic fatalism, and certain well-thumbed copies of Livy and Horace to leave to his four adolescent children. Of these four, the three brothers were alike sons of misfortune: Quentin drowned himself at the end of his first Harvard year; Benjamin was born an idiot ("A judgment upon me"—as were most things—according to his mother); and Jason IV grew into a petty, tight-fisted, and resentful man.

The sister of these three, Candace (or Caddy), likewise frustrated her life despite a spirit of rebellious hope and caring. The story really belongs to her, and to the emotions that criss-cross through her response to the family anguish. She plays a role of kindness, abandon, and clear-sightedness amid the confusion—loving Benjy, protecting Quentin and her father, rebuking Jason, keeping her mother's brittle self-pity at bay. She knows that the family pretense is a sham. Yet her insight into the vanity of those around her does not allay her own misfortune, since her protective loyalty to the others keeps her wed to their game of honor and position. In one sense, she remains tenaciously on the sinking family ship; in another, she elects to repudiate the family's values. And on both counts she is quite clear about what she is doing. The ultimate frustration for Caddy is the situation of her daughter, Quentin (named for the dead brother), who must grow up in the old family home. There is no civilized place in Caddy's exiled life for child-rearing; yet this means separation from her daughter and infuriating dependence upon the spiteful Jason, the last remaining head of the house. The unfolding of the story finally portrays the girl, Quentin, now seventeen, a reflection of her mother's frustration and conflict, bitterly rebellious against Jason and climactically stealing his hidden money-box in an escape from the Compson home.

In form and technique *The Sound and the Fury* is a masterpiece of character delineation and of combining four variant points of view into a gradually focussed portrayal of events. (That is, the four segments of the book give an account from the points of view, in turn, of Benjy, Quentin the son, Jason, and finally the universal-author.) Significantly, in respect to what we have said concerning narrative (above, p. 58), the story does not proceed in orderly sequence, but employs stream-of-consciousness in weaving past and present scenes together through the first two segments. Next Jason "tells" his own chapter in a continuous, running present, and the final chapter brings into increasing public focus via universal author the telling events of the last calendar day in the body of the novel. This last "objective" chapter uses as a touchstone the vision of Dilsey, the Compson's black servant, during Easter preaching service.

In the brief space available here, a full critical analysis of this rich and varied work is hardly possible. For our purposes, a limited analysis will follow based on the themes of time and order, an examination of style, and a concept of literary portraiture. This will be followed by comment on what theological sense or outlook is suggested by the novel.

First, one may comment that the theme of "time" is obvious and indeed almost overwhelming in the unfolding of Faulkner's saga. Time has dealt harshly with the Compson generations. Time therefore is a problem for each Compson, according to that member's particular outlook and circumstances. To examine the theme requires at least the well-known distinction between *chronos* (measured clock-time) and *kairos* (the "right" time, the "key" time) and certain possible relations between the two. Because of the Compson's deteriorating state of affairs, *chronos* plays the major role in the story, seeming to guarantee moment by moment the demise of all family dignity and significance. Oddly enough then, *chronos*, despite all its measured quality, increasingly signals chaos rather than order. Perhaps one should say that the hostile pulse of *chronos*, like a beat of judgment, renders chaotic whatever is not able to keep up, to endure. Thus, though classical qualities of time and fate appear, *chronos* in

Faulkner's story has the features of a distorted Calvinist deity in his condemning role. Very much the same allusion appears in the large billboard eye with its mechanical electric pupil that confronts Jason at the point of his lowest ebb (p. 327). The all-seeing eye of a Calvinist God here combines with the tawdry technical life of Jason's enforced punctuality at his job and the general sterility of his existence.

Quentin, the eldest brother of the four children, is conscious and articulate concerning clock-time. His father's gift to him of a gold watch was the occasion for a cynical speech on time:

> . . . It was Grandfather's and when Father gave it to me he said, Quentin, I give you the mausoleum of all hope and desire. . . . I give it to you not that you may remember time, but that you might forget it now and then for a moment and not spend all your breath trying to conquer it. Because no battle is ever won he said. They are not even fought (p. 95).

Quentin signals his suicide decision by twisting the hands off the watch, determined thus to overcome time by yielding to it (p. 99).

The novel itself is neatly laid out in segments identified by calendar time, though not in order: April 7, 1928 (Holy Saturday; Benjy's thirty-third birthday); June 2, 1910 (Quentin's suicide); April 6, 1928 (Good Friday); April 8, 1928 (Easter Sunday). The merger of mechanical time with Christian liturgical time provides a certain irony, especially since considerations other than the liturgical sequence set the order of the chapters. Also, within the first two chapters the order of calendar time is broken up by the stream-of-consciousness recall, first of Benjy, secondly of Quentin. For Benjy the idiot, time has become a jumble, the center of whose meaning is mostly past, but the center of whose experience is all present. The result is, as Faulkner tells us, that he does not remember his sister Caddy (whom he loved) but only the loss of her (p. 19). The direct sensory awareness that Ben has of things, so attractive in contrast to the formalized pretense of the family, is increasingly restricted; time imprisons him by the loss of his pasture, then the loss of his sister, then his castration, and finally his institutionalizing. Since he has no positive memory by which to deal with time, his association-links from the present pick up the "feeling" equivalent of things past; but these are signals of loss and pain. If he then cannot consciously span time, his only sense of it is as a single center of agony.

> . . . Ben wailed again, hopeless and prolonged. It was nothing. Just sound. It might have been all time and injustice and sorrow become vocal for an instant by a conjunction of planets (pp. 303–304).

In his own way, Ben's brother Jason knows a much more vacuous present, filled less with diffuse agony and more with known frustration. Indeed, present-ness appears to be his chief awareness, as indicated by the use in his chapter of "I says . . . he says . . ." throughout the dialogue. Jason's kind of absorption in the present is nevertheless not the sort that contradicts preoccupation with past and future. The *telos* or goal of his present activity is rather to correct the past and secure the future. Consequently, his sense of present-ness is mortgaged to those two commitments so as to render the present literal, definite, and utilitarian. In the terms of this study, past, present, and future are for Jason *only* present insofar as they are at all, with no sense of mystery involved or of the important distinction made between presence and the unfinished nature of "presentations." "Once a bitch always a bitch . . . ," he tells us at the opening of his account (p. 198).

Jason's treatment of inexorable time focuses in the box of money hidden in his room, cash stolen from his sister Caddy intended for her daughter. For years he has deceptively impounded checks and made of them a token of his persistent rage about the past and determination to control his destiny. When the girl Quentin successfully robs him and makes good her escape, Faulkner comments:

> . . . Of his niece he did not think at all, nor the arbitrary valuation of the money. Neither of them had had entity or individuality for him for ten years; together they merely symbolized the job in

the bank of which he had been deprived before he ever got it (p. 321).

With all the characters, the threat of *chronos* against life is so severe that efforts to allay it only serve to solidify its power. So Jason fortifies himself, but suffocates within his own citadel. Quentin clings to the family honor, which becomes his coffin. Benjy's incessant complaint brings not comfort, but reasserted isolation. The motif of order does emerge in each of these three, but the order that each pursues only guarantees the incapacity to deal with the realities of time. Quentin, for example, has intensified the family's aristocratic code to a point of purity that necessarily must carry him outside of time. All the burden of shoring up the family ruins has come down upon his shoulders in the one item of his sister's lost virginity. His fantasy of purifying the blemish is to pretend that her daughter was conceived in an incestuous relationship with himself. As Quentin's father states it,

> . . . you wanted to sublimate a piece of natural human folly into a horror and then exorcize it with truth. . . . [And Quentin's reply:] . . . it was to isolate her out of the loud world so that it would have to flee us of necessity and then the sound of it would be as though it had never been. . . . (p. 195).

The hellish purification that would "isolate her out of the loud world" could only be death by refinement, as over against death by disarray. Quentin's "order" of family honor no longer has the capacity to endure or to "contain" time and therefore must withdraw from time into gnostic self-obliteration. Jason's order of things is an abstracted utility based on a massive resentment of his lot in life. He cannot accept time; he cannot accept what history has given him. His strategy is consequently all the more vulnerable to time and contingency, as the purloined money-box testifies. Benjy's order is definite and public (never take him to the left of the town square —pp. 335–336), but infantile and personal. With normal adult help gone, Ben's small order has no strength against time and loss.

Only Dilsey "endured" (p. 14). The last chapter, told in the simple past by a universal author, features the ancient black servant's attendance at church on Easter Sunday and preaching by the Rev. Shegog. Dilsey's sense of time becomes explicit in Shegog's Easter sermon, which holds forth a vision of the world from its beginning to its ending seen through "de ricklickshun en de blood of de Lamb" (pp. 310–313). In effect, the climax of the preaching is a rehearsal of the biblical story at certain critical points (exodus, incarnation, crucifixion-resurrection, last day) that link the whole saga together from Genesis to Revelation. Dilsey weeps on her way home. "I've seed de first en de last," she says. "I seed de beginnin, en now I sees de endin" (p. 313). For Dilsey, the heavy rhythm of *chronos* is held within the bounds of an immense saga whose significance is divine. Such a framework is also one in which the beginning and the ending of the Compson household find their meaning. Perhaps one should say that the movement of *chronos* is given significance and *telos* by a series of intersecting moments or *kairoi*, key times, along the chronological line—exactly the key times featured in Shegog's sermon. Thus the exodus and the resurrection, for example, claim a significance that resists the sameness of *chronos* and pulls it into a hopeful future-oriented outlook. The *kairoi* make the difference, but of course they are not experienced as moments of existential decision by Dilsey herself but as time-worn, typical events of the Bible: the sacrifice of Isaac, the passover, the resurrection, the descending dove. What were once moments of crisis have become for her definite pathways out of sheer *chronos* and into the meaningful, divine time of God. They are indeed fissures in the regularity of *chronos* that glimpse beyond themselves a vast pattern of divine promise and fulfilment, solid and sure. Fully identified with that pattern, Dilsey finds in it the grounds of her healthy "common sense" amidst the Compsons, and her staying power against the erosions of time. Indeed the chapter is marked by bodily and facial images of time-resistance:

> ... The preacher ... began to walk back and forth before the desk, his hands clasped behind him, a meagre figure, hunched over upon itself like that of

> one long immured in striving with the implacable
> earth . . . He was like a worn small rock whelmed
> by the successive waves of his voice (p. 310). Dilsey
> sat bolt upright . . . Two tears slid down her fallen
> cheeks, in and out of the myriad coruscations of im-
> molation and abnegation and time (p. 311).

Dilsey and the congregation enter with great emotion and
re-enactment into Shegog's "ricklickshun" of the wonderful
history of the Lamb; but the moment is not a *kairos* moment
of crisis and decisive action, but of orienting vision and confirmation. For Dilsey, in that moment, time and order coincide on a universal scale. Her place-to-stand is over against
the larger divine pattern, to be measured by it and to participate in it. One does not, however, enter into Dilsey's stream
of consciousness as with Ben, Quentin, and Jason. The pattern may be a scheme for the spiritual geography of human
destinies, but it is not for Dilsey's people a hermeneutic of
secular, human existence. The tensions, yearnings, and ago-
nies of individuals relative to the pattern are otherwise revealed. Dilsey's role and experience are not therefore the final
key to the interior lives of the Compsons, which are of great
concern to Faulkner. An understanding of that concern is
provided by examining the character of Caddy Compson.

Faulkner's Portrait of Caddy Compson

What means the most may not be directly approached, but
should emerge of itself. The character of Candace Compson
is a study in literary portraiture because, despite its importance, it is not approached directly. Caddy has no chapter
peculiarly assigned to her. She must be conveyed through
three chapters that are stream-of-consciousness studies; in the
last, more "objective" chapter almost no references to her
occur. This means that the character must be etched through
the impressions of an idiot (who cannot really remember her),
the preoccupations of a brother who compulsively regards her
out of only one concern, and the selective memory of another
brother who hates her. That the character emerges with integrity and sympathy is no small credit to the author. Perhaps

he "cheats" somewhat in his literary reading of the idiot's brain, for it is in the first chapter that most of the compelling clues to Caddy come clear and strong. Nevertheless, the composite portrait works, and the complexity of Caddy is finally best read if it is read through those various angles that other different characters bring to it.

"Portrait" is a term borrowed from painting and therefore applies with a certain irony to Caddy Compson, since so little visual image of her appears. Language presents the person directly in certain respects, as painting presents the person directly in others. Visual and linguistic modes and values mesh—one cannot be thought entirely apart from the other— yet one may heavily dominate over the other, as the linguistic mode does in this literary "portrait." Caddy's person is thus built up by countless occasional incidents, remarks, attitudes, relationships, and moments of touching, smelling, and hearing as well as seeing. As a consequence, the person of Caddy stands somewhere "within" the body of the novel as if within a three-dimensional setting or housing. This living effect is analogous to the use of three or four transparent overlays, each of which includes parts or colors for a picture that emerges fully only via the combination. Thus the sense of Caddy richly accumulates through the "transparencies" of three or four other characters, until her presence becomes significant throughout the text. The result is to introduce the reader into relationships between Caddy and others and so to share in the directness of her life. Note that the result here contrasts importantly with Rev. Shegog's language that presents and "brings home" the human drama of biblical events; in that case a certain distance from the monumental occasions of Scripture is retained. It is another matter with direct and lively portraiture. More needs to be said of this further on.

Granted the variety of sensuous images presenting Caddy, the original one that caught Faulkner's fancy is heavily visual: that of the little girl with muddy drawers climbing the tree to look in on the death of her grandmother in the house. But immediately the sense of smell becomes also involved,

VII

and Walter Brylowski points out to us the recurring imagery in Faulkner associating trees with youthful virginity:

> . . . The history of this image suggests that long be-
> fore *The Sound and the Fury* Faulkner's imagina-
> tion had fixed upon an equation between virginity
> and straight, slim trees, an image further extended
> to include the odor of each as the identifying prin-
> ciple, the sense of smell being labeled by Faulkner
> as "one of my sharper senses."[2]

The result in *The Sound and the Fury* is the well known impression belonging to Benjy, that "Caddy smelled like trees"
(p. 26).

With such qualities in mind, it may be said that *chronos*
for Caddy takes on a more natural and less mechanical character, that time belongs more to the cyclical realm of nature
than to machinery. She does not lack, it is true, the tick-tock
sense of impending family doom shared by all the Compsons,
as in the scene with Benjy:

> I could hear the clock, and I could hear Caddy
> standing behind me, and I could hear the roof. It's
> still raining, Caddy said. I hate rain. I hate every-
> thing. And then her head came into my lap and she
> was crying . . . I could hear the clock and the roof
> and Caddy (p. 76).

But time for Caddy is also the seasons of nature and the time
of flourishing girlhood with its sexual directness. When
Faulkner says of her that she "accepted the doom without
either seeking or fleeing it" (p. 10), a certain inevitability of
the natural informs his words. Caddy's lostness is part of the
many-sided family agony; yet from another point of view it is
part of a "natural" emergence and decline.

Such a consideration of nature and time asks whether the
fall of the Compsons is not modeled on classical tragedy and
the *nemesis* that restores nature's disturbed balance. At the
same time, the style of the novel recalls the Hebraic and
"mixed" styles noted by Auerbach as biblical. That is, com-

mon folk in common situations handle affairs of high seriousness; the style is fragmentary, living, "unfinished," suggesting
much more than it explicitly says. If so, we are dealing with
historical time (the history of the house of Compson) reminiscent of the shape of biblical time as laid out in Shegog's
sermon. It is important to be clear about this: Auerbach finds
the biblical style (as noted earlier) to be characterized by a
certain rudeness of syntax and incompleteness, a multilayered
effect, a strong sense of "background," and a relational awareness of persons. He also finds that this style invokes universal
history and process as the arena for the events narrated, and
includes a certain striving "to overcome our reality." These
factors Auerbach contrasts with the Homeric style, in which
he finds the *personae* definite and unchanging, the whole
narrative fixed in space-time as if in a comprehensive present,
and the account having the nature of a clear, externalized,
syntactically precise foreground.[3] Surely the biblical, "mixed"
style and the Christian tradition have had the greater impact
upon *The Sound and the Fury*, though classical tragic themes
are present. In consequence of this biblical effect the every-
day-ish characters of the novel struggle with lofty issues of
guilt and responsibility in the midst of a social *and* natural
"order"—if it can be so called—that nevertheless appears to
fore-doom their efforts. The biblical framework is present insofar as responsible persons struggle in a world that evidently
aspires to a divine covenant or transcendent order, but finds
none. The frame of reference is Christian, but it is that of a
"disappointed" Christianity.

The strands concerning Candace now should be drawn together. The biblical pattern somewhat more informs her situation than that of the other characters, for added to mechanical time and natural cyclical time is an element of *kairos*.
That is, there are critical moments of decisiveness that promise to weigh heavily in how future matters will go. Caddy
evidently has the forthrightness to "grasp the time." The
model is in the prime incident of climbing the tree as a little
girl. She takes matters into her own hands in order to see for
herself. Faulkner comments,

> . . . they were three boys, one was a girl and the girl
> was the only one that was brave enough to climb
> that tree to look in the forbidden window to see
> what was going on.[4]

Thus it is Caddy's disposition to take matters into her own
hands, "see" what is the case, and act accordingly. The same
is true of her, even as a youngster, in her treatment of Benjy,
her sexual revolt, her decision to marry Sidney Herbert
Head, and her move to leave Quentin, her daughter, back at
the family home. Critical moments, the "makings" of *kairoi*,
occur and she responds to them. But though she has courage
and sees clearly, in the end the would-be *kairoi* do not draw
the span of time into a promising direction; *chronos* continues its downward path. Things do not change. Courage,
revolt, and compassion do not constitute eyelets into a redeeming providence, larger than herself. Time remains the
expression of a natural cycle and a chronological decline, and
the critical "times" end up only confirming what necessity requires. Indeed, the *kairoi* are *kairoi* only in that they illumine the inevitable, not that they are moments of genuinely
new possibility.

The success and power of the Caddy portrait lie substantively in this combination of inevitable situation with personal characteristics of courage, honesty, and compassion.
The one side does not cancel the other, as one would expect
them to do. The success of the portrait lies methodologically
in the indirection by which Faulkner allows the character to
emerge out of a countless accumulation of other's experiences
of her. What the author wishes most seriously to explore he
guards and gives by hints and fragments, so that only for the
most persistent reader comes the reward of emotional and
conceptual discovery.

Clearly, the Benjy, Quentin, and Jason chapters contribute
to the Candace figure, but does the final chapter with its
events of Easter Sunday? Here the Shegog sermon functions
not as the novel's confession of faith, nor as a panoramic view
of the biblical account, within whose terms Caddy is
"damned." Rather the Shegog sermon functions as an ironic

reference point for the shape of the Compson history, if the affirmation of God's special providence be taken out. Within its structure, Caddy "endures"—as indeed she did endure—reminiscent of Dilsey's "enduring" as if by a peculiar spiritual formation, but without belief that the structure is of God or incarnates God. If this is true, Dilsey's experience, as well as that of Benjy, Quentin, and Jason, reflects and refracts the character of Caddy, which is nevertheless uniquely different from all those four. In her, the various meanings suggested by the novel cluster to their most complex field.

Reflected Theology in The Sound and the Fury

Implicit in the above analysis are two general moves within one fabric of comment: one is the application of certain concepts, *"chronos," "kairos,"* "order," "portrait," "style," in an effort to see the response of the material to them; second is a certain gaming with the novel, by which it is judged that the axis of the significant "world" of the novel passes in and through the character of Candace. As regards "gaming" with the novel, recall what has already been said at the conclusion of chapter three (pp. 86–89). Appropriate technical and conceptual analysis is essential, yet views the literary work at the level of "object." It would ordinarily seem that setting forth the characters and their relative importance to the story is likewise a part of this more objective task. To a degree, such objectivity is appropriate in dealing with the character of Caddy. On the other hand, the elements of her portrayal in the novel are diffuse and indirect; more especially, assessing her character as the key to the whole work requires a risk in judgment. In approaching such a judgment the novel may become more a game than an object; and "gaming with" the book means temporarily participating in it *as if* a player and thus evaluating—in thought and feeling—the horizon of its general outlook. The judgment I have thus tried to make is that the "world" of the novel gathers around Candace and that the novel's strands of meaning flow through her and her relationships.

To do a theological reading of the novel requires further

that one allow its "world" to constitute an illumination of the real world, and to reflect upon how one's grasp of reality is focused and heightened for having "entered into" the literary work. In the case of *The Sound and the Fury*, what view emerges of what I have called the nature and meaning of the temporal process? Perspectives on time that occur in the novel have already been described and that should be of significant help. Comments will fall roughly under four topics: (1) the decline of the Compson house; (2) the destiny of consciousness in the decline of human affairs; (3) the bondage and demise of consciousness; (4) "friction" between a negative destiny and acceptance of that destiny.

First of all, in a novel about the decline and fall of a significant house, a view of the general, temporal process finds its primary standpoint in that fall. Time and process wear their guise of the fateful deterioration of all things. Reality may express itself as a mixed cornucopia of astonishing, even gratuitous flourishes; yet all this abundance apparently has no point to it, a fact underscored as time erodes the structures of human order that apparently set meaningful boundaries. These structures—family, school, class, religion—may have invoked the sanction of God; nevertheless, "God" himself evidently sweeps by in his own appointed way, setting off brilliant world-images of his presence that finally bespeak confusion. The nature of God (dropping now the quotation marks . . . ". . ." . . . and simply assuming reflected theology) invokes, then, both wonder and dismay, as God's fruitfulness in time exists only in order to wither and vanish. Reality gives, but then sinks back from what it has given.

Secondly, such a decline in affairs has a most significant impact upon human consciousness and its destiny, at least as emphasized in Faulkner's story. Indeed, the author's stream-of-consciousness technique shows his determination to keep this intimate closeness with his characters and to consider the direction that consciousness takes. This study has rather scrupulously avoided speaking of "consciousness" because to do so raises the spectre of privacy and solipsism; if everything belongs to consciousness, the implication is that consciousness alone exists. My point has been that everyday intentionality moves from a "situated" locus, and if situated, then situated within a setting of a certain kind and shape. Nevertheless, the first three segments of *The Sound and the Fury* make clear a tendency of consciousness to organize experience into increasingly private universes.

Thus the destiny of consciousness is in itself important. Something of that importance can be seen by contrasting the first three parts of the novel with the last, which is not written from the stream-of-consciousness point of view. There the biblical framework in Shegog's sermon outlines a meaningful scope of time, the very geography that is lacking elsewhere in the book. The different kinds of treatment that these two areas of the novel receive—the "consciousness" chapters and the sermon—are instructive in tracing the novel's sensibility. Shegog's vision of the biblical story (". . . I sees . . . I hears . . .") finds language that opens for the congregation the reality of the world-embracing account. The reader can know and feel the congregation's identification with biblical figures that are like and yet at the same time "larger" than themselves. But the reader does *not* identify with the biblical figures, at least not within the province of the novel. The account of Pharaoh's chariots, of the baby Jesus, of God's mighty judgments may have literary and symbolic value for the reader concerning sacrifice, endurance, and hope; but they are not the reader's account of actual history the way they are Dilsey's, whose consciousness is not immediately presented.

On the other hand, the author offers directly the consciousness of other figures, who are in turn immediate to the consciousness of Caddy. In earlier Western centuries each figure, and therefore each consciousness, would have been considered *within* the framework of the biblical account; but in this twentieth-century novel personal consciousness and the biblical framework stand separated. The latter can apply only ironically and symbolically to the former. For that reason, the novel can be termed specifically post-Dantean in character. Recall Auerbach's comment that in Dante himself the force of personhood begins to break the grand structure meant to hold it (p. 121):

> . . . The image of man eclipses the image of God. . . . The tremendous pattern was broken by the overwhelming power of the images it had to contain. . . . even in Hell there are great souls, and certain souls in Purgatory can for a moment forget the path of purification for the sweetness of a poem, the work of human frailty.[5]

Put in a position of choice, the novelist of course sets personal consciousness at the center and lets the "tremendous pattern" relate to consciousness however it may. In the bizarre play of time and process, the destiny of consciousness becomes of primary interest.

Thirdly, the end of consciousness is bondage and demise. The story discloses a progressive negating of consciousness as reality alienates the *personae* and forces them to abstract certain sparse elements to which they tenaciously cling. Thus Ben clings to his sense of Caddy's loss. Quentin clings to Caddy's lost virginity. Jason clings to his resentment incarnate in the money box. Caddy clings to the family even in its eccentric pattern and at the same time knows that the pattern is empty and defeated. Her conflict of rejection-affirmation sets up an impossible field of responsibility that must exhaust her resources. In this respect, God appears as the judgment of reality upon a consciousness that necessarily must cling to certain treasured elements and know all else as chaos. Then language becomes disordered and fragmentary in expressing temporal process—process now become a threat to those who must insist upon the past. The language of increasing privacy becomes appropriate to the alienated consciousness, for which there are fewer and fewer stable points of orientation "out there." That the healthy eccentricity of human knowing becomes exaggerated to a point of crisis and alienation is the judgment of God. Yet no assurance emerges that the judgments of God are "righteous altogether"; rather they appear to entail inscrutable ends.

Fourthly, a certain "friction" appears between one's negative destiny and acceptance of that destiny. This appears only with the character of Candace. An affirmation appears in her that is nevertheless interlaced with the negation that is taking place. At such a point, one comes to the angle of vision that motivated the author's novel. The language of the book must articulate alienation, the process of the negation of consciousness. Yet that language also articulates a certain awe. It is not that the language of crisis and disorder *yields* to a language of meaning and direction; that would be a false imposition. Rather the same language that articulates disorder means *also* something else: a new kind of excellence, a new *desideratum.* So the articulation of irreversible anguish and sterility may carry in itself a wonder. The point is reminiscent of the statement attributed to Kafka:

> No people sing with such pure voices as those who live in deepest Hell; what we take for the song of angels is their song.[6]

A way of holding to the world is gone, but in the delineation of its ruins something else appears. In *The Sound and the Fury* the language of brokenness, sterility, and death is also the language that sketches stroke by stroke the character of Candace. The result is that she, too, is found as exemplar of the family's decline. Yet the elements that gather in her also portray a certain beauty in pain and courage in desperation, and it is this that has caught the novelist's innermost eye. Thus a first-order effect with a certain amazement that "gathers" the world appears amid the portrayal of chaos. Something in Caddy's quality of acceptance makes the difference between simple deterioration and rich complexity; thus the metaphoric effect of the literature takes place at a point of conscious and knowing will in the central character. Her posture involves a kind of natural devotion of herself to a contradiction, and out of this comes the novel's sense of awe.

Theologically, the expression of inexorable time and of God's judgment finds a surprising turn at the novel's center, in the matter of Candace. That is, the first-order impact of the work offers a world of both disorder *and* wonder that co-incide. Consequently, the metaphoric work of the novel finds something excellent in and through the juxtaposition of factors that produce no ordinary hope. The "world" produced by this first-order clustering suggests that when time's process of decay involves a particular type of human being (in this case, Candace), an excellence of virtue appears. Thus God, the inexorable process, when incarnate in a certain metaphoric act, and thereby in a peculiar human being, reveals a component of excellence unseen except under conditions of conflict.

The story of the Compsons with Candace at the center thus turns out to include a reflection of theology, or if you will, a "reflected theology." The mystery of God is not resolved, yet to a degree the nature of God is present in language that invokes crisis and wonder at the point of a certain human condition. The virtue of Caddy is "given" more than "wrought"; it is beneficence through anguish. So on occasion, reality is capable of a certain splendor. Notice at the same time two things: no resolution is envisioned of the tension between the anguish and the excellence; secondly, the axis of grace is human life, whose destiny remains ambiguous. One may not speak therefore of a victory of grace, but of a "graciousness through agony" whose value requires the continuing contradiction that produced it. Reality is many-sided but still enigmatic; grace is informed by human life-in-process and relative human insight.

In the past, Christian commentary on Faulkner's work has suggested that the characters of Benjy and Dilsey are bearers of grace in the novel. But this is to give up the center of the novel to "sin and damnation" in order to find the redeeming Christian God in the book at some other point. Rather, Benjy and Dilsey share in the entire structure, which must be judged as a whole. A reminiscence of the Christian story is present; yet the theology is a reflection in which the lines between God incarnate and the general human condition are inconclusive.

In *The Sound and the Fury* God, as the reality of temporal

process, is glimpsed through moments of disorder and wonder, even as the human being—the "metaphor" of that process—emerges as a creature potentially of excellence, but always of tension and ambiguity.

NOTES

1. William Faulkner, *The Sound and the Fury* (New York: Vintage Books, 1929, 1946).

2. Walter Brylowski, *Faulkner's Olympian Laugh—Myth in the Novels* (Detroit: Wayne State University Press, 1968) 60. See *Faulkner in the University*, ed. F. L. Gwynn and J. L. Blotner (Charlottesville: University of Virginia Press, 1959) 253.

3. Auerbach, *Mimesis*, 6–7.

4. Gwynn and Blotner, *University*, 31. Also, Brylowski, *Laugh*, 61.

5. Auerbach, *Mimesis*, 202.

6. Quoted from an "unpublished letter" in Heller, *Disinherited Mind*, 231.

Kafka's The Trial   VIII

In turning from Faulkner to Kafka, an even greater discipline of resistance against the traditional lines of theological affirmation is encountered. Yet for that very reason Kafka may paradoxically offer a more direct engagement of broad theological concerns and of the questions theology raises.

It has been said of Kafka's fiction that it pressed contemporary irony to such a point that the dim outlines of ritual and myth, lost to contemporary secularity, began once again to emerge.[1] If that be so, the challenge of Kafka's work to theology may be two-fold: the challenge of secularity, and also that of a rival religious force. The two elements combine in a most extraordinary manner in Kafka's novels, stories, and parables. On the one hand, a deceptively simple, clear, and naturalistic style builds a sense of everyday reality. On the other, the fracture of everyday expectations within the stories suggests the presence of a hideous and unfathomable power. Assuredly, the twentieth-century imagination and competence of Kafka leave us with an enduring problematic.

Kafka's *The Trial*[2] is a curious, nightmare account of a man tried and found guilty, who nevertheless cannot specify what he is guilty of. Joseph K. simply awakens one morning in his boarding house to find himself under arrest at the hands of two "warders," who do not know the charge on which they are arresting him. Following this official procedure, his life as a junior executive in a bank is permitted to go on very much as before, though now he is evidently under obligation to a bizarre court, before whom his case is being tried. Alternate impulses to ignore the matter as nonsense, or angrily "get to the bottom of it" so as to dissipate the affair, are alike followed by moments of uncertainty. The sense grows upon him that something needs to be done to come to terms with the court—though what that may be is not clear. And each effort to gain information or to insure progress towards acquittal ends in a situation impossibly wearisome and absurd: court is held in an old tenement house in a large room the other side of a washerwoman's flat; the law offices are in a hot, dusty attic; the lawyer he secures is weak and slow, and K. succeeds only in falling into a distracting affair with the man's nurse.

As time passes, K. discovers that more and more individuals and agencies are either arms of, or are controlled by, the mysterious court—e.g., a priest in a nearby cathedral that he visits by chance. On one occasion, he discovers the two warders who arrested him being whipped by a third individual in an old storeroom of the bank where he is employed. One evening, after long deterioration of his confidence and morale, two roly-poly individuals in top hats come to his room and lead him away to a deserted rock quarry. K. has the opportunity to end his own life, but he cannot bring himself to the task. Instead he becomes preoccupied with a human figure leaning out of a lighted window, high up in a nearby building. Is it someone to help? Surely there are still possibilities for reprieve in his "case." But even as he grasps for straws, the two men are proceeding to kill him. He dies overwhelmed with a piercing sense of shame.

The style of Kafka in his weird tale is in fascinating con-

VIII

186

trast to that of Faulkner in the novel just considered. Rather than the broken and unpunctuated stream-of-consciousness in much of Faulkner's story, Kafka's narrative offers a clear and realistic "foreground" (as Auerbach would call it), evenly illuminated and objectively realistic. All the perceptual detail is recited in a calm, leisurely, and precise manner. Indeed the texture is so much that of objective story-telling as to omit virtually all stylistic metaphors or figures of speech. Kafka wished to approach each reader in the most common, everyday wakeful state of mind and observation, precisely so that his realistic surface would draw one into the absurd world of events that Joseph K. experiences. No metaphors are employed; rather the whole work becomes a metaphor of itself, capturing the attentive reader within its own peculiar universe. Consequently, with *The Trial*, we are immediately back into Beda Alleman's description of both antimetaphor and absolute metaphor, as commented on above in chapter two (pp. 60–67). Kafka's novel is antimetaphoric in that virtually no rhetorical metaphors appear; rather the tale works as a metaphor of the whole. Beyond that, the work constitutes an absolute metaphor in that the reality called up by it breaks our usual system of expectations. The everyday world portrayed moves into deep crisis. Reality seen through the novel thus uses familiar objects and situations to portray a world that draws away from us into its own bizarre consistency. The implicit threat to our well-being trades on both the familiar surface and its highly unfamiliar consequences.

Elements of Analysis

Roughly parallel to our treatment of Faulkner's novel, the brief analysis here of *The Trial* will consider the themes of time and order, the literary style of the work, and the character of Joseph K.

As regards time, there is no situation here of inexorable *chronos* that masters and reduces *kairos*; rather, both *chronos* and *kairos* become problematic. There seems, on the one hand, no "reason" to doubt their ordinary shape and efficacy; yet events render their clear applicability uncertain. Consider for a moment what happens to *chronos* in the course of the novel. One's general impression upon examining the story and its arrangement is that chronological time is straightforward enough. As is usual with stories, this one appears inserted into chronological time so as to occupy a certain segment of that continuing process. There is a beginning ". . . one fine morning," and an ending in the death of Joseph K. "on the evening before K.'s thirty-first birthday" (pp. 3, 279). In between these two landmarks a series of events occurs, in sequence, tracing the "progress" of the legal "case" and revealing a decline in K.'s fortunes as he moves towards his execution. All of this seems usual enough as structure, and the reader's only initial discomfort is that gaps exist *between* chapters; it is not clear how much time or action elapses from one episode to the other, more particularly between the last and the next-to-last chapters where the move to his actual execution takes place. It is also a bit disconcerting to find an appendix of "unfinished chapters," as if it were not clear how many episodes the author might have sandwiched in, given time and inclination. The question arises whether such a structure offers the economic and "inevitable" unfolding, the tightness of framework, appropriate to a good novel.

Further immersion in the story increases one's uneasiness about the time sequence. It turns out that each of the chapters has a similar formulation, even down to the last (presumably conclusive) one. In each case, a line of thought or action arises between Joseph K. and the mysterious "court," precipitating an initiative of some sort on K.'s part. Invariably, the initiative opens up a new level of complexity in his affairs; yet this level is just as inconclusive and problematic as any previous view of the matter. New revelations disclose a further range of possibilities that in turn must be sorted out and evaluated; but weariness, or indecisiveness, or distraction, or the sheer subtlety of the options leaves the matter still unclear, if indeed not more unclear than before. Attention to critical matters slips away into fantasy and preoccupation. For example, in chapter IX, a priest recites to K. the remarkable parable of the law, in which the petitioner seeking admission to the law waits many years only to have the door finally closed upon him. The parable appears to give new insight into K.'s situation, but then the priest begins rehearsing the wide accumulations of commentary upon it until all the various readings become a mere jumble of interpretations in K.'s mind.

The fact is that no chapter of the book makes significant progress on the chief questions of the narrative. Each chapter sheds some further light on the inner crevices and corners of the situation, but the assessment always remains the same. New scenes and characters appear, but fundamentally nothing "happens." With each segment Joseph K. is neither closer to nor farther from the solution of the matter than before. One is reminded of the dream of being unable to move one's feet, or of setting out on a journey only to find oneself arriving at the same—if somewhat expanded—locus where one began. Thus the chief project of the action is to clarify the relation of Joseph K. to the "court." Each effort to do so ends with the sense that clarity has been frustrated thus far, though progress seems possible.

The result of this pattern is that the reliability and reality of chronological time as a significant measure of events comes into question. "Before" and "after" bear significance only in a genuine sequence. Yet *The Trial* reads as such an account only at the initial level. The impression gathers that Joseph K.'s state of affairs is essentially no different at the end of the story from what it was at the beginning, even if we include his death. Clockwork time, in this case, has allowed the appearance of movement, but, like the pendulum that ceaselessly exchanges left for right and right for left, results only in stasis. The overpowering reason for this immobility is the lack of assurance, even at the very end, that there is a real judgment against Joseph K. In the case of a clear negative judgment at least one's situation is definite and can be responded to. With K., the outrageous nature of the court and its procedures is never justified. The whole matter may be as much a mistake as it seemed to be on the day of "arrest." *Chronos* therefore brings explication, yet with no advancement or conclusiveness. Chronological time fails of significance except as a pulsation that marks the locus of an enigma.

If time is seen in this light, then the unfinished chapters in the appendix and the spaces between chapters begin to find their significance. The number of inconclusive episodes one might compose in the saga of Joseph K. is really arbitrary. The chapters do not make actual progress, nor do they link over from one to the other as if the eventful results of one were to set the agenda and pursuits of the next. Indeed, the chapters build an image of chronological time in ruins, with the initial appearance of sequence and goal, but with heavy gaps that open between episodes and undercut the thrust toward sequential meaning. Immediately, Kafka's own story of the Great Wall of China comes to mind. According to this story, the state of the Great Wall ended in some uncertainty because different segments of it arose together and it was not clear that the operation successfully joined them all in the end. Kafka comments in his factual, informative manner:

> . . . In fact it is said that there are gaps which have never been filled in at all, an assertion, however, which is probably merely one of the many legends to which the building of the wall gave rise, and which cannot be verified . . .[3]

It may be that the wall is complete, but there is also reason to doubt it. In the same sly and tentative manner, the sequential meaning of the Joseph K. story becomes a problem; and once it becomes a problem, the sturdiness of chronological time is lost as a frame of reference.

In the case of *kairos*, the openness of real decision is stultified, not as in Faulkner by the outworkings of inevitable doom, but by the same uncertainty that abuses the significance of chronological time. Numerous instances arise in K.'s story in which some interjection or crisis calls for his response. His reactions to these moments are usually regarded unfavorably by the court—or so it is reported—but whether they are actually good or bad reactions is lost in a web of inconclusiveness. The source of this uncertainty is a contradiction within K.'s own feelings. On one hand, the matter of a "court" and an "arrest" seems the sheerest nonsense. Opportunities for decisive action are opportunities to scoff at the whole matter and get on with one's life. On the other hand, K. has an unaccountable, if limited, impulse to acknowledge the court, even if only to scold it for being preposterous. It is as if the court were a forgotten part of life, now inexplicably recalled despite scoffing disbelief. So at the very onset of the weird story, K. finds himself slipping unintentionally into a moment of subservience.

> ... "I must see what people these are next door, and how Frau Grubach can account to me for such behavior." Yet it occurred to him at once that he should not have said this aloud and that by doing so he had in a way admitted the stranger's right to superintend his actions ... (p. 4).

This ambivalence of denial-acknowledgment means that every *kairos* is only a new opportunity for acts that never have the requisite data for decisive assurance, and that never are fully convincing in retrospect.

Kafka's Theme of Balance

The form of chronological time that may be illusory and the instances of *kairos* that are unclearly posed both suggest a certain balance in affairs of an ennervating, wearying sort. To believe that the unfolding of time has no significance means at least to take a stand; to be unsure whether it does or not is to be caught among possibilities. This unhappy balance of circumstances, ultimately paralyzing in nature, is an essential motif in *The Trial* and should be kept in mind throughout examination of order, style, and character.

At least three notions of order emerge in the novel, each ending in some degree of the balanced uncertainty just noted. The first is the secular, rationalistic order of the city and of the bank where K. holds a position. The flavor of Kafka's bland, informational prose bespeaks the modern city and its calculated routine, its agency reports, its plans and appointments. The circumstances of K., an aspiring young banker, living in rented rooms and alone except for his mistress, is likewise a part of that vaguely numerical existence of the contemporary Western city. This form of order in the secular, urban setting fits well with the notion of chronological, measured time just considered. Just as it becomes uncertain whether chronological time constitutes a significant measure, so the order of secular rationality comes increasingly into question as to whether it is reality, or appearance only. Joseph K. confronts us as one schooled in the pragmatics of modern, organized life; the rules of survival are the rules of the bank, and he has learned to keep them well. The story of *The Trial* is precisely the story of an experience that nevertheless resists all the rules without definitively eliminating them. No matter how odious his experience of the "court," K. continues to ask whether there is not somewhere a rational explanation, a reasonable and illuminating course of action. Contemporary rationality moves into abject distress but is not obliterated.

The second concept of order is much less explicit in the novel, yet equally suggestive. It is in fact a romantic notion of order, an inclusive order of the world realized and participated in by a vision of the whole. The imposed, rationalistic order of means-ends to one side, the romantic view holds that if the wide, experiential phenomena of earth are given sufficient scope, the key to their unity will at length appear in a moment of unifying vision. Lacking such an order, the subject or protagonist will appear as quester, in search of the wisdom or insight that locates ultimate meaning. Although not obviously, Joseph K. is a near descendant of the romantic seeker, aiming in his disrupted circumstances to get at the source of meaning and resolution that will clarify and reconcile all things. Thus he strives either to get at the heart of the strange "court" or to demonstrate its true nature. He seeks, he struggles, to attain the Law. Thus the Parable of the Law and its unhappy petitioner, who waits and hopes for fruitless years, is applicable to him. That petitioner, as the darkness of his years of waiting close in around him, can glimpse through the entrance-way the radiance of the distant Law. Evidently the Law exists, and gaining access to it would seem possible. Yet the confounding uncertainty of the search makes the efforts to arrive of no more avail than a paralysis, or than a pilgrimage that returns always unavoidably to its original starting point. Yet evidently each individual holds a destiny of "arrival," even if never accomplished.

> . . . "how does it come about . . . that in all these years no one has come seeking admittance but me?" . . . "No one but you could gain admittance through this door, since this door was intended for you. I am now going to shut it" (p. 269).

Thus the quest for a romantic order ends in the bewildering affirmation-denial of destiny, which simply reduces the seeker to worn insignificance.

The third motif of order in the narrative is the order of the bizarre "court," if indeed "order" is the appropriate term. Certainly from one point of view, the phenomenon of the court is that of an alien and repulsive order impinging upon everyday affairs, and indeed already operative "behind the scenes." It constitutes an "order" in that the arms of its organized influence penetrate everywhere. An increasing number of figures that K. encounters turn out to be agents of the court, including the priest in the cathedral. On the other hand, the court is hardly an order in its own nature, for every approach to it presents chaos and frustration. Cramped, dingy, awkward, inconvenient circumstances permeate the court and its personnel; law books turn out to contain toilet-wall pornography (pp. 64–65); portraits of the judges lack dignity and show vain, enthroned men about to rise menacingly (pp. 134, 182); the emblem of the goddess of Justice is done as a Winged Victory (p. 182). Search for the court leads K. into tenement houses, washrooms, and dusty, choking attics. Evidently the court is approached through sheer corruption and decay, and is absurd. Yet again, it clearly maintains powerful control within its own domain. The court must be dealt with, and yet it amounts to nonsense. Again, the balance of possibilities becomes frustrating and counter-productive. In one sense, the theme of the entire novel is the intrusion of a hideous order that defies human attempts either to ignore it, or to come to terms with it.

Another important element of the novel is its literary style, and once more Auerbach's basic comments will serve well. Consider again the contrast between Hebraic and "mixed" styles, on the one hand, and classic Homeric style, on the other. A question may be raised as to whether the epic-like novel, *The Trial*, manifests clearly one or the other types. To the extent that I have already commented on style in Kafka's novel—its "naturalistic" surface—Auerbach's description of the Homeric "foreground" as clear, externalized, and syntactically precise certainly calls to mind *The Trial*. Kafka's anti-metaphoric discipline has produced a texture almost monotonous in its careful, even description of acts and thoughts and its fulsome reporting of dialogue. Further, when Auerbach finds in the classical epic a minimum of change and development, as if narrative and characters were fixed in a comprehensive, present space-time, again we may think of Kafka's work. K.'s destiny of absurd tension stands constant from "beginning" to "end." Change, development, and "outcome" are limited to rendering explicit what is present throughout. When Auerbach says of the Homeric style that it presents reality, but seeks "to make us forget our own reality,"[4] we think ironically of *The Trial*, which offers an objectively "realistic" surface, but in such a way as to carry us beyond objective realism—not only in "forgetting," but in nightmarish apprehension.

Does *The Trial*, then, fail to exemplify characteristics of the Hebraic and "mixed" styles? Surprisingly, such a lack is not the case—despite the reminiscences of the classical epic. Evidently Kafka has remarkably brought something of both styles into his novel, for characteristics of biblical style are not wanting in the work. Primarily, the sense of near-sacred mystery surrounding "the Law," the driving intent of K. to get to the "bottom of things," and the universal claims of the weird court upon all human affairs are features recalling biblical settings. As regards the effect more strictly upon style, the use of common language by everyday persons (who deal nevertheless with a massive question), the sense of multilayered mystery and of activities "fraught with background" bring us close to biblical literature. Kafka's own Jewish background and preoccupation with "the Law" in this work obviously have biblical attachments.

The combination of biblical and classical in the novel is a highly special construct. Kafka deftly combines them in a manner suitable to the essence of the work as a whole. One finds the biblical depth of the Law (God's righteous will) but without access or promise because of the quiet, persistent secularity of contemporary life. Our clear rationalistic surfaces cannot express their own depths, let alone the transcendent, except by simple decay and deterioration, and therefore by revulsion. On the other hand, clear illumination of "foreground" in a modern mode offers no reliable stability because the anguish of time and historical process suggests a power that underlies and consumes our affairs. In other words, Kafka has put the qualities of the two styles into the most difficult possible tension with one another. Calm rational information precludes biblical insight; biblical depth and passion undermine the techniques of contemporary order. The one cannot eliminate the possibility of the other. They hang in a balance of mutual impairment with only deterioration of meaning as end-in-view. A further part of the conundrum is that the entire situation can be read either as secular or sacred. Twentieth-century secularity, on the one hand, has rendered the "depth" of life into a tangled web of secular absurdity. Or, from the other viewpoint, the tradition of sacrality has thrust itself back upon us in a hideous form, penetrating and turning to confusion our well-tuned mechanisms of living.

With *The Trial* both rationalistic and romantic ideals of the modern West become problematic, while a new outlook upon the Western legacy and its components finds a balanced and irreversible sterility.

The Character of Joseph K.

The central character of the novel is an ironically and inappropriately suffering figure. In Joseph K. the ambiguities of time, order, and style all come to focus. The fictional "point of view" in dealing with Joseph K. is significant: the narrative is recounted from the viewpoint of the author, who is nevertheless not a "universal" author, but follows K. closely through all his doings, thoughts, and conversations. The story is therefore strictly K.'s story and presents him intimately, although not by stream-of-consciousness approach nor through the eyes of others (except where K. himself is spoken to by someone about his own conduct). The result is a type of objective portrayal of K., even in a sense a clinical rendering, in that we lack no significant present information about him during the episodes of the story.

At the same time, K. does not stand out for us as a rich "personality." He could be any average individual of middle-class circumstances with perhaps some excessive degree of self-doubt; his actions in the novel are largely *re*actions and are normal, granted that they are reactions to highly abnormal occurrences. Indeed, the story of K. is really the story of the events that crowd in upon him and the reaction of a heretofore successful intelligence in trying to cope with these events. Thus the account is an objective narrative of circumstance and character, with the proviso that the character largely derives from the circumstance and takes on its hue. K. attempts, certainly, to take initiative, but his initiatives end only in confirming the general pattern of events already underway. K.'s responses and his external circumstances are part of the same warp and woof, but it is clear that what is going on externally tips the balance in determining the interlocking of the two.

With all this "objective" portrayal, it is of high credit to Kafka's skill that he nevertheless succeeds in telling a tale that could be an interior psychic study of personal deterioration. As already noted, the meaning of a narrative *as* narrative is a cumulative meaning. The self-contained character of a story builds from its beginning to its end; the richest approach to its meaning is simply to read it. Kafka has pursued the narrative effect of his novel by presenting it as a sequence of affairs from a beginning to an ending. K. thus becomes a contemporary "everyman" in a self-contained, objective story, in which person and affairs clearly illuminate one another. At the same time, Kafka has adroitly broken the sequential narrative into repetitious segments that give the whole account a meandering quality. This secondary effect, under the initial appearance of linear narrative, reveals Joseph K. in a loose chain of events analogous to one another and entirely frustrating of any "progress." From this perspective, playing especially upon its weird happenings, the novel takes on the dream-like character of a living nightmare. In such a manner Kafka opens up interiority without ever leaving his objective mode. He can present the alienated consciousness, a saga of subjectivity, without employing stream-of-consciousness or losing his naturalistic style. Joseph K. may be a sensible man increasingly victimized by real cosmic forces, or he may be a painfully estranged spirit who has mentally lost touch with reality. The novel can read either way.

In effect, the same option that faces the reader faces the character of Joseph K. within the story. Is he dealing with a corrupt, objective force in things against which his isolated sanity must stand? Or is some weakness, a compulsion within his own consciousness, endowing absurd and banal events with an importance they cannot possibly claim? A crucial passage that tends to pass by as a routine transition stands at the beginning of chapter III:

> During the next week K. waited day after day for a new summons, he would not believe that his refusal to be interrogated had been taken literally, and when no appointment was made by Saturday evening, he assumed that he was tacitly expected to report himself again . . . (p. 61).

In the "realism" of the novel, why make such tacit assumptions? Why not ignore the whole matter? K. risks generating his own compulsions in the situation and becoming increasingly preoccupied with the court throughout. He does so because he will *not* risk what the court may do to him should it have the genuine authority it claims. What he further risks, however, is being pulled apart on the horns of a subjective-objective dilemma: an inability either to resolve the problem by treating his own attitude toward it (a "subjective" view), or to resolve it by dealing successfully with the court itself (an "objective" view). Certainly, from what has already transpired in this study, it is a misstep for anyone—including K.— to cast the problem in purely subject-object terms. Perhaps K. attempts to avoid doing so by taking the course of action that he will somehow "get to the bottom" of the matter, clarify it, make sense of it. Such a "making sense" would entail relief of his own preoccupations plus a clarifying of the court's nature. Reality would be in some way "of a piece."

K. never gives up the possibility that some clarity and justice will illumine the situation; and that is the key to the novel. Nevertheless, all the elements of ambiguity that we have cited in this review conspire against him and make it *seem* unlikely that clarity can ever emerge. Time apparently takes him nowhere closer to his goal, but always returns to the same starting point. Everyday human order and the "order" of the court cannot finally resolve their contest. The linguistic styles of K.'s story prevent one another from reaching full traditional integrity. Nevertheless, when he comes to the moment of physical execution, K. cannot shake off the possibility that something has been overlooked, that liberating clarity somewhere exists. His final impulse in this regard is triggered by a chance incident at a window some distance off:

> . . . His glance fell on the top story of the house adjoining the quarry. With a flicker as of a light going up, the casements of a window there suddenly flew open; a human figure, faint and insubstantial at that distance and that height, leaned abruptly far forward and stretched both arms still farther. Who was it? A friend? A good man? Someone who sympathized? Someone who wanted to help? Was it one person only? Or was it mankind? Was help at hand? Were there arguments in his favor that had been overlooked? Of course there must be. Logic is doubtless unshakable, but it cannot withstand a man who wants to go on living. Where was the Judge whom he had never seen? Where was the High Court, to

which he had never penetrated? He raised his hands and spread out all his fingers.

But the hands of one of the partners were already at K.'s throat, while the other thrust the knife deep into his heart and turned it there twice. With failing eyes K. could still see the two of them immediately before him, cheek leaning against cheek, watching the final act. "Like a dog!" he said; it was as if the shame of it must outlive him (pp. 285–286).

K.'s last opportunity for decisiveness and dignity lay in the option of suicide in the quarry, which opportunity his executioners offered him (p. 285). But he stumbled awkwardly to the very end as he had done throughout the entire narrative. Distracted at the last by a chance image of hope and reasonableness, he falls again into uncertainty, as he has done so often throughout. At that swaying moment of weakness, his life is ground out "like a dog's," so that death resolves nothing; his unhappy posture lives on in the "shame of it."

Those who suppose that the bleakness of Kafka is ameliorated by such images as the human figure in the lighted window fail to note the consistency of the novel's texture from first to last. Too often a remark falls that Kafka does not paint an entirely dark picture; he leaves a ray of hope at the end. The "ray of hope" is by no means a softening. The bleakness of Kafka is that there seems always just enough hope and possibility to cause uncertainty. Indeed, a ray of hope *completes* that picture of uncertainty, and uncertainty is the state of hideous "wasting away." Joseph K. dies in a balanced condition of possibilities that has throughout robbed him of decisiveness. Hope and the desire to gain clarity have played an essential role in his ineptness, which is the final mark of who he is. Thus a figure who has not lacked for initiative and struggle discloses that his very initiatives have played into the pattern of balanced possibilities, or balanced sterility, which has finally rendered him pathetic.

Reflected Theology in The Trial

Finding a "reflection of theology" in Kafka's novel means almost a complete inversion of the substance of theology proper. Obviously the work puts under the most severe strain any traditional theological affirmation. At the same time, the novel recalls many theological interests and categories, as our survey of its stylistic indebtedness—Hebraic and Homeric—has already indicated.

Let us assume without further comment our "gaming" entry into the novel as a vision of the real world, as we have already attempted with the Faulkner piece. In that case, what is the world like, as we find it refracted through *The Trial?* And what content is given to such theological categories as God, incarnation, and grace, if they do have analogues in the Kafkian narrative? Bear in mind the literary approach to reflected theology. If the nature of "God" is the general nature of process, then the articulation or "unfinished" presentation of that process takes place via the large "metaphor" or first-order clustering that *is* a novel. In the case of *The Trial,* that metaphor, as pointed out, is in fact an antimetaphor and an absolute metaphor; but that constitutes no disturbance of the art-work's basic first-order function. What then may be said of "God" as disclosed in the world of this fiction?

Clues to the process of things in *The Trial* turn out to set up certain ambivalences in a reader's response, as might be expected. Conflicts in images are ready to hand: imagery of law, courtrooms, banks, judges, guilt and innocence abounds; at the same time heavy imagery occurs of dust, stale air, darkness, nausea, pornography, cramped quarters, torture. The presentation of the novel would hold that order is an inescapable question, but that all approaches to order seemingly mire down in stultifying, pointless effort on our part. God, or the process of things, invariably provokes the question of order and leads toward a search for order, while finally frustrating the search into which he has drawn us. A sense of progress may turn out to be no progress; analyses of detail may only intensify the range of problems raised.

Yet what has just been said, though a generalization about the novel's content, stands as a comment made from outside the reality of the novel's world. Since what is being dealt with bears the nature of an absolute metaphor, an attempt at theological reading must include a certain willingness on the reader's part not to comment from an alternative position, but to find a place of "under-standing" from which to speak, much as the world of Faulkner can be understood and spoken "out of." In other words, the "incarnation" of God in the novel must be permitted and entered into. Now when this takes place, the very imaginative act of the reader starts abrasively to become its own undoing and to "loosen" the customary reference points of intelligibility. That is, if something like the strange court does begin to make its claim within Joseph K.'s world—of which the reader momentarily is a part—what is the assessment? Human posture and dignity are called into question at once on obscure grounds. The nature of reality becomes devious. What route would we ourselves follow?

"Reality has no meaning." Such quiescent acceptance of the new "order" moving in would most evidently surrender all sense of dignity from the start. Are human beings to become metaphysical slaves? "Take action"—even if only to declare oneself stoically "free." Say that reality includes the possibility of human dignity, even if that dignity is created by an act of our own will. Such an act calls back all the human virtues of courage, self-esteem, and just dealing, but now on the basis of an ungrounded act of will in the midst of vanity. It is at this juncture that the enigma of Joseph K.'s world reaches its most acute point: if one revolts to create dignity by an act of will, then one admits that the kind of world given us is a world that allows *such a possibility* and is therefore not without meaning or favor. In other words, one cannot adopt a posture of dignity, even on a continual *ad hoc* basis, without slipping into making of this posture a universal or cosmological principle. (In this sense, Kafka anticipates and transcends the advocates of existential revolt, such as Camus and Sartre, who presumed in some sense to have taken Kafka into account and gone beyond him. Existential revolt taken seriously slips back into an ironic confidence in reality that disallows the radical autonomy the revolt assumes.) When Joseph K., in modest fashion, sets out to assert himself and his rights, he unavoidably involves himself in a proposal flying in the face of the tangled and decadent "court" (reality). Such frustration leads us back again to the impulsive cry, "Reality has no meaning." In that event, either we passively acquiesce or seize upon our own inner stamina as a kind of defiance. But this defiance is once again the stance of revolt, whose possibility entangles us once again with the world and its nature. One wonders if there is no final recourse for our character as human beings, and so the entire non-productive sequence starts over again and again. Thus the state of affairs in *The Trial* may be seen under the image of a "balanced wheel" of reality's potential interpretations.

To enter Joseph K.'s world is to experience a cycle of reflections and orientations that never allows a stability of attitude. The individual is simply worn to insignificance by the shifting conundrum. Much of this effect is brought about by the "double-image" possibility. That is, in the case of images or concepts usually considered desirable or "good," the story is told such that these become evil parodies of themselves. Then it remains forever unclear whether the virtues in question are valid or illicit. All established criteria of evil and good fall subject to this anguish of doubling. For example, with Joseph K., the "sin" he committed was to hope for a resolution, which led him only deeper into the morass. His personal "hell" was the fact of possibility, in this case the possibility of acquittal, which robbed him even of his last opportunity for dignity in suicide. Ordinarily, hope and possibility are counted positively in human experience. If with Joseph K. they become sin and perdition, then the doubling effect renders all affirmation uncertain. The "grace" of God in this situation—what is "given" as the ground of human life—is a relation in things that throws the human being, including the human mind, into an irresolvable dilemma with itself.

If a theological reader of *The Trial* enters into reality through Joseph K.'s world, then all that can be said is that theological reflection itself begins to fracture and dissipate. All initial viewpoints begin to shift and all thought projects become private impulses. Within the world of *The Trial* theology is terminated by the nature of its object, which evidently yields no *logos* of meaning, yet disallows the view that it never will so yield. Were a reader to pursue imaginative entry without qualification, no return would be possible to the usual world of meanings and decisions. One gains the sense of setting out to pursue evil "in itself," which can only mean the cessation of the very instruments of inquiry.

At the same time, the novel is an excellent, if not monumental, work of art. I have argued that the form of an artwork, affording a renewal of excellence even in the midst of a crisis of ordinary materials, is reminiscent of the Christ story with its suffering and recovery. Kafka has undoubtedly offered a splendid work out of the most unpromising of human experiences. Is there in the very fact of art a reflection of theological affirmation, even when the experiential substance of the work undoes the very distinction between meaning and meaninglessness? Kafka himself evidently doubted it, since he left behind at his death explicit instructions that all his works should be destroyed, thereby presumably bringing them into accord with the thrust of their own content. (Kafka's friend and editor, Max Brod, reflected that such a destruction would include the destruction of the author's message to destroy! and therefore decided that he was not bound to it.[5]) We are left, in any case, with a severe theological puzzle in the assessment of a work which, on the one hand, affords excellence, and on the other, proposes that all affirmation of excellence drowns in obscurity. That *The Trial* nevertheless urges itself upon us is undeniable.

As for the author Kafka himself, I do not propose here to describe his position as an independent person on theological questions. That would mean taking into account his aphorisms as well as his fiction, and it is not my purpose to pursue here the difficult relation between the fiction and the aphorisms. Kafka's fiction, or in this case one piece of it, should bear its own weight and hold its own integrity.

VIII

The preceding two chapters discuss two instances of the examination of literature by the measures of "reflected theology." In the first of these, the work as a whole admitted of an analogue to the ancient Christian account of crucifixion and grace, though with great irony and a shift to human-centeredness in employing the categories. In the second, the author's approach to reflected theological concerns is clear enough, but the material is handled in such a way that entry into "reality" via the world of the novel precludes constructive thought and rather dissipates it into flaccid weakness.

This latter result with the examination of Kafka is of the utmost importance in the consideration of language, reality, and reflected theology. This study's experiment has proposed that to consider language from a standpoint "situated" *within* language, on the basis of everyday motivations and commitments is to find that language does present reality to us through a first- and second-order rhythm. Such knowledge of reality misses finality because of the double movement of "presentation" and "sinking back." Nevertheless, this very "eccentricity of disposition" as between ourselves and things is in itself salutary in that it lets language, and therefore knowledge, "be" in the gap. It has seemed that to ponder this serviceable gap of "eccentricity" has been a good rejoinder to the rather wooden terminology of "subject-object split" so prevalent and presumably threatening in modern thought. To be eccentrically disposed in the full pragmatic and temporal situation is no counsel of evil but to the contrary a situation conducive to purposeful direction. Should the gap be widened to proportions of crisis, the literary work of art often encourages us that metaphoric recovery is a strong function of language in time.

With Kafka, however, a debilitating option has emerged which suggests that the regaining of a constructive grip on reality through linguistic crisis and recovery is no air-tight procedure. We may not have returned to the simplistic subject-object split, but have discovered that a situation of ungovernable frustration and estrangement can arise despite recourse to "situated" thinking and even despite the usually renewing articulation via a work of art. With *The Trial* reflected theology finally loses all affirmative analogues with its sister category of theology proper and translates theological concepts, with a final irony, into a continuing tension between the meaningful and the meaningless. Full moral reflection on the human situation in the modern West may therefore appear to stave off *anomie* through linguistic first- and second-order rhythms; but a tendency also exists for the double order of language to engender a paralytic circumstance in which metaphoric participation (in, for example, the Parable of the Law, let alone the entire novel of *The Trial*) yields only desperate passivity.

Kafka's novel "accomplishes" this unnerving feat by developing the theme of a certain excess of feasible responses to human existence. Joseph K.'s dilemma is that reality as he faces it numbs the closing down of sufficient options to clarify a consistent affirmative posture. If he could decide that the court is not "real" and has no claim on his consciousness, so that he could turn his back on it; if he could avoid distracting influences and relationships; most particularly, if he could surrender the possibility of a rational solution; if he could do any of these things, the frittering away of effort and energy would come under harness. But the situation virtually decrees that there is no way so to exclude. The responsibility for closure becomes unbearable when the reality around him appears to offer no clear confirmation for any particular such move. The modern human situation has relativized the accepted boundaries usually considered as applicable to a significant, fruitful life.

If the modern "reflection" of theology in literature is thus so ironic in Kafka, is it possible to say nevertheless that *The Trial* is only one of a few instances in which such "unleashing" occurs and that much reflected theology in modern cultural products is affirming in some way of human dignity and meaning? It is possible certainly to say so, and with just cause through citing instances. Still, *The Trial* is a kind of Pandora's box. Once opened, its range of doubts begins to invade many literary regions. Everywhere one turns in modernity, the appropriate boundary-limits for shaping existence increasingly turn out to be a function of contemporary human convenience and arbitrariness. That is, Western humanity has more and more taken upon itself the setting of its own limits. That has rendered the limits relative to the shifting human situation and in effect uncertain as limits at all. Even where traditional lines of behavior are drawn and affirmed, it is not tradition that finally gives them their authority, but the fact that someone now has chosen to elect "the tradition," perhaps for a variety of motives.

No one should oppose the dignity of human choice and election, but such choice requires a setting or structure of reality in which decision takes place. Modernity has rendered the setting problematic, forcing more and more burden upon choice. The question is one of reality, not desirability. Are there in reality theological limits upon daily human choice, to which that choice can be responsive? Reflected theology has ended in some uncertainty as to whether even analogues of the tradition are not creatures of contemporary human autonomy, with all the ambiguity of human circumstance necessarily involved in their assertion. The question remains whether "theology proper" promises to any better degree to resist the debilitating plurality of options so unforgettably portrayed by Franz Kafka. And if it should so promise, does theology proper then dismiss reflected theology as a treacherous and pale imitation of the "real thing"? Or is some feasible relation between the two at least plausible? The final venture of this study will be to attempt to consider these questions.

NOTES

1. Frye, *Anatomy*, 42.

2. Franz Kafka, *The Trial*, trans. W. and E. Muir (New York: Random House, 1956).

3. From *Selected Short Stories*, trans. W. and E. Muir (New York: Random House, 1952) 129.

4. Auerbach, *Mimesis*, 15. Note pp. 13–15 generally.

5. Leonard Michaels, "Life, Works, and Locus" in *The New York Times Book Review* (November 21, 1971) 1.

VIII

Part Three
THEOLOGY PROPER

Theology and the Gospel Portrait of Jesus IX

The aim from the very beginning in this book has been to carry forward a case study in the relation of theology to contemporary Western culture, a case study involving theology and imaginative literature. It has been stressed that even in the most modern of terms language may and does articulate reality as a rich, moral field, inclusive of pragmatic orientation and of isolable, factual states of affairs. No one need feel compelled by contemporaneity to limit the real objects of language to reduced, analytical components. Indeed, even when language employs itself in such a reductive, public manner, it carries a first-order impact at another level—on occasion suggesting, for example, a searching moral anxiety that may actually impel elaborate technical precision. Certainly the claim that reality comes to presence dynamically within a tensive two-order relation need not bow its head to any view of reality that drives single-mindedly toward either one of those orders taken alone.

In other words, an important concern has been to point out a moral, and implicitly theological, valence in language, insofar as language is fully "permitted" and appreciated and not pointedly segmented or reduced. Furthermore, such "permission" of language takes place in no self-contained and isolable universe of discourse, but within a historic stream of language with its rude characteristics and unresolved minglings of utterance. Even the most generalized commentary on the nature and force of language assumes and emerges from a historic tradition. If what has been done in this study often has about it the generalized character of a philosophy of language, still the appeal to the peculiar Western historical tradition out of which that language has come renders the frame of reference theological. It has been possible, for example, to cite a theological potential in the formal and substantive processes of modern Western literature just because the language involved remembers the theological shape given it from its inception. Theology is reflected in contemporary artistic works because they are the descendants, though distant, of a theologically shaped linguistic past.

Pursuit of the "meaning" consequences of those theological shadows or reflections led to the illustrative examples in Faulkner and Kafka. From the standpoint of theology *per se*, the "reflection" has not been able to propose a theological confession of faith in the full, classical sense of that term. No objection arises for that reason to the works of art. Their excellence is strictly their own, and their images of theological meaning are appropriate to that excellence. Nevertheless, from the standpoint of the professional theologian, the ambiguities that remain require that cultural theology yield to other kinds and levels of theological work. That is, this case study of theology and culture through literature clarifies that more than one perspective on the literary data must obtain if the full theological task is done. It is necessary to do theology "in its own right" as well as to trace its reflected cultural images.

This study has said that a theology in and for literature cannot finally do that full theological task because, taken by itself, it falls subject to ambiguity. Now the ambiguity found in theology reflected through literature is the ambiguity of unlimited relational possibilities. That is, with ancient lines of doctrine dissolved, the God of temporal process shows many faces, some of them, for example, through the persons of admirable, anguished characters of literature. In such figures, the possibility of wonder exists, even in a chaotic world. We think not only of Candace Compson, but of Dostoevski's Prince Myshkin, O'Neill's Josie, Shaw's Joan of Arc, as well as Camus' Meursault and Elie Wiesel's Michael or Pedro. And, of course, a mingling of wonder with degradation occurs in many works where singling out one "admirable" character is not even to the point. What occurs is either one of two things. The wonder-in-degradation subtly becomes for the reader (if not the author) a universal principle, a "confession" that really transcends, if it does not belie, the very conditions of ambiguity that gave the confession its substance. That is, the tension that gave the wonder its "life"—a tension of courage or compassion within a hopelessly tangled web of affairs—is resolved by the "confession," or by the positing of a general principle. Or on the other hand, the paralyzing possibility of wonder in degradation—now not a "confession" but merely a continuing experience—by its ambiguity numbs the nerve of decision and of a claimed identity. Uncertain *hope* simply ennervates the human being, who is worn away by the immense burden of keeping options open (Franz Kafka, Samuel Beckett). In the first case, the human beings involved "make the difference"; human compassion or sacrifice or even simply suffering becomes what ancient God-in-Christ "talk" was really all about, once demythologized; the human being becomes the center of the confession and must carry the immense vocation of becoming the man-God. In the second case, turning a "cool eye" on inescapable and unlimited ambiguity means gradually wasting oneself in frustration. Of course, in some works of literature a historic confession of faith is either assumed or "overheard," as with Eliot, Auden, Georges Bernanos, and Flannery O'Connor. These are special cases and serve only to affirm, not to deny, the dilemma of ambiguity in the scope of modern Western literature.

"Theology proper," in claiming its own identity and vocation, must differentiate itself from the kind of ambiguity described above. If Kafka has portrayed the demise of reflected theology in a complete weariness of spirit, theology cannot, in turn, confess the wonder of "human being" as an alternative, lest the humanity of the human be lost by becoming a new divinity. The ambiguity associated with open-ended human relationships gives theology proper no place to stand. At the same time, no claim is made that traditional theology can resolve all ambiguity. The difference nevertheless lies in theology's central affirmation. If theology's affirmation of the Christ holds firm, this Christ becomes a peculiar and eccentric element that throws "off-balance" the even-handed ambiguity of human-centered relationships. Like an irritant that demands resolution, the particularity of Christ brings its own frustrations, but definitely not the ones associated with a religious human-centeredness. That is, the nature and setting of the "Christ-ambiguity" differs from that of reflected theology. For the ambiguity confronted in Christian confession is the tension of working out the relation between *two* historical centers, Christ and the self, even if one (the Christ) be counted divine as well as historical. The former ambiguity (of reflected theology) is the ambiguity gathering around and through *one* historical center, viz., that of the human self (or of the human community); for the "Christ" of reflected theology is either a paradigm of the human situation or is God "trapped" within the antinomies of the flow of nature. The "advantage," on the other hand, of confessional ambiguity—as between two centers—is the ultimate limit placed upon the human, giving human possibilities some boundary line, which renders those possibilities fruitful by affording them a certain discipline.

Theology proper must therefore make a different start from a theology for literature. Does this mean that theology proper must thereby give up its literary or poetic side? No indeed. It means rather that theology will take a different approach to literature by way of emphasis and perspective. Let us therefore turn to the question of what is specially involved in the literary foundations of essential theology.

IX

214

The Election of Certain Documents

The aim of this section will be to give some description of theology's special concern for documents of the New Testament, over against reflected theology's even-handed interest in literature across the board. In effect, I am speaking here of adopting two different viewpoints toward the general body of Western literature. In the first, the corpus of Western literature, including biblical material, is considered together. That is, the same general canons of criticism and principles of hermeneutic apply to all documents. In the second, the body of Western literature is considered, excluding at least certain biblical materials, which receive separate treatment. In relation to these biblical materials, the usual canons of criticism apply, but they are applied with different emphases, and hermeneutical principles are reduced to a minimum. The first is appropriate to reflected theology; the second, to theology proper.

In pursuing this second viewpoint and therefore the core of theology, certain New Testament narratives concerning the life of Jesus of Nazareth will stand at the focus of attention. Initially, a strongly objective mode of literary critical analysis is appropriate for examining the narratives. Indeed, the argument has been throughout that careful object analysis is initially appropriate for any literary work and does not impede "meaning," but opens the way for it. The case for objective consideration will be made all the stronger in scrutinizing the Jesus narratives as groundwork for theology. Once the object analysis has proceeded, then the questions of meaning and truth may be very carefully raised. At such a point it may become clearer as to why, of all the pieces of literature the West has found significant, so few pages of a given life-story should command priority. On the other hand, the terms of the question "why" are problematic. In the final analysis, all answers to the question "why these documents" will fall short of being conclusive reasons. In any event, if the force of the narratives is dealt with, then one should be ready to state the role that the narratives play in theological affirmation and reflection. Obviously, it will be important to ask specifically

the function of these narratives as first- and second-order instances of language and the styles of response they evoke to
their own broad metaphoric nature. As might be anticipated,
I shall wish to argue that certain interpretive responses to
these narratives assume a different theological shape from
what is to be found in reflected theology.

In all of this work I can make no claim to originality but
am attempting to follow suggestions emerging from the work
of Professor Hans W. Frei. In this regard, two things must be
said: the risk of misunderstanding the work of another is
great, especially when that work is still in progress. I alone
can bear responsibility for what follows; Frei's work is to be
evaluated only by reading it directly. Secondly, the theological point of view that I finally adopt includes certain moves
that I am sure Frei would be unwilling to make, despite my
initial dependence upon him. I can only hope that I have not
distorted his achievement, and that my departures from his
own viewpoint are sufficiently clear.

Frei's first published work on the Jesus narratives is en-
titled "Theological Reflections on the Accounts of Jesus'
Death and Resurrection,"[1] a summary of his careful literary
consideration of the Synoptic Passion narratives, more particularly that found in Luke. What is initially striking about
this and other of Frei's works is his disciplined consideration
in literary terms of the Jesus portrait, with no movement at
all into historical-critical questions or into a pursuit of "the
historical Jesus." Biblical and theological studies have for so
long and so consistently been dominated by historical-critical
moves that it is worth calling attention, at a minimum, to a
study concerned with the literary "character," Jesus, as he
emerges within the edited biblical text—apart from questions
of historical sources, redactions, or "forms" that manifest the
Sitz im Leben of the early Christian movement. Frei's central
preoccupation is with the *identity* of the literary Jesus-figure,
a motif that he has sustained and further developed in a recent study, *The Identity of Jesus Christ—the Hermeneutical
Bases of Dogmatic Theology*.[2] Frei's argument is that the
portrait of Jesus in the Gospels is, on the one hand, a realistic

portrait of a specific person within specific circumstances, on the order of the realistic nineteenth-century novel. On the other hand, the portrait incorporates the stylized pattern, "Son of God." As Frei sees it, the individualized person and the Son-of-God pattern precisely merge within the narrative account of Jesus, denoting that Jesus' identity indissolubly weds the one to the other, or indeed, defines the one through the other.

> . . . the story of salvation is completely and exclusively that of the savior Jesus from Nazareth in Galilee. . . . The form of the Gospel story is sufficiently novel-like that we have to say that the pattern of redemptive action exhibited in Jesus is so identical with his personal story that he preempts the pattern. It is *his* story and cannot be reiterated in full by the story of anybody else—just as any particular person's story, whether fictional or real, is exclusively his own and not also that of somebody else.[3]

What Frei means by the Jesus story includes the full sweep of the synoptic Gospels (with, apparently, certain important linkages to John's Gospel), but actually the heart of the matter is found in the passion-resurrection narratives. There the critical factors emerge; there the portrayed identity of Jesus comes to its own. In this connection, Frei locates three stages of the Jesus story as a whole: (1) birth and early life; (2) ministry, with his baptism by John as the transitional act; (3) passion-resurrection, with his decision for him and the disciples to go to Jerusalem as the transitional act. In the first of these Frei finds Jesus heavily dominated by images of his prophetic fulfilment of the nation Israel. In the second, the Jesus-figure emerges more in its own right, but still is virtually defined by the reality of the Kingdom of God. In the third, Jesus by his initiative becomes increasingly and freely his own person; and even though this initiative leads paradoxically to his helplessness, nevertheless, the direct result (in the resurrection) is that he himself comes to define the community of Israel and the active Kingdom of God.[4] This third segment is obviously the critical one for Frei, as regards the literary-Christological identity of Jesus. The narrative in this portion is "history-like"; character and circumstance are realistically themselves. At the same time, the account is reminiscent of fiction (we are privy, for example, to Jesus' prayer in Gethsemane). In and through this history-like narrative the identity of Jesus comes most clearly and truly to literary representation. The question is, how shall this identity be described? And further, what status or claim upon reality do we understand that identity to bear?

Having thus summarized the nature of Frei's literary interest in the Gospel narratives, I shall consider more closely how he arrives at his position, bearing always in mind that the concern is ultimately to examine the literary foundations of "theology proper."

The Identity of Jesus: Two Modes of Identity Description

Frei's work with Jesus as a literary figure finds his character or person most surely and fully expressed in the accounts of his passion, crucifixion, and resurrection. (It is notable that Frei does not find the portrayal of Jesus' prior ministry the most penetrating as regards his own person; that segment of the Evangelists' account shows Jesus, in Frei's judgment, dominated by the reality of the Kingdom of God, as we have briefly noted.[5]) Who Jesus is emerges definitively within the narrative from passion to resurrection, in the relation between Jesus' person and his circumstances. It is of the highest importance to Frei that the essential identity of Jesus does come to expression in the culmination of his story; for the story itself not only stands or falls with the climactic presentation of its central figure; beyond that, the story includes a divine pattern of meaning whose *universal* significance can come clear only if it does so through the full presentation of Jesus as embodying person. Clearly, everything of critical importance to the story must focus in the explicit character of Jesus, lest the story itself forfeit its nature and function. Therefore, more is involved in the clear identity of Jesus, within the story's own terms, than merely Jesus' individual figuration. The complex of affairs that centers upon his person is seen to bear the highest significance for the story's "world" in that world's ultimate relation to God.

Since the identity of the Jesus figure claims chief concern, Frei spends considerable time and thought on what he calls the "formal elements" or "tools" of identity description. How is identity to be expressed in such fashion so as to be genuinely available in and through language? At this point, Frei impinges upon questions of the linguistic presentation of reality, of the same sort that have been noted in so many previous pages of this study. How is the essential character of Jesus to be genuinely explicated through narrative, and through narrative considered both as to form and matter? The position taken here as a general view affirms the linguistic presentation of reality, but with an element of concealment, or of reality's "receding," coincident with disclosure. Recall my earlier suggestion that language gestures arbitrarily limit "present-ness," or the real (giving it a distinct or particular shape before us) in the very act of allowing it to come to light (see above, pp. 35–36). That position was taken without prejudice towards the question of what may be called "moral crisis" in language, when the element of concealment in all language strangely passes over into alienation and distortion. The notion of the linguistic human being as "eccentrically disposed" in the general setting of reality admits of an *occasion or circumstance* into which evil may enter, resulting in destructive isolation; but the element of concealment in language *per se* means no initial prejudice towards or "wrong-ness" within language (see above, pp. 129–30).

Now Frei undoubtedly agrees that no language on any occasion exposes all mysteries; words of his to that effect will be noted shortly. Nevertheless, in the tension of language between disclosure and concealment, Frei most evidently is attracted by those instances in which disclosure or expression is uppermost and concealment is most contained or "manageable." Such a view becomes clear in Frei's dealings with the tools of identity description, especially as they are applicable to the climactic portion of the Jesus story. In brief, the instruments of identity description Frei finds most appropriate to the Jesus story are those by which character is chiefly disposed through outward, "readable" acts, or those by which the agent subject (in this case, Jesus) is most truly embodied in an outward form. By assuming such a position, notice how Frei completely distinguishes himself from the pervasive modern mood of seeking out the "historical Jesus" through some kind of subjective interpretation of objective data—the attempt to read Jesus' own historical consciousness. Not only is his Jesus initially literary rather than historical; even *within* this body of literature, Jesus is minimally "subjective" and maximally articulate in outward forms and events. Little of consequence remains of private self-consciousness. Thus a greater departure from historical speculation about Jesus is hardly conceivable.

The two methods Frei finds most congenial for dealing with matters of self-identity are, first, "intention-action" and secondly, "subject manifest in difference," or simply, "self-manifestation."[6] His strongest and climactic appeal is to the first, but consider initially for a moment the second. "Self-manifestation" implies the penetrating pursuit of "who" someone is (not only "what that person is like," which Frei associates with intention-action). The "who" question is difficult because it pursues the *consistency* of one's identity through and across all the separable episodes of deciding and acting. Frei must allow such a "who" question as valid; yet it troubles him because it stands on the edge of admitting the self to be "behind" outward affairs, or not available. Frei must admit that the self is "elusive."[7] Nevertheless, he is ready to say that consistency of self-manifestation does occur in a human life. Examples chosen are self-manifestation in "word" and self-manifestation in "body."[8] The paradigmatic instance of self manifest in "word" is a person's name, a linguistic object with which one identifies and to which one responds throughout life. As regards the body, one both *has* a body and *is* a body. One's name and one's body are "different" from the self *per se*; nevertheless, the self can be clearly manifest in them.

Frei sharply distinguishes self-manifestation from "self-alienation description" so often associated with modern romantic and existentialist works. In the "alienation" model the self is reflected in distortions of itself or by contrast to its true nature, and must thereby venture through a myriad of inconclusive events in unsuccessful quest of itself. Our examination of Kafka's *The Trial* is a case in point. Frei is convincing in his reluctance to become entangled in the web of self-alienation seeking. Yet the reader senses that in his commitment to stand against self-alienation Frei overdoes his resistance to any "seeking" or "questing" element present in the self-manifestation he does espouse. Surely the self manifest in "word" or "body" is from one point of view in process, despite life-long self-consistency, or indeed as a part of it. Such a process of emergence need not in itself suggest the fate of endless alienation.

Frei appears on much surer ground with the tool of intention-action analysis—at least as concerns Jesus. To put it perhaps too simply, intention-action proposes that a person becomes manifest in decisive acts that carry through a self-disclosing intention. How better to arrive at a person's identity than through those actions that are in and of themselves clear to all? Thus Jesus' intention to go to Jerusalem and his portrayed purpose to carry through God's act of salvation are clear enough in the third segment of the Gospel narrative. Surely Frei is accurate in declaring that this "intentional" Jesus of the Passion narrative offers the fullest and truest disclosure of who the literary character, Jesus, is. With Frei, intention-action further broadens into character and circumstance, such that Jesus as person and that which goes on around him are eminently articulate in one another. Frei comments:

> By means of . . . pathetic or ironic ambiguity or detachment between Jesus and the Kingdom, the focus of the story's last part falls more and more on him in his unadorned singularity. He is simply himself in his circumstances.[9]

The portrait of Jesus reaches its conclusive form as expressed through cross and resurrection, just as cross and resurrection gain their meaning only from his unsubstitutable and unique personhood. Intention finds its act, just as act has embodied a decisive intent—or thus the story relates it to us.

Even when Frei undertakes to speak of the second sort of analysis, the consistent self-manifestation of Jesus throughout the entire scope of the Evangelists' accounts (including birth and ministry), this broad method yields to the passion sequence and its predominantly intention-action view.[10] Of highest importance is the manifesting of Jesus' identity through this sequence; for if his identity is thus manifest, interlocked with circumstance, then *within the structure of the story* self-alienation—or subject-subject and subject-object "splits"—are overcome. As the narrative has it, the person of Jesus and the set of affairs around him are fully manifest through each other, and the purposes of God are fully manifest through this unique occurrence. Jesus is identified as his own peculiar person *and* as Son of God, Savior. Nor is the narrative form of the literature that tells this story an incidental feature. Since the meaning of a narrative is cumulative within its own telling, and its "objective" character reduces to a minimum the questions of "understanding" between author and reader, then the realistic, history-like narrative is the perfect vehicle for articulating the express unity of intent and act, of character and circumstance, *within* the story. Literature can honor the mystery of selfhood while at the same time, through the "objectivity" of narrative, tell a story in which all the elements—even that of universal, divine providence—come to clear articulation through one another.

Four Patterns of Meaning within the Jesus Narrative

Thus far it should be clear that not only is a literary portrait of Jesus more readily available than a historical one, but that the particular portrait at hand renders the identity of Jesus with high clarity, by intent and action, as his own unique person. Immediately an objection arises to the uniqueness of the Jesus figure, since the ancient world found dying and rising gods quite common. Frei's treatment nevertheless sharply sets the Jesus account apart from the many cultic stories associated with vegetation or with Gnostic fall and return. The identity of Jesus in his death and resurrection is marked by certain patterns of meaning that put the Gospel narrative into a different category from other dying-rising accounts. Those patterns illumine the realistic figure of a central person, who takes the patterns to himself and dominates them. Speaking specifically concerning the resurrection event, Frei comments:

> . . . the resurrection story, as a narrative description, is anything but mythical, no matter what one may think of its factuality or non-factuality. Unsubstitutable identity is simply not the stuff of mythological tales. Jesus identifies [his] titles rather than they him.[11]

It is appropriate, then, to examine more closely the patterns of meaning that give content to the portrait of this realistic person, so uniquely himself. Frei responds with four such patterns of meaning that he considers "embedded in the narrative itself."[12] These are (1) Jesus' obedience, (2) the co-existence of power and powerlessness, (3) the transition from one to the other, and (4) the interrelation of Jesus' and God's intention and action. In the first, not Jesus' "consciousness" or self-understanding—for example, the quality of his own "faith"—but rather his obedience to the Father's purposes, stands uppermost and is clearly explicit through the narrative events. In the second, the image of Jesus moves from one who seizes initiative and power to one who is powerless upon the cross; yet in another sense, thirdly, a kind of power and authority characterizes even his most helpless moments. In the fourth, the question of power and activity is complicated by the activity of the Father God, whose work increases in and through Jesus' loss of initiative, while nevertheless not contradicting the centrality of the Jesus figure.

In the brief space possible here, justice cannot be done to all four of Frei's patterns. Perhaps something further can be said, however, about the relation of power and powerlessness in the Jesus figure. The Jesus who goes to Jerusalem is one who wields a certain charismatic authority and holds a conviction of what his role must be under God. A deliberate decision to exercise his power in the capital city results in an inevitable clash with the authorities. Frei does not comment so, but at least in the Gospel of Luke, one has the sense of a Jesus who is sure that the city and its people are doomed, that the city is perverse beyond hope of recognizing its own plight, and that his own deliberate sacrificial activity intends a kind of salvage operation for whatever can be redeemed from the Jews' crumbling history. In any event, Jesus initiates a confrontation with the authorities that leads finally to his own powerlessness and indeed virtual isolation. Ironically, this condition of powerlessness does not defeat his purpose of redeeming Israel, but turns out to enhance it. Such is the case because God's intent is to work out his own aims through this powerlessness, climactically in raising Jesus on the third day.

Jesus' exercise of his intention sets in motion a complex of events that strikingly reflects his identity, just as his identity is also shaped by those events. Frei states:

> . . . the enacted intention of Jesus—to obey God and to enact men's good on their behalf—meshes with external circumstances devolving upon him. That is to say that the exact circumstances climaxing his story were not completely initiated and executed at his behest. On the other hand, he did not passively await and accept them. In fact, his identity is revealed in the mysterious unity of his own decision and determination with the circumstances and events of his passion and death. He is identified as well by his initiation of circumstances, his response to them and by their sheer impingement upon him.[13]

The interaction of character and circumstance comes to the point where the presumed savior is helpless in the hands of those seeking to destroy him. Frei notes that the chief priests' mockery is ironically true of the savior and his saving act: "He saved others; himself he cannot save" (Mark 15:31).[14] The transition to helplessness, more particularly in light of Jesus' innocence, Frei finds essential to his identity as savior. Thus, innocent powerlessness becomes a critical factor in distinguishing Jesus from gnostic descending-and-returning savior figures. Frei indicates that the gnostic "primal man" or redeemer actually falls into the same plight as those whom he ventures to save ("fleshly ignorance," "sleeping"). Nevertheless, an organic scheme or destiny joins the gnostic redeemer's "fall" to its inevitable outcome in successful "awakening" and renewal. Jesus, on the other hand, truly dies; only an exceptional act intruded by God in raising him turns loss into gain.[15] The transition to powerlessness is thereby real, yet it also coincides with another level of power, a saving efficacy in innocent helplessness, because God himself elects to work through the powerless figure. Still another level of coincidence (the powerless with the powerful) occurs in that the abandoned Jesus, helpless though he may be, bears a lordly authority even in suffering and death. Thus he turns questions back on his interrogators, reassures a dying thief, and commends his own spirit into the Father's hands. The interfaces of power and powerlessness turn out to be manifold and suggestive.

In Jesus' resurrection, the pattern of meaning is complete, and indeed is not complete apart from the resurrection. The power of the Father reaches its peak; nevertheless, in the act of resurrection itself it is the powerless one, Jesus, whose figure is central and commanding. All the titles and associations with the Kingdom of God that bleakly had fallen away from Jesus in his final distress, he himself now redefines and consummates in his resurrected person. Thus Luke notes that the resurrected Jesus is able to correlate the full tradition of Israel with his own now explicit identity:

> And beginning at Moses and all the prophets, he expounded unto them in all the scriptures the things concerning himself (Luke 24:27).

The intention-action sequence is complete, involving interlacing lines of power and powerlessness through Jesus and the Father and culminating in the challenge to belief in Jesus as the surprising fulfilment of Israel's hopes. The portrait, though rich with mystery, stands finished.

*The Identity of Jesus and the Question of 'Presence' within
the Narrative*

The above section has been all too brief a summary of
Frei's reflections regarding the identity of the person of Jesus
within the literary structure of the Gospel narratives. As literature, the Gospel story presents in realistic, narrative terms
person-and-event as uniquely themselves. ("Realistic" and
"history-like" as applied to the passion-resurrection account
refer to the fact that persons, events, and affairs in the story
stand directly for themselves in an ordinary sense, and are not
ciphers for something else.) The anti-mythical, everyday concreteness of the story is the ground of its uniqueness, in the
sense that any event in a particular time and place is unique.
But that everyday, historical uniqueness is lifted within the
story to a further uniqueness in that the central character is
found to coincide with the schematic, universal Son of God;
indeed, the person of Jesus comes to *define* who and what the
Son of God is, and thus conforms the title to his peculiar self.
It is of the highest importance, then, that the personal identity of Jesus be made clear, that the self who *is* the savior not
be hidden "behind" a mask of words and acts, the object of
private speculation. The form of narrative literature with its
event-ful, cumulative, and self-contained meaning is thereby
ideally suited to such an expression. Dilemmas of hermeneutic and interpretive appropriation are held to a minimum as
the figure of Jesus focuses itself through situation and action,
with little strain over "subject" and "object."

Frei has undoubtedly done us a great service in calling us
to read the passion-resurrection sequence once again as narrative literature with its own integrity, centering upon the commanding central character, Jesus. Before moving on, one may
well ask how his considerations fit the general position of Part
I of this study. In particular, does Frei's eagerness to point
out the availability and clarity of Jesus' identity contradict
my previous concern to note that language does indeed present reality but in a manner that includes an element of concealment or "receding"? It is true that in his work with sub-

ject- or self-manifestation Frei understandably strives to see the "who" of a person at the point of its maximal availability. Although he refers to the self as "elusive," he is most reluctant to get involved in the notion of the self as seeking or "in quest" of itself. But to avoid doing so requires him to press towards manifest evidences from point to point in life of the "essential self," or the abiding reality of who one "really" is. To attempt this with Jesus inevitably results in stressing the passion-resurrection sequence over previous segments, since it is there that the identity of "who" Jesus uniquely is (not merely "what he is like") comes to the fore.

Perhaps it would be best simply to see the full scope of the Gospel narratives, from the ancestry and birth accounts, as presenting Jesus in a kind of quest for final self-manifestation —without prejudice in any way against the Gospels' confession that he "was who he was" from the beginning. That is, the process of coming to a manifest self-identity in the portrait of Jesus need not predispose the account towards contemporary Western alienation. The assertion in this study of a "present-ness" that nevertheless conceals a deeper level of "presence" within itself (and without necessary hostility between the two levels) can serve as framework for a Gospel account in which manifestations of "who Jesus is" become increasingly explicit to the end. Thus, the new-born Jesus, the infant king (as Frei notes) is the culmination of his people's history and hopes, but is virtually defined by that tradition. The resurrected Jesus, at the culmination of an extended process, has taken that tradition to himself and redefined it through his personal identity! The process from the one to the other has even passed through the most intense alienation (the crucifixion), but with no loss—at another level—of his actual identity as savior, rather indeed with a more profound affirmation of it.

The unbiased notion of "presence" as both real and concealing not only gives framework to the process of a culminating self-manifestation; it can also allow for Frei's own statements of the continuing "mystery" of Jesus, even in the midst of the most explicit clarity of his person (for example, at the

IX
———
227

resurrection). Frei himself comments concerning self-manifestation:

> In the first form of subject description, that of the subject manifest in differentiation from himself, the naming question points to an *illuminating mystery* rather than a *haunting problem*.[16] (Italics ours.)

Frei notes that just the reverse is true with subject-alienation. An "illuminating mystery," therefore, does not contradict the resolution of ambiguity enacted in Jesus' person, supremely in the resurrection. Frei states in his moving "meditation" at the end of the *Identity* book:

> . . . The everlasting veil remains between him and us, but the story we have heard again today is that of a Lordship, a life and a love embracing both sides of the veil.[17]

The language of a story can therefore provide both "presence" and "mystery" coincident with one another without the language being accused of acute ambiguity. And surely even the explicit identity of Jesus in the Gospel story looks forward, in the story's terms, to a wider manifestation at the end of history. The point is undoubtedly obvious that Frei's "mystery" can fit in with our deeper-level "presence"; yet the point bears stressing—partly because our scheme here is an adaptation of Heidegger, whom Frei may easily associate with the existentialist, subject-alienation approach. Nevertheless, Frei refers by way of opposition only to "Heidegger's early philosophy."[18] In any event, Heidegger's final philosophical position may be affirmed as "reflected theology" without denying the validity for general theological work of his insight concerning language and "presence."

Language, even with its "concealing" side, can be profoundly adequate to "presence" and therefore to community. The point recalls Frei's own fascination with Erich Auerbach and the latter's analysis of biblical "types," which both realistically are their historical selves and yet bear with them a reality not yet fully explicit. Indeed, Frei appeals to Auerbach in support of the "realism" of biblical narrative generally.[19] All the same, we recall that for Auerbach, Hebraic or biblical style is suggestive rather than complete, rude of syntax, engaging, demanding, and rich with "background." Surely it is most significant that Frei has elected to employ classical, objective-descriptive literary critical methods on a piece (the Jesus story) that by Auerbach's own stylistic estimate must be denominated rich, suggestive, and full of "becoming." In other words, the story of the sacrifice of Jesus, like that of the sacrifice of Isaac, may offer itself to a variety of interpretations and even applications by its suggestiveness, its first-order metaphoric "aura." Yet Frei's whole program is to treat this account so as to hold interpretation to a bare minimum!

Perhaps the basis and appropriateness of such a move lies in what I have broadly termed the "discipline of metaphor." That is, suggestive, metaphoric power of a peculiarly biblical sort finds itself under the most tensive of disciplines in the realistic "object" narrative of Jesus' last days. The narrative form and the explication of Jesus' character in a rapid series of outward events moves the literature to be strongly self-contained in meaning. The narrative tends to mean, cumulatively, "what it says." The identity of Jesus, even with its mystery, unfolds clearly *within* the structure of the story and in and through the story's terms and objects. First-order suggestiveness is held maximally within the simple lines of the literary object. In other words, the passion-resurrection sequence turns out to have the discipline of an antimetaphor, as that phenomenon has been previously described (see above, pp. 61–62). The story, without rhetorical metaphors, binds and contains its power within deceptively simple, everyday terms and objects. Thus the multilayered, impassioned quality of biblical style is not erased; yet the story comes to a clear explication of Jesus' character and person within its own disciplined lines and structure. Identity, presence, and mystery all find portrayal.[20]

Jesus' Person Described and Affirmed as Real

Up to this point the tracing of Frei's literary work with some comment upon it has remained strictly within the structure of the Gospel narrative, within the well-disciplined and self-contained story and its internal relationships. To approach theology from literary criticism requires, however, that one ask whether Jesus' person is only *described* as real by literary criticism, within the story, or whether Jesus' person so identified will be *affirmed* as real within the world as experienced from day to day. Surely the move from delineation of a reality within a history-like narrative to the affirmation of that reality within the world is a matter of great moment. The resurrected Jesus abides within literature. Does he abide in reality? The central affirmation of Christianity is that he does. Despite Frei's own great reluctance to do so, I shall venture to ask in what frame of mind the move to affirmation is possibly made.

First, it may be well to clarify the kind of move that is *not* being suggested here. Surely it is not adequate to the issue being raised to apply simply the model of "gaming" with the literature, as was suggested earlier in connection with possible "reflected theology." With "gaming" a moment transpires when the reader enters into the literary piece *as if* a player-participant and thereby gains a perspective by which to make a judgment on meaning. The shared meaning between the reader and the subject matter then becomes a particular horizon within which reality is glimpsed afresh. Lest this act of "sharing" become simply a subjective appropriation, careful objective analysis of the literary piece must precede "understanding"; and even beyond that, when the gaming is done, the literary piece "withdraws" into its own disciplined form as object with still untapped possible meanings.

Nevertheless, even these safeguards are not entirely relevant to the matter of reading "reality" in the Jesus narrative. To do "gaming" with the passion-resurrection narrative, with whatever safeguards, would necessarily end with a "shared" meaning that by virtue of being shared would have to be confined to a human, historical meaning. One might find, for example, that the story of Jesus encourages entry into the antinomies of existence, the scandal and crisis of living, with confidence that some deeper level of life or of renewal lies hidden within these. This would not be an entirely inappropriate "shared" meaning; but it would not avoid the final ambiguity of history and human life that has been seen as the end of reflected theology—with the consequences either of frustration or of the confessional divinization of ourselves. Such a move would hardly support the setting aside of the Jesus narrative from other literature, a distinction already cited as the mark of essential theology.

Indeed, grasping the real in and through the Jesus story involves no ordinary safeguards such as literature may commonly offer against illicit appropriation. Within the terms of the story itself, the reality of the God-world relationship comes clear in a special set of circumstances in a particular time and place. Thus the identity of Jesus as unique savior puts no ordinary literary restraints on interpretation; rather that identity draws a marked limit upon interpretation at the point where the human meets the divine and knows itself distinctively different from the divine and unable to penetrate it. The portrait of Jesus emerges as that of an actual human being, but at the same time as that of the divine Son of God. There may be imaginative participation in the humanity of the Jesus character, but there can be no direct "gaming" or participation in the divinity. Thus the terms of the story set a boundary on ordinary formalizing, generalizing interpretations of the Jesus figure. Gaming towards reflected theology falls short of the full terms of the story itself.

In such case acceptance of reality on the story's own terms can only mean affirming a unique set of events of which Jesus is the center, and indeed affirming his resurrected presence as the story insists upon it. No way is open to read reality as this account fairly would have it and avoid the unique element of the resurrected savior. The only alternatives are to construe the story as symbolic of a general human divinity that belongs to us all (an option upon which we have already commented), or to decide that the story is "just" a story, that it is idle to suppose a final, particular meeting between God and world. This latter option would mean the account falls short of genuine literature.

At the same time, it becomes specially offensive to the modern sense of historical reality to affirm that the passion-resurrection narrative is substantively true. Surely the physical simplicities of a crucified and risen one are not really as much unbelievable as they simply seem irrelevant and distant. Frei comments only charily about this difficult move to "belief," the affirmation that Jesus' identity and presence are real in the story's terms.[21] Perhaps his most helpful insights occur, in any event, in his historical study, *The Eclipse of Biblical Narrative.* Here Frei takes us back to examine the power and function of biblical accounts prior to the onset of modern critical-historical study. Undoubtedly, his most serviceable insight points out that in the Reformation days, for example, *the explicative sense of biblical narrative and its factual, historical reference were not separated from one another.* Frei speaks of this "older" approach to biblical reading in a variety of ways but in none more usefully than when he uses the word "render" to describe the unified literal and historical function of narrative. For example, he describes the

> . . . old realistic sensibility . . . in which the narrative itself *rendered a world at once real and meaningful,* which was identical with the narrative, while serving also to orient men's dispositions.[22] (Italics ours.)

Or he speaks of

> . . . the precritical cohesion of historical reference with literal sense, rendering directly accessible the world literally depicted . . .[23]

In other words, modernity made a fateful move in deciding to inquire "behind" the literal text for firm, historical reality ("how it really was"), rather than allowing the text to retain in itself, indivisible, the literal and historical senses. The move was equally fateful whether made for conservative, supernaturalist reasons ("it really happened") or for progressive, rationalist reasons ("it didn't happen as it is recorded to have done"). Either way the integrity of the narrative text as "rendering" at once both explicative sense and historical reference was broken.

Frei has in no way suggested in the *Eclipse* book that such an integrity of the biblical narrative still stands, despite the intervening centuries of historical-critical study. If I do so here, it is strictly my own responsibility. What is intriguing, in any event, is the suggestion that the first move toward wisdom in dealing with the passion-resurrection narrative is to respect the text, that is, to keep the functioning integrity of the textual language, and not seek to penetrate "behind" the words themselves as a move towards "reality." One may indeed experiment in reading the Jesus story to see whether in any sense the account does "render" a reality both explicative and historical. What sort of mind-set, then, is involved in such a reading?

There is no question but what Auerbach is right, that the central biblical narratives are autocratic in their bearing; they were born to rule (see above, p. 107). The story of Jesus makes a singular, divine claim focused in his person, which furthermore refracts history and tradition through itself. For that reason, the Jesus narrative is not only an antimetaphor, as I have suggested; its sparse and intruding nature makes it a kind of absolute metaphor as well, with the simplicity of its disciplined lines disturbing our ordinary human-centered realism and asking either to command or be dismissed. Its everyday, history-like affairs create a most non-everyday reality and claim. And at many levels the claim seems seriously unreasonable and out of proportion. For example, if the narrative indeed renders historical truth within the integrity of the text, does this mean that one must read as *at least* factual (whatever other than factual may be involved) such items as the figures in dazzling apparel standing beside the tomb, the risen Jesus eating fish, or Jesus at Emmaus vanishing from the sight of his disciples?

No doubt the narrative means and involves a factual state of affairs; otherwise the claimed reality of the human person Jesus, dead and risen, would be in vain. On the other hand, just this factual state of affairs is portrayed as absolutely unique. A factual, historical state of affairs that coincides with the once-for-all self-manifestation of the God of Israel belongs strictly to itself. Facts are at our disposal, but the God of Israel is not at our disposal. The coincidence of the two must necessarily disturb our ordinary canons of judgment. The central point is this: an incomparable occurrence must include a communicable state of affairs in the world, yet can finally be judged only from the standpoint of its own reality. Obviously, our usual approach to historical judgment from a present standpoint (by the principle of analogy with the present) will not do. Suppose, then, we were to "yield"—give up our usual critical acumen—and take all the fact-like statements in the resurrection account as simply factual (fundamentalism). Again, we would surprisingly be putting the matter *at our own disposal,* at a certain level of our ordinary experience. We would in fact be affirming an "objective" infantile structure of factual resurrection as an unwarranted security around ourselves, against the everyday contingencies of life. On the other hand, were we to say that the fact-like statements are symbols of a deeper, formalized "meaning," then we would reduce the whole occurrence to a generalization and find ourselves in the ultimate dilemma of reflected theology. Finally, what can be said is that the passion-resurrection narrative renders a natural and historical reality, including a level of particular factuality, but also including an incomparable presence that resists generalizing canons of judgment. Beyond this, for the time being, reflection cannot go. The important thing is to have recognized that the passion-resurrection narrative makes a reality claim which, because of its peculiar content (an incomparable occurrence of divine presence), stands apart both from reduction to *mere* factuality and from the more generalized penetrations of the human world.

If the above comments seem a counsel of despair as regards human reason, consider that reason functioning usefully in any field needs salutary limits, and not only open-ended possibilities. Reason functioning in historical study, via historical-critical method, builds usefully only within a specified contract or field of investigation. When historical method investigates history as the medium of revelation and faith, end-

IX

less subjectivizing ambiguity sets in. Within the field of the Christian faith, historical inquiry that is to be humanly fruitful requires a salutary limit or a feasible contract, lest its researches move toward an even-handed balance of possibilities, whose stultifying effects we have already considered. The salutary limit, that point at which the divine meets human everyday-ness, is precisely the limit on historical reason that leads it into disciplined fruitfulness. Apart from that limit, historical study must either become mysticism, or turn to the burdensome and frustrating task of building the Kingdom of Humanity in lieu of the Kingdom of Heaven. Since neither of those options is attractive, historical study has tended to separate itself from the issues of Western Christian faith entirely. Historical work is done within manageable contracts or fields in which the significance for or against "belief" is not broached—perhaps, for example, a history of "religion." It is no derogation of achievements in the latter to say that the abandonment of any rapprochement between historical study and the tradition of Christian faith bodes ill for the stability and generative power of both. But that is another topic which to pursue in detail would take us far off course.

Some distance has been covered in this survey of the literary foundations of essential theology, or theology proper. Literary criticism can describe the meeting of identity and abiding presence in the person of Jesus, from the viewpoint of the Gospel narratives; faith and theology alone can affirm their actual reality. At the same time, such an approach to essential theology rests heavily upon a literary and linguistic act, namely the articulation of the passion-resurrection narratives. From the literary-critical standpoint, and finally from the standpoint of faith, no way opens to go "behind" the text, to reach what imagination might conceive as a firmer and more complete understanding of the Christ. Thus, while we have proposed that literature does present reality, nevertheless the climactic narrative of Jesus puts certain limits on imaginative participation *in* that reality, which we do not find in literature generally. It is true that Jesus as portrayed may be paradigmatically suggestive. But beyond that, and more important, the text claims a historical reality both divine and human in the actual occurrences it presents, and not simply a panoply of symbols. If one returns to the text frequently, it cannot be only for meanings applicable to oneself and one's situation. It must finally be in order to trace and re-trace the lines and patterns within the account itself, presenting us with a reality that usefully resists at a crucial point incorporation into our current world of meanings.

Such is the literary foundation of theology proper. It means that the primary task of theology is to scan again and again the identifying lines of who Jesus was, and to call attention to his consequent continuing presence—who Jesus *is*—with all the manifold implications of that reality.

NOTES

→ 1. Hans W. Frei, "Theological Reflections on the Accounts of Jesus' Death and Resurrection," *The Christian Scholar,* XLIX, 4 (1966) 263–306.

2. Hans W. Frei, *The Identity of Jesus Christ—the Hermeneutical Bases of Dogmatic Theology* (Philadelphia: Fortress Press, 1975).

3. "Reflections," 263.

4. "Reflections," 292–297. *Identity,* 126–138.

5. *Identity,* 130.

6. *Identity,* 86–91, 126–127. "Reflections," 278–283.

7. *Identity,* 95.

8. *Identity,* 95–98.

9. *Identity,* 134.

10. *Identity,* 132–138. Frei makes a later comment on his own use of the second type of analysis; see the Preface, *Identity,* x.

11. *Identity,* 136.

12. *Identity,* 126.

13. *Identity,* 105.

14. *Identity,* 113.

15. *Identity,* 56–58.

16. "Reflections," 285.

17. *Identity,* 173.

18. *Identity,* 98.

19. For example, *Eclipse,* 3, 15, 28–29.

20. If my own tendency is to give more scope to presence and self-unfolding in the narrative, Frei in his late Preface, *Identity,* viii–x, moves away from them.

21. For example, *Identity,* 145–147.

22. *Eclipse,* 156.

23. *Eclipse,* 220. See also pp. 34, 80, 84, 91, 192, 270, 278, etc.

Theology as 'Proper'
And as 'Reflected' X

The program of inquiry pursued here has at length discerned a relationship between essential theology and its literary foundations that is significantly different from the relationship between general literature and "reflected theology." Most obviously, theology proper yields to the special claims implicit within the Gospel narratives of Jesus—precisely because the divine-human events there presented resist transformation into a cluster of symbols, while the literature as literature resists outright dismissal. The appropriate literary treatment of the passion-resurrection stories thereby requires much more emphasis upon literary "object" analysis than upon hermeneutical "gaming" or communing. If reality as presented in the Gospel sequences is to be taken seriously, then it must be attended to on the terms those sequences employ. Critical reading therefore stresses internal analysis of what the narrative is saying and how the narrative is saying it rather than "interpretation" or "understanding."

An objection may arise that the passion-resurrection stories have no more right than any other narrative to insist that their fact-like assertions be taken seriously, at some level, as factual. Is it not just as easily said that the narrative of *Moby Dick* or of *Main Street* or of *Slaughterhouse Five* requires that its fact-like assertions be honored as factual in order that the book be taken seriously? Yet clearly such an insistence would simply damage the effectiveness of fiction as fiction. A novel offers a certain horizon on the world, and what happens in it is the *kind* of thing that happens in the world, or *can* happen seen from the particular viewpoint of that horizon. (See above, p. 95). Should not the Gospel narrative be the same? Should not its theological depth be suggested and symbolized by the *kind* of thing that is recorded as happening to Jesus, regardless of a particular level of factuality? But to the contrary, the Gospel narrative requires different handling because the theological "depth" is no longer, in Jesus' story, simply a generalized "depth." That is, the theological element or "divinity" within the account emerges precisely in this, that it coincides with a given real person and a given set of events, and not with a *kind* of person or *kind* of event. There is no avoiding this focus when asking whether the Gospel narrative, fairly considered, presents reality to us. Modern fiction does not and should not—as regards its theological dimension—follow such a model. Likewise the Gospel narrative does not (in this particular matter) coincide with the model of modern fiction.

Evidently, therefore, I have with rather a severe line drawn the difference between the nature and task of theology and the nature and task of "reflected" theology. Indeed, has not the latter been almost banished in favor of the former? Is reflected theology after all an actual theology in any true sense of the word? Or is it merely a shadow or image of real theology that renders a service only by disclosing its own inadequacies and by somehow managing to point us toward the "real thing"? What is the actual relationship between theology and its reflection? The aim of this final chapter is to consider this highly important question. By way of anticipation, the purpose will be to show that a kind of affirmative relation

X

does obtain between the two theologies and that therefore theology and modern literature (and perhaps, by implication, theology and contemporary culture) need not be impoverished by some final alienation from one another.

Two General Schemes for Viewing Literature

It will be recalled from the Introduction and also from the last chapter that it has been the purpose in this study to set side by side two different over-arching schemes for reflection upon literature. One of these schemes considers the general body of Western literature (including the Bible); the second considers the same general body of Western literature *except* certain biblical narratives distinguished from and set over against the remainder of the corpus. We have at least to a degree executed the second of these schemes. That is, the Gospel narratives of Jesus' life, more especially the passion-resurrection accounts, have claimed for themselves a special category apart from the remainder of the literary corpus in our tradition. Presumably I have also worked at length within the first of these schemes through Parts I and II of this study, pursuing the theological implications of literature generally, though with admitted attention specially given to modern literature. A particular aspect of the first scheme, however, has remained virtually untouched. The purpose in that plan was to consider the general body of Western literature, *including the Bible.* Yet we have spent considerable time in Part III indicating that at least certain portions of biblical literature must stand apart from the rest of literature generally. Is there a scheme or a framework within which even these portions of the biblical material, the Gospel narratives of death and resurrection, take their place by both nature and treatment along with the wide, general corpus of literature in the West? To say that there is would seem to undo everything attempted in the chapter immediately preceding this one.

Certainly a boundary appears that separates the Jesus narratives from the rest, as has been argued, and that separation is primary. At the same time, I have hinted and allowed at points that though final justice to the Jesus story must set it apart, nevertheless in a more preliminary manner that narrative, even in its realistic or history-like qualities, does offer paradigmatic implications or wider fiction-like overtones, on the order of any number of fictional texts. That is to say, the hermeneutical, "gaming" approach to the Jesus story—the reader's search for a humanly *shared* meaning or perspective on the world as between oneself and the narrative—almost inevitably occurs, even if the narrative itself at length resists it. One can hardly expect otherwise. Certainly the story *is* about a human figure. In considering the crises, the crucifixion-resurrection experienced by that figure, one may be led to reflect upon the severe crises of life generally, which, when faced with strength, turn out to bear within them the stuff of surprising recovery. Or perhaps in the light of Jesus one reflects upon the price a person pays for challenging strongly entrenched, conventional institutions, and ponders whether a well-timed self-sacrifice results in a kind of triumph at another level, just as, for example, Thomas Becket finally won a martyr's victory over Henry II. "What does the story mean to you?" "How does Jesus function as a cipher?" These will not soon be banished questions. Indeed, the Christian faith through the New Testament exhorts that we take up our own vocations and "follow him." That the story of Jesus functions at one level as a paradigm for Christians is thus embedded in Christian teaching itself.

Finally, if Auerbach is correct, and our argument in Part II stands, then much of Western literature and thought reflects or "images" incarnation, crisis, and renewal because of having borrowed on the suggestive outline of the Jesus account. This formalizing and generalizing construction of the story may finally not be fair to it, as we have shown; but it would be another matter to declare such reflections totally inappropriate. Application to and from one's own life will certainly occur, more specifically within Christian commitment. Furthermore, even the most careful "object" analysis of the Gospel narratives will not be entirely free of existential turns of thought. Our imperfection as critics means that a continu-

X

242

ing element of "appropriating" the story must be acknowledged.

The point of view that I wish to adopt here is that, with
regard to the passion-resurrection narratives, much that has
been laid out in Part II of this study is applicable in an admittedly secondary, though important, manner. Such a statement must, of course, recall the very stringent remarks concerning the discipline of metaphor. Indeed, the possibility has
already been raised of referring to the climactic Gospel narratives as an absolute metaphor, with all of the disciplined tightness of "address" to our ordinary situation thereby implied.
Surely no interpretation of the story at the broad human level
will come short of challenging bland conventions concerning
our existence.

If the Jesus story is thus grouped with other literature in a
secondary move, then we can say that in this unusual situation reflected theology is applicable to it. An odd situation:
secondary theology incorporates into its own tenuous nature
the foundations of that other more assertive discipline that
gave it being. Reflected theology's comment at this point may
take numerous forms, but all will undoubtedly find in Jesus
a figure of wonder, whose bizarre prepossessions and contingencies give birth to an ironic glory—probably of a sort not
clear to Jesus himself as protagonist. Regardless of just the
outcome of applying "theology for literature" to the Jesus
story, a broad and more important principle emerges thereby:
inevitably and invariably, attempts to interpret the story, orthodox or progressive, and to find its applicability to our existence will move into construing its meaning much after
ourselves and our own way of life.

Any attempt simply to deny all "applicability" in order to
avoid distortion must founder on the necessity of relating
one's life to whatever chosen or favored religious meaning.
On the other hand, the disturbing prospect always attached
to applicability is that we shall conclude the exercise, perhaps
broadened, but essentially having reduced the narrative of
Jesus to who and what we ourselves were prior to the interpretive task. Thus the two schemes for dealing with the core

Christian literature apparently result in a dilemma. The primary approach stresses the exceptional presence of Jesus, but leaves matters of interpretive discipleship much open. The secondary approach hermeneutically construes the narrative in relation to our existence, but risks absorbing the Jesus figure into the set of categories brought to him. Is there any way that theology itself can assist in making sense of this problem?

The Larger Rhythm of Inclusiveness-Separation

In this section the possibility should be considered that the two ways of regarding the Jesus narrative, primary and secondary, will find relation to one another in a rhythm or movement of inclusiveness-separation. The attempt here will be to revert to a principle adopted in Part I in relation to language and reality and see if an expanded implementation of that principle will assist us in resolving our dilemma of the two literary orientations of the Jesus material.

In the early consideration of language, literature, and reality, a notion from Heidegger of two levels of presence became highly useful in the effort to construe the rather complex field covered by the designation "reality." Indeed, the same principle was referred to in the immediately preceding chapter in the discussion of the continuing mystery of Jesus' person, even as a part of the high clarity of his identity (p. 228). The idea of two levels of presence thus identifies what takes place when language presents reality, which nevertheless in the same instant recedes "a step back" or partly conceals itself. Immediate presence always intimates the full richness of presence as a whole, which somehow must nevertheless recede a bit even from its own widest and most imaginative expressions. Now this sense of movement in the "present-ness of reality" suggests a rhythm through time of inclusiveness-separation already alluded to in connection with Heidegger. (Recall Walter Lowe's comments on Heidegger's movement toward wide explanatory contexts, followed by a moment of ontological discontinuity.—p. 38). First-order suggestive inclusiveness is accompanied by a movement of "separation" in reality; such separation invites increased second-order sorting-out activity until a certain fragmentation precipitates a new inclusiveness, and so on. This pattern provided us a means of reflecting upon reality as process and thereby suggested a formal outline for reflected theology.

What I wish to propose is that this same principle be elevated to a different level of our conversation and see if, with quite a different content—indeed a content inclusive of the stuff of theology *per se*—it can assist us in locating some order between the two approaches to the Jesus material.

Surely there is a sense in which the force and shape of the passion-resurrection narrative move towards an inclusiveness of reality. More than once Auerbach has been alluded to on the autocracy of biblical narratives. The Jesus story was "born to rule." When the beginnings of Western civilization elected the Gospel account as its chosen sacred story, there was no question but that all phases of culture and social existence would feel the impact of that narrative in one form or another. Indeed, our entire case for the existence of a "reflected" theology has been grounded in the pervasive effect of both the form and style of the New Testament account upon literature and thought in the West. The reigning force of the Jesus figure as the New Testament portrayed him inevitably moved towards a wide cultural inclusiveness within such a civilization that proposed to acknowledge New Testament authority. To that extent, what is being said is hardly different from the usual situation of religion and culture reflecting one another. What did tend to be different in the West, however, was that the religion was not primarily ontocratic, symbolizing a wide reality of Being as its foundation, but rather acknowledged the exclusive, particular person Jesus as ruler. Often as not, the exclusiveness and particularity were hardly well understood, but the principle implicitly remained.

With the inclusive reign of the Jesus figure came nevertheless a wide cultural appropriation of who he was and what his story was taken to mean. An obvious example in the medieval period was his identification with the papal "Vicar of Christ" and attendant hierarchy of clergy. An example from the Calvinist movement was his identification with the dynamic Lord of history who would found the reformed commonwealth of the elect on earth. Inclusive dominance almost necessarily involved cultural manifestations that, while defensible, nevertheless circumscribed the person of Jesus within a given socioreligious system. The vision of a purified church born in the mind of a Gregory VII, or the vision of a reformed community born in the mind of a Calvin had the imaginative force to "read" the world in the light of Jesus, died and risen, and his peculiar reality. But even as these first-order presentations took hold, something of the incomparable portrait of Jesus and his personal "presence" receded or took "one step back," even coincidentally with the newly proffered rulership. No construing of the Jesus story in and through culture could refrain, in the nature of the case, from leaving less than explicit some mystery of the singular person. To acknowledge the deeper mystery of "presence" is indeed appropriate and to the point. Yet the very distinction between Christ explicit and implicit became the *occasion* for an unhappy division in things, as the first-order insight of Jesus as manifest gave way to an increasingly strict "sorting out" of institutional forms and relations. The lines of meaning, coherent *within* the Jesus narrative itself—the patterned integrity of the story—began to separate from the cultural expressions previously derived from them.

When the articulate "presence" of Jesus in his narrative begins to separate from the cultural inclusiveness originally derived from that presence, a crisis in Christianity as a historical movement sets in. The recourse then is to make a return to the original narrative and its unsubstitutable figure, to rediscover that narrative's own cumulative meaning or pattern and thus to attempt to come to terms with the presentation of reality that has "separated itself" from its own current derivatives. One cycle in the rhythm of inclusiveness-separation is complete, having worked itself out within the framework of a specific double-sidedness of "presence" in reality. The rhythm goes on; but each approach to fresh enlightenment must *re*-approach the same closely disciplined narrative and its clear lines of portraiture, with nevertheless its mystery of "presence."

Thus the two frames of reference respecting the Jesus narrative—the one generally hermeneutical-interpretive, and the other specially analytical-descriptive—can find relation to one another within the model of an inclusiveness-separation rhythm, *bearing always in mind* that the perspective of "separation" ever holds the upper hand. The clear and yet complex narrative of what happened to Jesus and who he was again and again stands judge over the apparently inexhaustible constructions of inclusiveness that interpret and self-appropriate him.

The rhythm as described and the two sorts of pursuit of the Jesus literature bring to mind their reflection in two centers of existence, fundamental to Western Christian faith throughout its many centuries. One recalls, for example, the two centers as described in the theology of Augustine: the center that is oneself, which determines one's true destiny by how it relates to that other center, which is God. Shall one's self-center be the world-center (inordinate self-love)? Or shall God be the world-center (love and acknowledgment of the deity)? The same tension informs, of course, Luther's thought. John B. Cobb has helpfully suggested a contemporary comment on the matter of two centers, as over against just one. He distinguishes in effect "personal" existence from what he calls "spiritual" existence. In personal existence the self realizes itself as will, responsible for that which it chooses from its own self-center. The self realizes its freedom, responsibility, and authority. In spiritual existence, however, the self becomes responsible for *the choice of the center from which it* organizes itself, and not only for what it chooses.[1] What is applied in this comment to the individual self can in a more complex way be applied to both self and culture. The spiritual existence of a culture means its situation of choice as to what center it will choose to live from—its own (the historic "spirit" of its people) or another. Traditionally, the West made its choice to live out of the center in Christ. That very commitment, however, tends finally to identify the Christ with the civilized order itself and to locate the Christ center within the culture's own center. No way of avoiding this risk is possible if the people take seriously the claimed rulership of Jesus. But in the "fallen" consequences of ending up with, in effect, only one center, a limit upon cultural autonomy is severely needed in order that the relational violence of "all things becoming possible" can be constrained.

The power of the Jesus account to separate itself in integrity from cultural expressions offers that other "center," limiting and chastening, that traditionally has called Western autonomies to task. On the contemporary scene, not only does the question of choosing an outside center become difficult, but the question of whether an outside center is any longer real in order to be chosen is more serious still. Theology finds the separating out of the Gospel narrative of primary importance in the crucial rhythm of asserting another center, in order that the culture may recognize the continuing terms of its existence.

Revelation and Theology: Two Perspectives

Considerable groundwork has now been laid for asking more closely the relationship that obtains between theology proper and reflected theology. Already it has been stated that the passion-resurrection narrative finds a special place in theology proper, while admittedly the more general human concerns of reflected theology may reach out to embrace that same narrative if opportunity arises. The two kinds of literary-critical approach have then been related to one another by means of a rhythmic inclusiveness-separation model, with the stipulation that as far as theology is concerned the moment of separation claims priority in the continuing historical movement.

It should be clear, then, that the above analysis will provide marked implications for the two theologies and the kinds of revelation they entail. Perhaps initially the two theologies can simply be related to the inclusiveness-separation model set forth in the last section. Just as the figure of Jesus tends to be both inclusive and separate, so theology as a structure of meaning tends to follow the same pulsation through its history. Theology proper, distinguishable in its particular confession, tends to communicate its themes throughout the culture that articulates it. In other words, theology proper tends to become reflected theology, as its particular and quite eccentric shape more and more becomes identified with what a culture comes to think of as "normal." The move toward reflected theology may become so pronounced that the peculiar historical intrusion of the Christ simply acculturates into a multi-leveled system of "symbols"—clues that point towards the general human condition vis-a-vis God and world. At that point, theology becomes philosophy of religion—or as we have termed it "reflected theology," since the structure of its thought remembers its foundations in the Jesus story.

At such a moment, theology proper, if it can find the wit and the will to do so, separates itself from its own descendants and calls marked attention to the special imbalance that the Jesus figure sets up in any even-handed history of humanity. Theology makes the move of separation and critique. But does it thereby repudiate and disown—and thereby dismantle —reflected theology, that broad outline of its own image? Would doing so be equivalent to renouncing its own lordliness, its ironic authority implicit in the story of the crucified and risen Jesus? For reflected theology was in one sense the result of theology's claim to set foundational motifs for all of life.

In an exceptional manner theology and reflected theology may require one another, even if theology proper holds definite priority and cites the foundations both for itself and its "imaged" partner. That is to say, theology proper may not be complete without some established thought on the manner in which its categories and its authority illumine nature and history. From the opposite perspective, reflected theology may ultimately require theology proper in order that its processes may arrive at a result other than wavering and ambiguity. The ideal proposal may indeed be approached that theology proper and reflected theology are necessary to *complete* one another. *Yet no way at all emerges* by which their single, "seamless" unity comes clear. They must function through time in tension with one another, with the move of "separation" as that which clarifies best their mutual identities.

Or another approach to the difficult relationship may lie in proposing that, of theology proper and reflected theology, each is complete in itself, but that each *implies* the content of the other, or suggests the inclusion of the other within itself, even though this inclusion can apparently not be clearly and conceptually stated. How is this the case? The account of Jesus crucified and risen draws towards itself not only those events and personages that are in some way of a *type* with Jesus' character but also the broad, "secular" culture we have glimpsed through modern literature. Not only Abraham "going out" by faith, and Isaac being sacrificed, but Melville's Ahab and Joyce's Dedalus become objects of concern and significance within the universal scope of the Jesus story. The claim of the personified Son of God, whose divinity is universal, suggests that in some manner modern, secular reality responds, even if faintly and formally, to the pattern of singular incarnation and life through death. The world seen from the standpoint of the cross and empty tomb must at least suggest such affirmative response to the Christian story, else the implicit universal claim of the crucified king becomes void. Thus the images of incarnation that have been allotted to reflected theology come distantly to view if essential theology but scans its periphery.

On the other hand, reflected theology likewise includes the distant locus of essential theology as the implied goal of its questing. This is not to argue that reflected theology consciously seeks to find its way through to a classical Christian confession; but at least the *absence* of that confession is known, which may include the view that in fact that confession is no longer possible. Insofar nevertheless as reflected theology involves some affirmation, that affirmation "remembers" the gracious complex of limits and possibilities realized in the surprising nature of Jesus as Messiah. Reflected theology implies, somewhere on its boundary-lines, the classical form of incarnation that made possible its own structures;

X

and by an inherent teleology or tendency those structures of reflected theology incline toward their own consummation in the uniqueness of Jesus, even if thought decrees that such is impossible.

In the above manner, the two theologies may imply an area of their own "overlap," where each one draws something of the other towards itself, though one is never able to view the content of both equally in balanced unity. Rather, a position must be assumed always in one, with the other seen only as a distant prospect. The center that theoretically joins the two theologies, and their two fields of experience, is hidden from the concrete processes of time and observation in which we live. We must be content with the indirect implications of their unity, and with the manifold and dynamic movement of experiencing their inclusiveness-separation rhythm in passage from one to the other. At the same time, when priority is called for, theology proper emerges as the ground of the full enterprise.

The mutual relation of implication and overlap in the two theologies recalls the pattern of two sorts of knowledge of God—as creator and as redeemer—set forth in the theology of John Calvin. Careful study of Calvin's theology—at least in the judgment of one important specialist, Edward A. Dowey, Jr.—suggests that knowledge of God as creator rests not only on general revelation in nature, but overlaps into special biblical revelation, whose primary purpose is, of course, redemption.[2] The implication is that a broad, rational knowledge of God includes a notion of the eternal Logos-Son and really presupposes (we have more ambiguously said "reflects") the redemptive knowledge of God in Christ. At the same time, knowledge of God the redeemer comes via Christ alone; yet redemption is not valid unless *creation* is presupposed, that is, unless the Father of Christ is in fact the original creator God, maker of all. Thus the two views hold a mutual inter-relation. The primary purpose of special revelation (redemption) presupposes knowledge of God the creator. On the other hand, knowing and glorifying a beneficent creator presupposes saving knowledge of the redeemer. Nevertheless, despite this mutual entailment, the two forms of knowledge may not be rationally reduced into one. Dowey finds Calvin posing them in a dialectic relation of implication or, more strongly, presupposition of one another. To move in thought from creator to redeemer, or vice versa, is to "jump to another starting point theologically."[3] The gratuitous intrusion of redemptive love, necessitated by the fall, precludes a unifying, intellectual resolution of the two kinds of knowledge into a single perspective.

Likewise in our relating of theology and literature's reflected theology, no way emerges to "see" directly the transition from one to the other. No conceptual model of the link between them is possible, and if such were to appear, finally it would belong to one side or the other. Thus the theologian must live in process, seeing the range of the theological field from one "end" and then from the other, even if theological "home" locates finally at the classical, confessional locus. And above all, in these circumstances, the theologian must resist the "ontologizing temptation"—the impulse to probe for a general ground or foundation in being that will somehow underlie the two sides of the enterprise, lest only the projection of an ontologizing imagination results. True, the theologian never ceases to inquire whether greater clarification is possible, seeing that general reflection and confession of faith do entail one another and must finally be one. Yet the conditions of temporal theologizing are such that the common, joining language remains elusive.

The Theological Reading of Literature

It remains only to comment upon where the theological position as summarized in the last section leaves us with respect to the reading of imaginative literature. At the same time, the richness of modern Western literature is so extensive that one is overwhelmed at the prospect of making adequate generalizations. This study would have to anticipate another full volume, employing a much broader inductive method for commenting theologically upon literary works. Furthermore, Part II has been devoted to setting forth in a

X

formal manner a theology for literature. That effort will have to stand regarding what a theological level of literary criticism broadly entails. The theological horizon as drawn in Part II is wide enough to include the plurality of humanistic perspectives offered by literature's great variety. Yet, since matters have been complicated by approaching a tentative relation *between* the two theologies, reflected and proper, something further needs to be said to suggest the implications of the above section of this chapter for theologically sensitive reading.

I have already proposed that the theology reflected in literature is finally an ambiguous theology. Yet if, as stated above, theology proper implies reflected theology or suggests the latter as already implicated within a classical Christology, then we must draw the surprising, if not disturbing conclusion that all Western literature of aesthetic merit belongs finally within the sphere of the Christ. The theologian must admit that statement, while knowing that it cannot be defended with clarity. Such is the tension of the theologian's confessional posture. Thus the Christian significance of all meritorious literature must hold, apart from any overt Christian imperialism or any arbitrary Christian "discrimination." Nor does much relief of this situation derive from the incarnational model of aesthetics espoused earlier, i.e., realistic things of earth penetrated by the artist's imaginative insight so as to imply a renewed "world." As already noted, that model can produce a substantive outlook highly ironic or quite contrary to original Christian confession. How is it meaningful to propose that all Western aesthetic strength belongs somehow to the Kingdom of God when the works themselves are heavily alien, if not contradictory, to the peculiar ascriptions of the Jesus story?

No theological solution as such offers itself, since the link that joins the two theologies into one is hidden from scrutiny. Want of a final solution does not, however, prevent moving *toward* that solution by a few steps. Initially, it may be fruitful to consider the sort of works that seem either clearly in harmony or clearly in disharmony with Christian confession, at least in appearance, and see if by pondering these the field of the problem is somewhat narrowed.

First of all, one group of works is an exception to the rule of inclusion within the Christian sphere because it can be dismissed on valid theological *and* artistic grounds. That is, there is a classification of literary pieces that poses no challenge to confessional theology because its vision leads its members into aesthetic failure. These are works that resort to a mythology, no matter how contemporary in style, that may be termed positive or confessional gnosticism. Such a work is an aesthetic failure because the author has deserted the task of imaginatively penetrating the stubborn materials of experience, in favor of certain fancies. An example is *Slaughterhouse Five* by Kurt Vonnegut.[4] The story contains many pungent critiques and comments on existence, but the author admits that he was simply at a loss to know how to deal in fiction with the bombing of Dresden. Invoking the imaginary realm of the Tralfamadorians provides a dreaming release in which evil is not real, and indirectly comments on the ungovernable horror too grisly to imagine or portray. The book therefore loses aesthetically, though it remains a biting comment on contemporary experience. Much futuristic writing and science fiction also surely fail as art because of the lapse into gnostic speculation. Such a popular work as Robert A. Heinlein's *Stranger in a Strange Land* falls into this category.[5]

To turn from certain non-candidates to presumed allies, one supposes that some works are both artistically excellent and so clearly espousing of a Christian world-view that their affirmative relation to theology is clear. The names of T. S. Eliot, W. H. Auden, Georges Bernanos, and Flannery O'Connor have already been mentioned. Some have been ready to argue nevertheless that the aesthetic strength of Eliot's and Auden's poems has been diminished by their requiring that language and experience speak from within a Christian confessional mold. Rather than argue that point, I wish to pose just the opposite thought: that the force of Christian confession may alter its own nature precisely by being expressed within an artistic work. That is, Christian confession within

X

an artistic work is not so much "heard" as it is "overheard." The confession may appeal to the reader as the keystone of the true way of life, or it may function simply as an "idea" providing framework for a powerful aesthetic piece—as Francis Fergusson has pointed out about the Christian framework of Eliot's play *Murder in the Cathedral*.[6] Life according to Christian confession may be portrayed, but the enthusiastic reader need not be included within that outlook; response may be legitimately aesthetic and that only. Something about the self-contained serenity of an art-work means that a confession of faith is not directly addressed to us, and a direct response of the reader is not required.

Thus even the literary works that are "friendly" to Christian avowal are not unequivocally so, and that is as it should be. A certain removal separates them not only from direct confession, but also from directly calling for confession. The matter is clear in many of Flannery O'Connor's stories, such as "A Good Man Is Hard to Find."[7] To game with the story is to enter a world in which the claim of Jesus as Lord is fiercely presented; or, on the other hand, the world of the story may simply reveal the impact of a distorted criminal mind. The claim of the story's world is not finally limited to only one of these two. Such tension is appropriate to current "Christian" art. Works friendly to Christian theology should not be unequivocal friends, lest the lively tension between the aesthetic and the theological be blandly dissolved. Any espousal of faith bears the marks of human limitation by virtue of who states it. "Friendly" artistic works, by their element of ambiguity, and by not "giving in" entirely to the stated confession, help to recall the human limitation and incompleteness of any statement of faith. If we are concerned as to how these works of art "belong" finally to Christ, then we must remember that a certain strand of *not* belonging is essential to a good relationship, as is the case with actual human relationships that we daily experience.

The situation of works that appear as "opponents" of Christian theology also turns out to be complex, as with those considered "friendly." There is a good deal to be said for certain kinds of opposition that clearly surface, as in a human nuclear family—where one suspects that antagonism signals a deeper common interest that simply cannot be disclosed or expressed for the time being. Many pieces that offer existential or metaphysical revolt or secular "confession" may belong in this class. The poems of a Robert Lowell or a Wallace Stevens or a Sylvia Plath, the plays of Eugene O'Neill, or the plays and novels of Sartre and Camus may offer that avowed independence of Christian belief that nevertheless has the ring of age-long and familiar issues about it. Western-rooted opposition to Western Christian faith knows that the issues at stake are indigenous to a common, age-long civilization. The quarrel is between cousins, or even more agonizingly, between parents and children. Such a quarrel may be tragic and destructive, but it is a quarrel within a recognizable relationship and therefore within a known circle of love and hate. Richard Wright in his novel *The Long Dream* portrays Mississippi blacks agonizing over the body of one of their number, mutilated by a white lynch mob. One of them comments,

> . . . You have to be terribly attracted toward a person, almost in love with 'im, to mangle 'im in this manner. They hate us, Tyree, but they love us too; in a perverted sort of way, they love us . . .[8]

And Sartre comments on the grotesque parody of love that took place many times in World War II between the torturer and the tortured.[9]

Yet gross physical acts of violence are not the point here, but rather aesthetic works that lay claim to excellence. Their implicit theological outlook may be hostile to classical Christianity; yet they bear a sense of human nobility or at least hard-won achievement. Their negativity and anger toward faith and its objects means not only a common reference point of altercation with theology, but an element of love-hate that has been turned to positive aesthetic account. There is no question but that the theologian must finally oppose their implicit viewpoints; but opposition does not mean that the theologian will refuse to hear. Nor does hearing mean conde-

X

scending, but rather entering in; for something lies in common between theology and these "secular" works, even if it is not possible to cite hard conceptual links between the two. That commonality is signaled by a common culture, but lies deeper than culture. It is a sharing between aesthetic excellence, on the one hand, and clarity of faith, on the other, though this sharing be extremely difficult to specify. The commonality may have to do with the disciplined solitude of the creative artist, risking opposition, and the solitude of the Jesus figure that resulted indeed in total opposition, yet turned to creative account.

In any event, the theologian-reader "enters into" the plays of an O'Neill, with his agonized inversion of Catholic teaching, or the novels of a Faulkner, born of collapsed and desiccated Southern Calvinism, with a complex of notions and sensibilities: there is excellence here, and it is to be enjoyed. The plays and novels somehow belong to the theologian's economy, even though theology's cultural "reflection" is all that can be specified. At the same time, a certain venture into the unknown is involved. To "enter in" means that at some level one's own confession of the Christ is vulnerable. Theology as a disciplining *of* faith may have to be the result of fresh reading and experience. But finally and more importantly, the theologian's avowal of Christ's identity as a gracious limit or frontier for all human meaning actually liberates. That is, the avowal of Christ all the more frees the theologian to "enter into" the human complex implicit in an art-work, precisely because the burden of joining its meanings with that of theology proper has been lifted. Knowing the limits of that proper field opens the theologian to the vast array of human affairs without the constant drag of a theological "ax to grind." Something exhilarating and appropriate informs such dealing with literature when meanings of clear opposition to theology emerge. Better a known and measured hostility between two antagonists than the coming of an opponent who wears the uncertain guise of a friend.

In this latter case, that of ambiguous friendship, clarifying aesthetic appreciation depends first of all on revealing the antagonism that appears at first as the approach of an ally. In such a category is most literature that proposes to portray and interpret Christ himself, either by retelling his story or by introducing him into the story of others. The designation of Christ-figures in literature is well known, and it is beyond our purposes to open the subject significantly here.[10] Suffice it to say that whether Jesus himself, as it were, or a Jesus-like character emerges in a literary work, the portrait either covertly or clearly offers an interpretation of Christ. Here the inclusiveness-separation model we have discussed above is applicable. Paradigms of Jesus will forever suggest themselves. Even the most disciplined and objective reading of the Gospel narrative varies the image of Jesus we carry in our heads, every time we review the story. The response to paradigms, whether derived from Kazantzakis, Dostoevski, or St. Luke, is that of laying them once again beside the New Testament narrative text to see whether the "separation" effect of the original Jesus figure takes place. Only in this way do endless fictional, ideological, and even historical images of Jesus find some limit and perspective of evaluation.

Especially by this procedure various contemporary versions of Jesus readily turn out as new offerings of ancient interpretations proposed long ago. Such an ancient succession does not negate their current descendants, but does help get them into perspective. For example, a novel by Peter DeVries, *The Blood of the Lamb*,[11] employs a tragic-comic theme that at length offers an image of Jesus as the crucified clown, patiently wiping from his face a smashed pie—or in this particular case, cake. Christ, the fool, suffers infinitely within the world's outrageous adventures. DeVries' metaphors in this intriguing interpretation resonate with much that is contemporary; at the same time, they bear a surprising resemblance to Christ as portrayed for the young Augustine of Hippo by the North African Manichees in the fourth century.[12] The passive Christ, whose image accords with an acute sense of the world's evil, and with that sense primarily, contributes an insight, but asks also to be measured again by the Gospel narrative portrait. On the other hand, it is possible for the Christ to be intro-

X

258

duced into fiction with such subtlety as to involve neither imposition nor distortion. Robert Detweiler has helpfully suggested concerning John Updike's *The Centaur*, for example, that

> Christ is manifestly present, not paradigmatically but theologically. Precisely because he is not the model here (as in some other recent fiction) he can be the cumulative and culminating meaning of the fiction.[13]

A Christ-meaning—one of many possible amplifications of Christ-confession—may be far more appropriately handled and criticized in a piece of fiction than the influence of a direct Jesus figure.

As we have noted, "opposition" of literature to Christian theology is variously complex. Dealing with it is not unlike dealing with the opposition between Christian and Jew. Though the difference between the two is potentially dangerous to both, far more dangerous is the *denial* of the difference, as by appealing to a supposed common cultural ground. Each position implies a universal claim, and thereby implies the dissolution of the other. Paradoxically, however, the Jew is highly important to the Christian theologian as the living, effective sign of the limits appropriate to the theological discipline. In the same manner, essential Christian theology *implies* that all Western cultural worth somehow belongs to it; yet the conceptual establishment of that belonging dare not—indeed *can*not—come to clarity and application under the conditions of time and process, let alone conditions of evil. By some such model of clear, disturbing, and yet oddly beneficent opposition, the theologian deals with admirable literary antagonists, bearing within himself or herself the requisite tensions that result.

The ultimate dilemma in these matters is nevertheless not the opposition that is clear, but that "deteriorating" opposition which has no certain case to make as to whether affairs and questions are meaningful—including questions of literature and theology. Some of the most striking artistic contributions of the twentieth century have been of this sort, generally characterized as the literature of the absurd. As has been increasingly noted in the last few years, the telling point of such work is not that existence is meaningless, but that the distinction meaningful-meaningless lacks decisive applicability. Apparent *anomie* does not convince us that all significant boundary-lines are impossible; yet in practice no such boundaries maintain themselves. Or, again, the more closely any problem is defined in the bid for clarity, the more complexly frustrating the results become—which is nevertheless not a conclusive result. "Gaming" with such art is participation in an erosion of all motives, questions, and intentions. Thus evil is most itself when the very questions of good and evil decline in force and effect.

It has been suggested that Samuel Beckett is an advance upon Franz Kafka, since his characters are crumbling in paralysis, while Kafka's continue to struggle and seek. But undoubtedly Kafka's work carries the epic force of evil for current sensibility. Much of Beckett's work poses clear excellence of aesthetic form (*Waiting for Godot* invites the most careful analysis of its balanced shape and structure). What disturbs about Kafka is that his very aesthetic form falls into question, though remaining entirely appropriate to what he is doing. Gaps, infinite regress, drowning in detail threaten his novels and culminate in the author's own ironic imperative that his works should be posthumously destroyed. The theologian stands in some wonder before the secularized, Jewish, and yet oddly familiar spectacle of Kafka's world. His work is a monument the theologian acknowledges. Yet it is not possible finally to oppose the world of his fiction by Christian theological assertion, just as good and evil themselves cannot be conceptually opposed. The two spheres are in different categories; they are not definable as direct opposites. That is why the world of Kafka's fiction is threatening; once inside, we find it all too familiar and complete. The theologian can only acknowledge the wonder of this art at the boundary line of the theological economy, and then quietly leave it.

X

As stated in the Introduction, the purpose in this case study has been not only to outline the two theologies, reflected and proper, but to suggest the sense in which they may be related to one another, and the degree of that relationship. We have been forced in the final result to appeal to a relationship of mutual implication, and thus to a relationship that lacks for the time being a clear conceptual model of how that implication points in fact to reality. Certainly the task of the Christian theologian is to persist in the search for a rational solution that will join the unyielding particularity of Jesus to the universal applicability of a lordly, yet rational faith. Yet even as the theologian persists, it is clear that this goal is an ideal limit for reflection which in practice, and under the conditions of existence, cannot be reached. Mutual implication provides a certain overlap of proper and reflected theologies, but not a joining. Nevertheless, the full rationality of faith is pursued; the hiatus can be reduced and variously qualified, if not finally eliminated.

At the same time, it is clear from this study that a major task of theology—perhaps *the* major task of theology currently —is to recall, declare, and *affirm* the hiatus. The most difficult and the most essential move of theology today is the movement of separation, in the inclusiveness-separation rhythm. That is, theology in the nineteenth and twentieth centuries has heavily and systematically participated in numerous cultural trends, social and intellectual. While such participation is inevitable and indeed just, theology has also found itself participating in the deeper ambiguities of culture and in fact the ambiguity of the general human situation, as we know it. The separation motif thereby presses itself upon us. One irony of the situation is that classical modern liberal theology, the work of systematic apologetics, emerged for the sake of greater flexibility and freedom between faith and culture. Today the separation motif oddly promises a more cogent freedom—the freedom that belongs to a confessional identity, and that does not feel called upon to provide systematic theological underpinning for every meaning or wonder cast up by day-to-day life.

Thus confessional statement and a true process of religious

questing really belong together, in fact are essential to one another in the character of Western Christian experience. Confession proposes by anticipation and indirection the limits within which significant seeking takes place. On the other hand, questing for meaning presupposes a goal already somehow implicit in the quest. The essential relation of the one to the other is strangely overlooked in much current sensibility. Most intellectual proposals in religion are devoted to flexibility, process, and increasing options. That these in and of themselves swiftly mount to an infinite regression and thereby to a static uncertainty appears lost on many, especially the secularized, upwardly mobile elements in Western society. Change and process, apart from quality assertions of identity, weirdly coincide with a grotesque parody of confession in any case—namely, the sterility of a pervasive mediocre sameness— so that in our rapidly moving world the "confessional" element will have its due, whether for good or for ill. On the other hand, productive free process in experience does not contradict genuine Christian confession, rather it is nourished by it. Indeed, the disclosure of valid confession marks those lines of identity that give significance to seeking and questioning, to opposition and debate, and to fruitful discussion.

Theology's inability, for the moment, to join conceptually its two levels (proper and reflected) is an allowable price to pay for the resultant "living rhythm" in its on-going pursuits. The continuing conversation of confession and quest affords a hope of vitality even in these days, which are most perilous for all human affairs and assuredly for productive theological work.

NOTES

1. John B. Cobb, Jr., *The Structure of Christian Existence* (Philadelphia: Westminster Press, 1967) 123.

2. Edward A. Dowey, Jr., *The Knowledge of God in Calvin's Theology* (New York: Columbia University Press, 1952) 41–46, 146–147, 238–240.

3. Dowey, *Knowledge,* 147.

4. Kurt Vonnegut, *Slaughterhouse Five* (New York: Delacorte Press, 1969).

5. Robert A. Heinlein, *Stranger in a Strange Land* (New York: Capricorn Books, 1961).

6. T. S. Eliot, *Murder in the Cathedral* (New York: Harcourt, Brace, and World, Inc., 1935). See F. Fergusson, *The Idea of a Theater* (Garden City: Doubleday and Co., 1955) 233.

7. Flannery O'Connor, *Three* (New York: Signet Books, 1964) 129–143.

8. Richard Wright, *The Long Dream* (New York: Doubleday and Co., 1958) 78.

9. Sartre, *Literature,* 211–213.

10. See Theodore Ziolkowski, *Fictional Transfigurations of Jesus* (Princeton: The University Press, 1972). Also, Frei, *Identity,* 63–84.

11. Peter DeVries, *The Blood of the Lamb* (Boston: Little, Brown and Co., 1961).

12. For example, Peter Brown, *Augustine of Hippo—a Biography* (Berkeley: University of California Press, 1969) 46–53.

13. Robert Detweiler, "The Protestant Risk in Updike's *The Centaur*" (unpublished paper, Emory University, April 1974) 17. See also Detweiler's *John Updike* (New York: Twayne Publishers, 1972). Also, John Updike, *The Centaur* (New York: Knopf, 1963).

Index

3/79

About the Author

William Mallard, of Georgia descent and residence, holds the B.A. degree from Randolph-Macon College (Ashland), the B.D. degree from the Duke Divinity School, and the doctorate of philosophy in religion from Duke University. He has been a Gurney Harriss Kearns Fellow in Religion at Duke University (1953–54), a Dempster Fellow in Religion of the national United Methodist Church (1954–55), a Faculty Fellow of the American Association of Theological Schools for research at Oxford, England (1962–63), and a Cross-Disciplinary Fellow of the (then) Society for Religion in Higher Education for research at Yale University (1969–70). He also received an Outstanding Faculty Award at Emory University in 1968.

Among Professor Mallard's published studies are "Method and Perspective in Church History: a Reconsideration," *Journal of the American Academy of Religion* (1968), "Clarity and Dilemma: the *Forty Sermons* of John Wyclif," in *Contemporary Reflections on the Medieval Christian Tradition*, edited by George H. Shriver (1974), and "Secularist and Traditionalist," *Religion in Life* (1973), "A Perspective for Current Theological Conversation," in *Toward a New Christianity*, edited by Thomas J. J. Altizer (1967), in addition to other articles and reviews.

Currently a professor in the History and Interpretation of Christianity, Candler School of Theology, Emory University, Professor Mallard is also a member of the university's Graduate Faculty in Religion and of the faculty of the Graduate Institute of the Liberal Arts.

271